PHILIP'S

CU00405381

STREE

Huddersfield

Batley, Brighouse, Dewsbury

www.philips-maps.co.uk

First published in 2007 by

Philip's, a division of
Octopus Publishing Group Ltd
www.octopusbooks.co.uk
2-4 Heron Quays, London E14 4JP
An Hachette Livre UK Company

First edition 2007
First impression 2007

ISBN-10   0-540-09172-3
ISBN-13   978-0-540-09172-0

© Philip's 2007

Ordnance Survey®

Photographic acknowledgements:
VIII Stephen Dorey / Alamy
IX Tom Curtis / Dreamstime.com

Printed by Toppan, China

Contents

II **Key to map symbols**

III **Key to map pages**

IV **Route planning**

VIII **Illustrated guide to visitor attractions**

2 **Street maps** at 4½ inches to 1 mile

96 **Street maps of central Huddersfield**
at 7 inches to 1 mile

97 **Index**

126 **List of numbered locations**

Key to map symbols

Roads

(12)	**Motorway** with junction number
A34	**Primary route** – dual, single carriageway
A40	**A road** – dual, single carriageway
B1289	**B road** – dual, single carriageway
	Through-route – dual, single carriageway
	Minor road – dual, single carriageway
	Rural track, private road or narrow road in urban area
	Path, bridleway, byway open to all traffic, road used as a public path
	Road under construction
	Pedestrianised area
	Gate or obstruction to traffic restrictions may not apply at all times or to all vehicles
P P&R	**Parking, Park and Ride**

Railways

	Railway
	Miniature railway
	Metro station, private railway station

Emergency services

◆ ◆	**Ambulance station, coastguard station**
◆ ◆	**Fire station, police station**
H ✚	**Hospital, Accident and Emergency** entrance to hospital

General features

✚ PO	**Place of worship, Post Office**
i	**Information centre** (open all year)
	Bus or coach station, shopping centre
	Important buildings, schools, colleges, universities and hospitals
	Woods, built-up area
Tumulus FORT	**Non-Roman antiquity, Roman antiquity**

Leisure facilities

⚊ 🚐	**Camping site, caravan site**
▶ ✕	**Golf course, picnic site**

Boundaries

• • • • • • •	**Postcode boundaries**
▬ · ▬ · ▬	**County and unitary authority boundaries**

Water features

River Ouse	**Tidal water, water name**
	Non-tidal water – lake, river, canal or stream
〈 ┃	**Lock, weir**

Enlarged mapping only

	Railway or bus station building
	Place of interest
	Parkland

Scales

Blue pages: 4½ inches to 1 mile 1:14 080

0	220 yds	¼ mile	660 yds	½ mile

0	125m	250m	375m	½ km

Red pages: 7 inches to 1 mile 1:9051

0	110 yds	220 yds	330 yds	¼ mile

0	125m	250m	375m	½ km

62   **Adjoining page indicators** The colour of the arrow and the band indicates the scale of the adjoining page (see above)

Abbreviations

Acad	**Academy**	Mkt	**Market**
Allot Gdns	**Allotments**	Meml	**Memorial**
Cemy	**Cemetery**	Mon	**Monument**
C Ctr	**Civic Centre**	Mus	**Museum**
CH	**Club House**	Obsy	**Observatory**
Coll	**College**	Pal	**Royal Palace**
Crem	**Crematorium**	PH	**Public House**
Ent	**Enterprise**	Recn Gd	**Recreation Ground**
Ex H	**Exhibition Hall**	Resr	**Reservoir**
Ind Est	**Industrial Estate**	Ret Pk	**Retail Park**
IRB Sta	**Inshore Rescue Boat Station**	Sch	**School**
		Sh Ctr	**Shopping Centre**
Inst	**Institute**	TH	**Town Hall/House**
Ct	**Law Court**	Trad Est	**Trading Estate**
L Ctr	**Leisure Centre**	Univ	**University**
LC	**Level Crossing**	Wks	**Works**
Liby	**Library**	YH	**Youth Hostel**

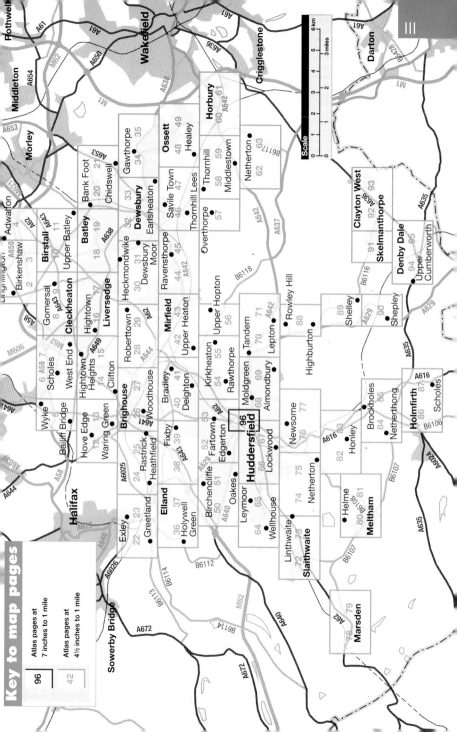

Key to map pages

Atlas pages at
7 inches to 1 mile

Atlas pages at
4½ inches to 1 mile

96

42

Scale

0 1 2 3 4 5 6 km
0 1 2 3 miles

Fothwell
Wakefield
Crigglestone
Darton
Middleton
Morley
Horbury
Ossett
Gawthorpe 34
Gawthorpe 35
Bank Foot
Chidswell 20
Batley 21
Upper Batley
Birstall 10
11
Adwalton
Birkenshaw 2
3
Dewsbury
Dewsbury Moor
Earlsheaton
Savile Town 46
Thornhill Lees 47
Thornhill
Overthorpe
57
58 59
Healey
48 49
Netherton
62 63
Clayton West 92 93
Skelmanthorpe
Denby Dale 91
94 95
Upper Cumberworth
Heckmondwike
Ravensthorpe
44 45
30 31
Mirfield
Upper Heaton
Upper Hopton
56
Rowley Hill
Shelley 89
Shepley 90
Highburton
Gomersal 9
Cleckheaton 8
Hightown 16
Liversedge 17
Robertown 28
Hightown 29
Scholes 5
West End
Hightown Heights
Clifton 14
15
Brighouse
Woodhouse
Bradley 40
Deighton 41
Fixby 38
39
Rastrick 25
Heathfield 26
Wyke
Bailiff Bridge
Hove Edge
Waring Green
Halifax
Exley 22
Greetland 23
Elland 36
Holywell Green 37
Birchencliffe 50
Oakes 51
Edgerton 52
Fartown 53
Leymoor 64
65
Wellhouse
Linthwaite 72
73
Slaithwaite
Marsden 78
79
Kirkheaton 54 55
Rawthorpe
Moldgreen 66
68 69
Almondbury
Lepton 70
Tandem
71
Lockwood 67
Newsome 76
77
Netherton 74
75
Honley 82
83
Helme 80
81
Meltham
Brockholes 84
85
Netherthong 86
87
Scholes
Holmfirth
Huddersfield 96

Sowerby Bridge

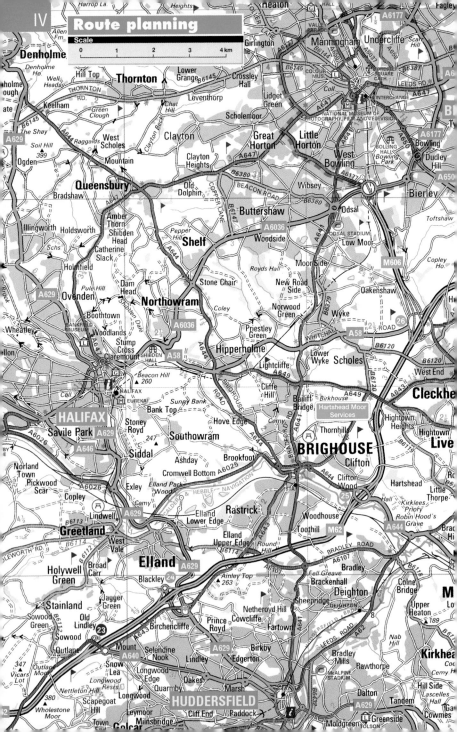

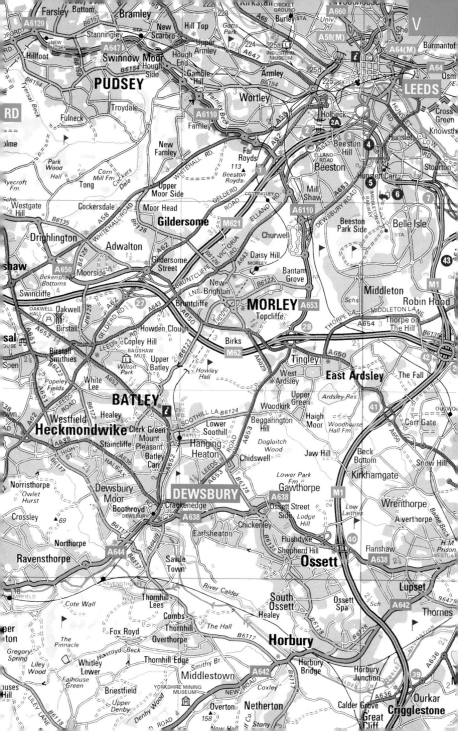

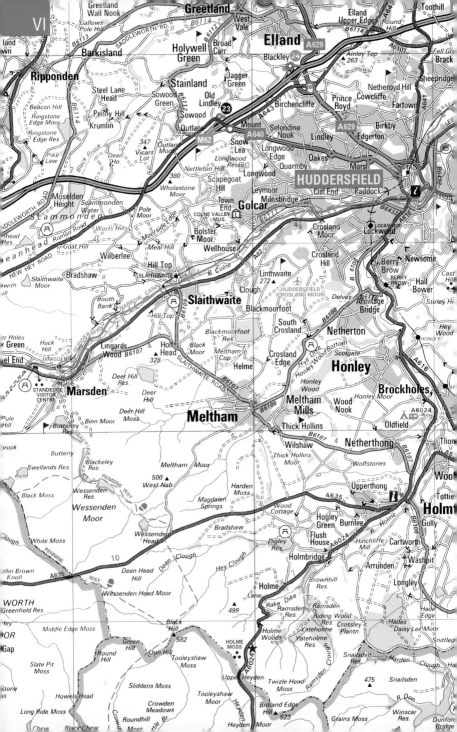

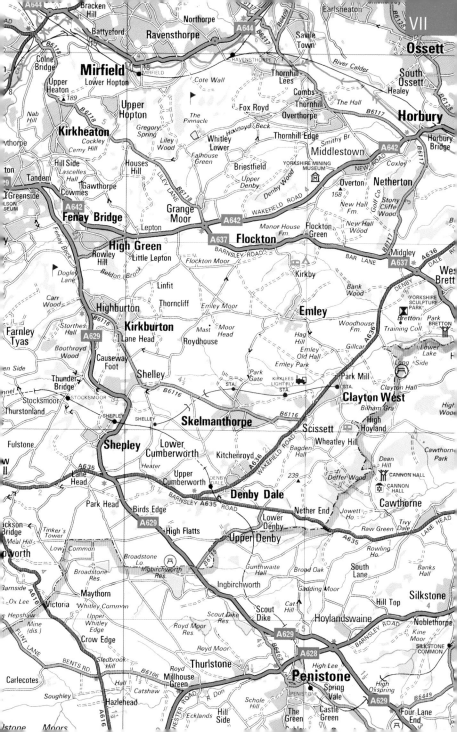

Visitor attractions

Museums and galleries

Bagshaw Museum *Wilton Park, Batley, West Yorkshire.* The dramatic Victorian home of a former mill owner in 36 acres of parkland and ancient woodland (see Wilton Park), this Gothic house became a museum in 1911 and was named after its first curator, Walter Bagshaw. Subjects include Egyptology, the Amazonian rainforest and decorative arts from India, China, Africa and Japan. 📞01924 326155 🖥www.kirklees.gov.uk 11 A2

Colne Valley Museum *Cliffe Ash, Golcar, Huddersfield.* Small local museum set in traditional 19th-century weavers' cottages furnished in period style. Spinning, weaving and clog-making demonstrations, children's corner and temporary art exhibitions. 📞01484 659762 64 C2 🖥www.colnevalleymuseum.org.uk

Dewsbury Museum *Crow Nest Park, Heckmondwike Road, Dewsbury.* A museum of childhood concentrating on the lives of children through the 20th century, including a 'Growing Up in Dewsbury' exhibition, toys gallery and temporary exhibitions and events. 📞01924 325100 🖥www.kirklees.gov.uk 32 A1

Huddersfield Art Gallery *Princess Alexandra Walk, Huddersfield.* In a dedicated area of the central library, the galleries house a rotating collection of 20th-century and contemporary art. 📞01484 221 964 🖥www.kirklees.gov.uk 96 B1

National Coal Mining Museum for England *Caphouse Colliery, New Road, Overton.* This museum gives a unique opportunity for the over-fives to travel

▼ *The Wrinkled Stocking, Holmfirth*

140 m down a working mine and see the machinery and conditions from the last two centuries. Pit ponies, exhibitions and pit-head baths. 📞01924 848806 🖥www.ncm.org.uk 62 A4

Last of the Summer Wine Exhibition *The Wrinkled Stocking Tea Room, Huddersfield Road, Holmfirth.* Exhibition about the popular sitcom, in Compo's house. 📞 01484 681408 86 A3

Red House Museum *Oxford Road, Gomersal, Cleckheaton.* A red-brick house, built in 1660, now chiefly known for its Charlotte Brontë connections, with interiors as they might have looked in the 1830s. Outdoors are recreated 19th-century gardens, a Brontë exhibition and interactive exhibitions on the 1950s. 📞01274 335100 🖥www.kirklees.gov.uk 9 B3

Skopos Motor Museum *Alexandra Mills, Alexandra Road, Batley.* A small motor museum run by enthusiasts, with a variety of cars from most of the history of motoring, bicycles and some motorcycles. 📞01924 444423 20 A2

Smith Art Gallery *Halifax Road, Brighouse.* Fine art museum chiefly of 19th-century works, including works by William Frith, Augustus Egg, Frederick Lord Leighton, John Grimshaw, Francis Danby and Philip Calderon. 🖥www.calderdale.gov.uk 📞01484 719 22 213 A1

Tolson Museum *Ravensknowle Park, Wakefield Road, Huddersfield.* An extensive local museum with collections on Huddersfield and its people from the prehistoric to the present, telling the story of the development of the town through archaeology, biology, clothing, art, weaponry, social history, transport and music. 📞01484 223830 🖥www.kirklees.gov.uk 69 A4

Places of worship

All Saints *Stocks Lane, Batley.* Although there was a church on this site before the Norman Conquest, the earliest part of this building is the south chantry chapel which was founded in 1334. The rest of the building was begun in the late 15th century, in the Perpendicular style. 🖥www.batleyparishchurch.org 19 C3

Church of the Holy and Undivided Trinity *Church Street, Ossett.* An ambitious piece of Victorian Gothic completed in 1865 in the form of a Greek Cross, with a central tower and spire that soar to a total height of 69 m (226 ft) 35 A1

Holy Trinity *Towngate, Holmfirth.* Looking quite dark and dour on the outside, inside this is a beautiful 18th-century church with side galleries and a classical simplicity. 🖥www.holme-valley-anglican.church.org 86 A3

St Michael and All Angels *Church Lane Thornhill, Dewsbury.* There has been a church here since Anglo-Saxon times and has elements from almost every era of medieval English architecture, including Saxon crosses and fragments of Norman and Early English carvings. Chief among its glories is the surviving medieval stained glass, in particular the Jesse window in the chancel. There is also a range of tombs and monuments. 🖥www.thornhillparishchurch.org.uk 58 A4

Other sights

Oakwell Hall *Nutter Lane, Birstall, Batley.* A pretty Tudor manor house set out as it would have been in the 1690s, with painted panelling, kitchens and furnishings and period garden, set in 100 acres of the original estate. Exhibition. 🖥www.kirklees.gov.uk/museums 📞01924 326 240 3 A1

Standedge Tunnel and Visitor Centre *Waters Road, Marsden, Huddersfield.* The longest, deepest canal tunnel in the UK. Boat trips in summer. Falconry centre. 📞01484 84429 🖥www.standedge.co.uk 79 B4

Victoria Tower and Castle Hill *Off Lumb Lane, Almondbury, Huddersfield.* The site of an iron age hill fort, as well as a medieval castle. The Victoria (or Jubilee) Tower was built to commemorate Queen Victoria's Diamond Jubilee of 1897. Check for opening days/times. 📞01484 223830 🖥www.kirklees.gov.uk 77 B2

Green spaces

Beaumont Park *Meltham Road Lockwood, Huddersfield.* Huddersfield's first public park, which opened in 1883. As well as woodland walks and empty open spaces to enoy, facilities include 5-a-side football pitches, a ball wall, basketball courts, children's play area and ornamental gardens. 📞01484 221000 🖥www.kirklees.gov.uk 75 C3

Crow Nest Park *Heckmondwike Road Dewsbury.* Opened to the public in 1893, these landscape gardens includes ornamental and wildlife gardens, terraced and woodland walks, a cricket ground, tennis and multi courts, bowling green, playground, allotments, a lake, a small football pitch, conservatory and Dewsbury Museum. 📞07966 455890 🖥www.kirklees.gov.uk 32 A1

Greenhead Park *Trinity Street Huddersfield.* The main park in Huddersfield, Greenhead Park opened in 1884. Facilities include the only paddling pool in the area, tennis courts, skate park, miniature steam railway, bowling greens, crazy golf course, 5-a-side football, basketball courts, bouncy castle and children's play area, ornamental

gardens and donkey rides. Major events, such as the Huddersfield Mela, are held here in summer. ☎07814 387426
🖳www.kirklees.gov.uk 67 A4

Peak District National Park *Aldern House Baslow Road, Bakewell, Derbyshire.* Located south-west of Huddersfield and accessed via Meltham or Marsden, the first national park in Britain covers 1,438 sq km and has more than 2500 km of public rights of way. The scenery is spectacular and visitors can undertake some of England's finest climbing, caving, walking and cycling. ☎01629 816200 🖳www.peakdistrict.org

Ravensknowle Park *Wakefield Road Moldgreen, Huddersfield.* A small park, with ornamental gardens, ball wall, 5-a-side football pitches, basketball court, bowling green, children's play area, multi court and the Tolson Museum.
🖳www.kirklees.gov.uk
☎07814 387420 69 A3

Wellholme Park *Bradford Road, Brighouse.* Landscaped park with play area, woodland walks, tennis courts, bowling greens, skateboard park, putting green and crazy golf. It is well known for its formal bedding displays. ☎01422 393215
🖳www.calderdale.gov.uk 13 B1

Wilton Park *Bradford Road, Batley.* Acquired by the Batley Corporation in 1909, the park includes formal grounds, a large lake with lots of wildfowl, the Kirklees Butterfly House, the Bagshaw Museum, bowling greens, tennis courts, children's play area, flower gardens, 5-a-side football pitches, crazy golf course, orienteering course, basket ball court and woodland walks. ☎07814 387415
🖳www.kirklees.gov.uk 11 A2

Activities

Batley Baths and Recreation Centre *Cambridge Street Batley.* Swimming pool, sauna and fitness suite. ☎01924 326167
🖳www.batleybaths.co.uk 19 C3

Batley Sports and Tennis Centre *Windmill Lane, Howden Clough, Batley.* Two swimming pools, a gymnasium, a large sports hall, a fitness suite and a specialist tennis centre. ☎01924 326181
🖳www.batleysports.co.uk 11 B3

Dewsbury Sports Centre *Longcauseway, Dewsbury.* Swimming pool, fitness suite, children's gym and spa. ☎01924 325020
🖳www.dewsburysports.co.uk 46 C1

Dewsbury Covered Market *Cloth Hall Street, Dewsbury.* Covered market open Mondays to Saturdays (half-day closing Tuesday), selling food, clothes and household goods. ☎01924 325011
🖳www.kirklees.gov.uk 33 A2

Dewsbury Open Market *Cloth Hall Street, Dewsbury.* General market on Wednesday and Saturday, antique and second-hand market on

Friday, car boot sale on Sunday mornings.
🖳www.kirklees.gov.uk ☎01924 325011 33 A2

Galpharm Stadium *Stadium Way, Huddersfield.* Home of Huddersfield Town AFC and Huddersfield Giants RLFC, also stages concerts. ☎0870 44 44 677
🖳www.htafc.com 🖳www.giantsrl.com
🖳www.galpharmstadium.com 53 C2

Huddersfield Open Market *Brook Street, Huddersfield.* General market, Monday, Thursday and Saturday, second-hand market Tuesday and Saturday
☎01484 223195
🖳www.kirklees.gov.uk 96 A3

Huddersfield Sports Centre *Southgate, Huddersfield.* Health suite, climbing room, fitness suite, sports hall, squash courts, combat room and bowling hall
☎01484 223630
🖳www.kirkleesactive.co.uk 96 B2

Kingsgate Shopping Centre *King Street, Huddersfield.* Nearly 50 shops, selling electricals, fashion, shoes, music, books and sportswear. ☎01484 542777 96 B2
🖳www.kingsgateshoppingcentre.co.uk

Kirklees Light Railway *Park Mill Way, Clayton West, Huddersfield.* Steam railway that runs on a 7-km track between Shelley and Clayton West. Stages days out with Thomas. ☎01484 865727
🖳www.kirkleeslightrailway.com 93 B4

Lawrence Batley Theatre *Queen's Square, Queen Street, Huddersfield.* In a former Wesleyan Chapel, presents drama, dance, comedy, music and exhibitions.
☎01484 430 528 🖳www.lbt-uk.org 96 B1

Packhorse Shopping Centre *Packhorse Walk, Huddersfield.* Shopping centre with a variety of outlets. ☎01484 533898
🖳www.packhorsecentre.com 96 B2

Piazza Shopping Centre *Princess Alexander Walk, Huddersfield.* Shopping centre with a variety of outlets.
☎01484 534594
🖳www.piazzacentre.co.uk 96 B2

The Picturedrome *Market Walk, Holmfirth, Huddersfield.* Cinema and music venue.
☎01484 689 759 86 A3
🖳www.picturedrome.net/home.htm

▲ *The entrance to Standedge Tunnel at Marsden*

Queensgate Market Hall *Princess Alexandra Walk, Huddersfield.* Large market, open Monday to Saturday.
🖳www.kirklees.gov.uk 96 B1
☎01484 223732

Spenborough Pool & Sports Complex *Bradford Road, Liversedge.* Two pools, dance studio, fitness classes, athletics stadium. ☎01274 335140
☎fitness suite 01274 335 145
🖳www.spenboroughpool.co.uk 16 C3

Stadium Pool & Fitness Club *Stadium Way Huddersfield.* Small pool and jacuzzi, two gyms, sauna and steam room, dance and aerobics studio. ☎01484 234110
🖳www.kirklees.gov.uk 53 C1

Whitcliffe Mount Sports Centre *Turnsteads Avenue, Cleckheaton.* Two sports halls, bowls, gymnasium, squash courts, tennis courts, activity area, floodlit pitches. ☎01274 335130
🖳www.whitcliffesports.co.uk 7 B2

Information

Tourist Information
🛈 **Batley** *Bradford Rd, Batley*
☎01924 426670 20 A3
🛈 **Holmfirth** *Huddersfield Rd, Holmfirth*
☎01484 222444 86 A3
🛈 **Huddersfield** *Albion St, Huddersfield*
☎01484 223200 96 A1
Kirklees Metropolitan Council *Civic Centre 3, Market Street, Huddersfield*
☎01484 221000
🖳www.kirkleesmc.gov.uk 96 A1
Car parks (council) ☎0800 731 8765
🖳www.kirkleesmc.gov.uk/transport/parking/parkingmenu.shtml
West Yorkshire Metro
☎01132 457 676 🖳www.wymetro.com
National Rail Enquiries ☎08457 48 49 50
🖳www.nationalrail.co.uk
First Calderdale and Huddersfield
☎01450 26 00 99 🖳www.firstgroup.com/ukbus/yorkhumber/caldhudd/home/index.php

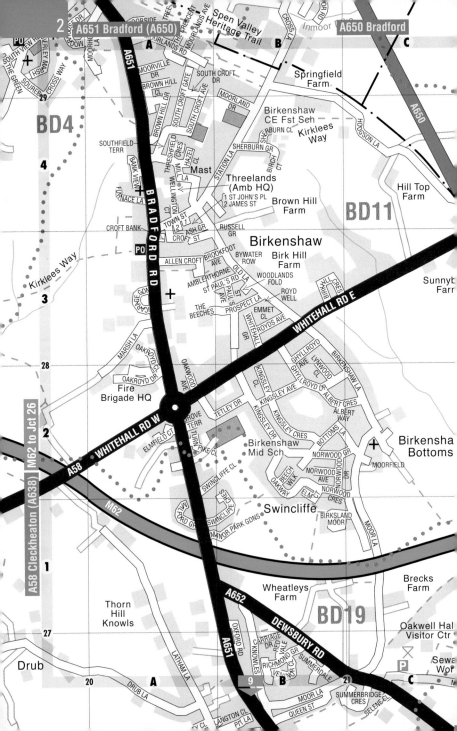

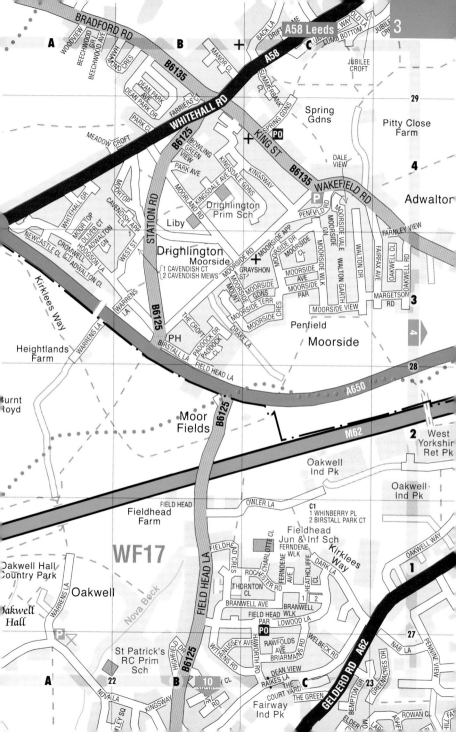

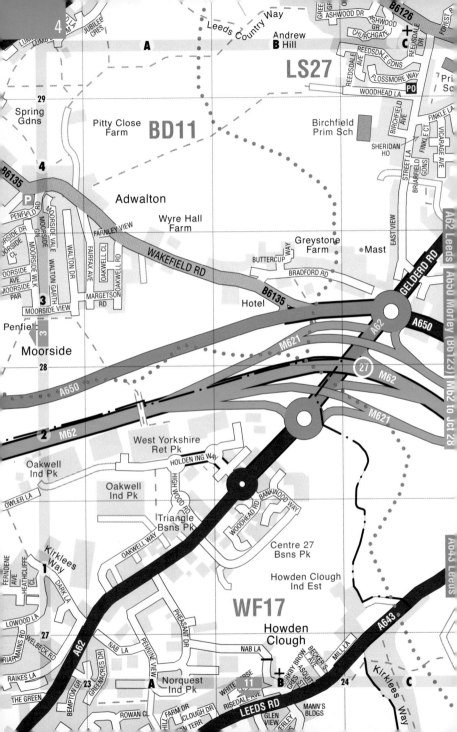

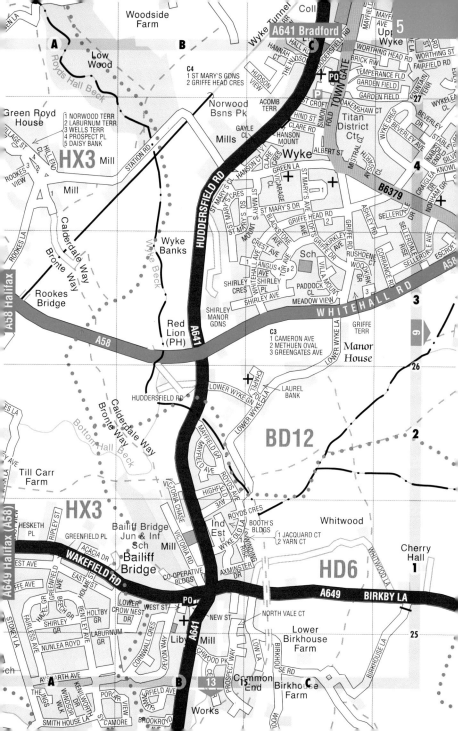

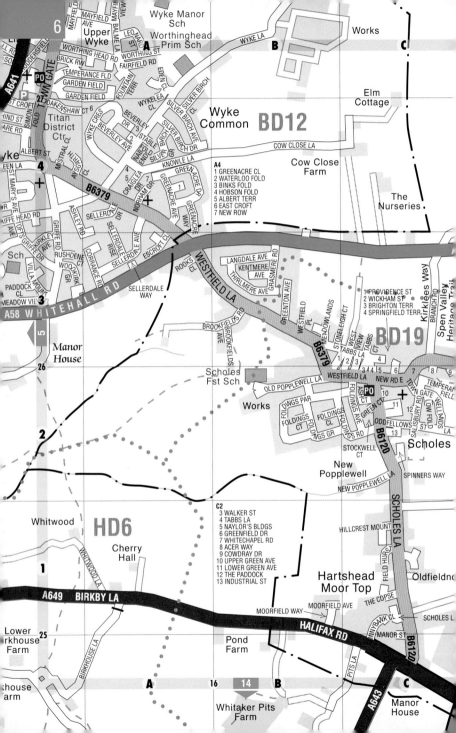

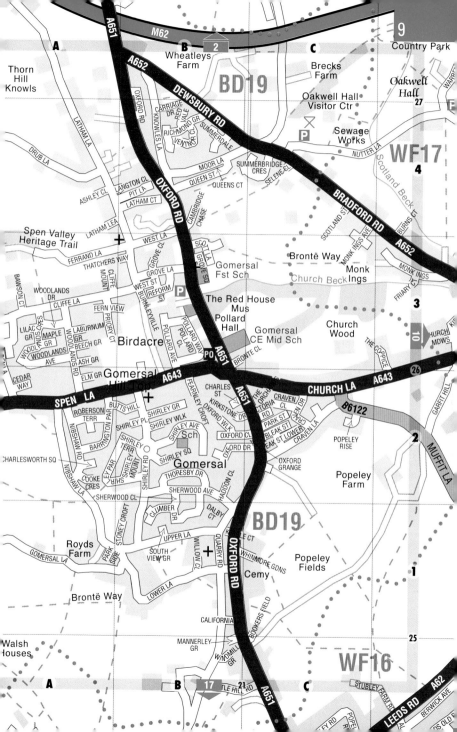

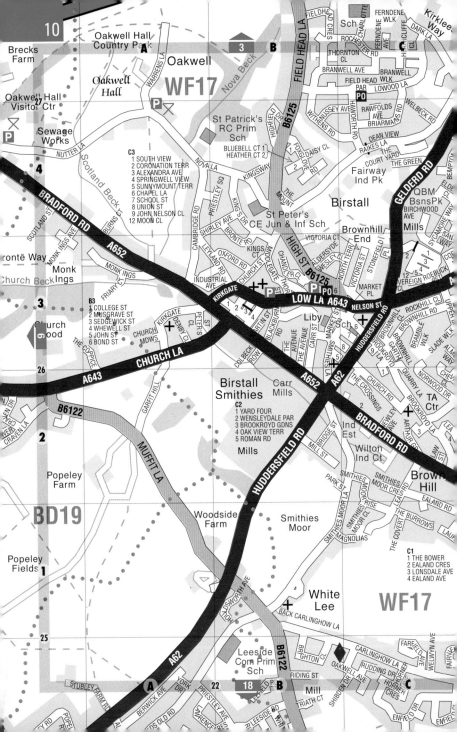

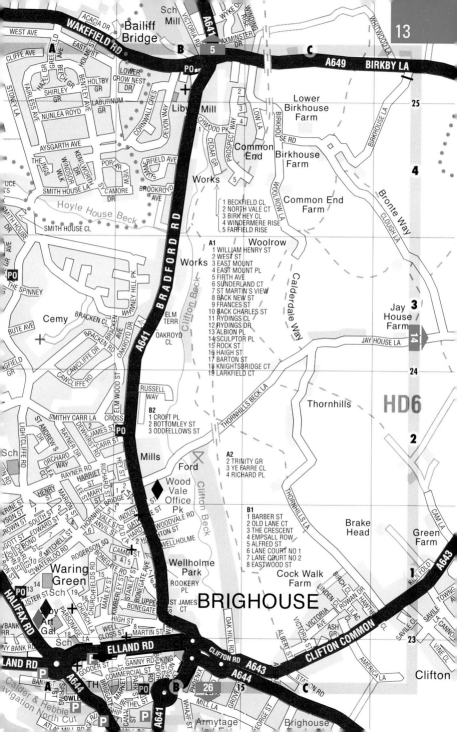

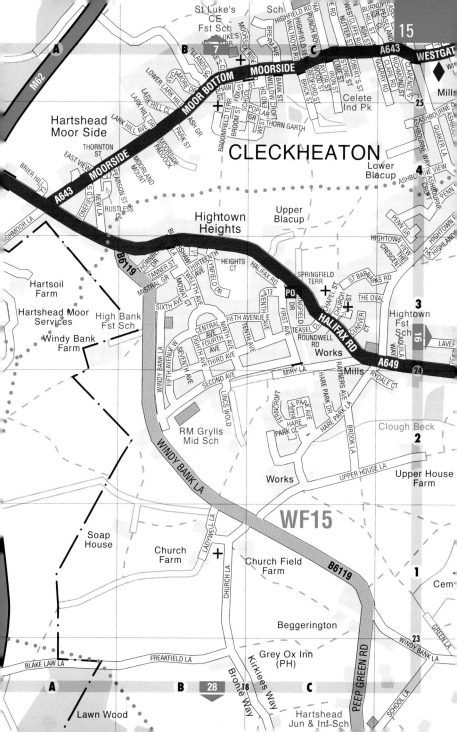

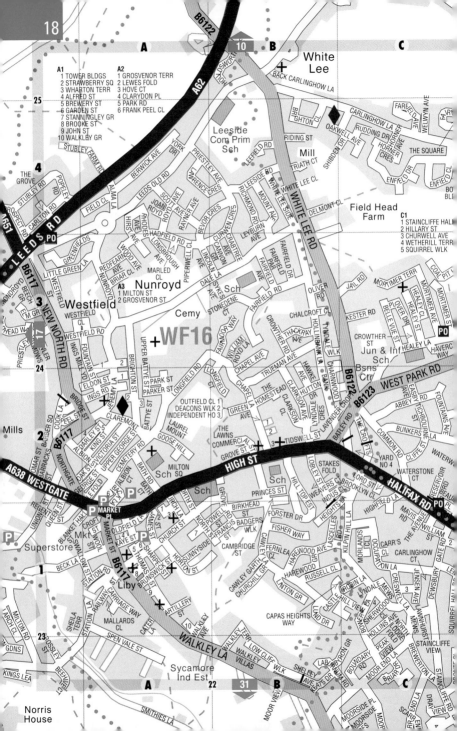

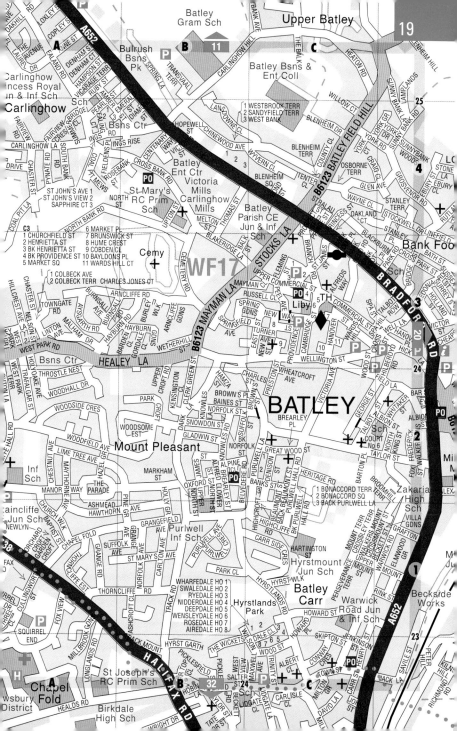

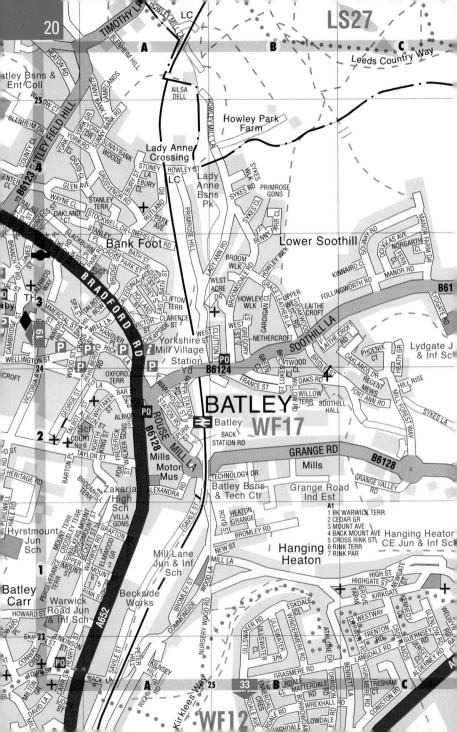

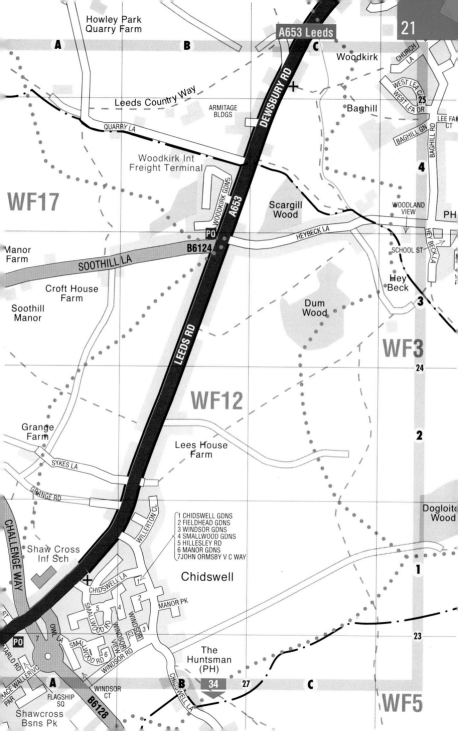

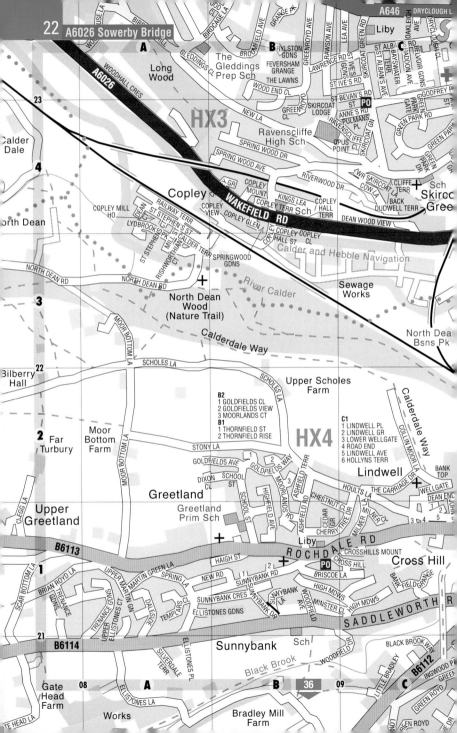

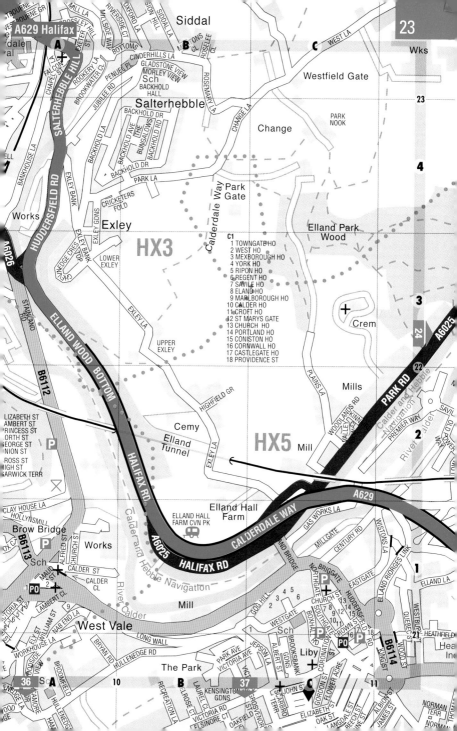

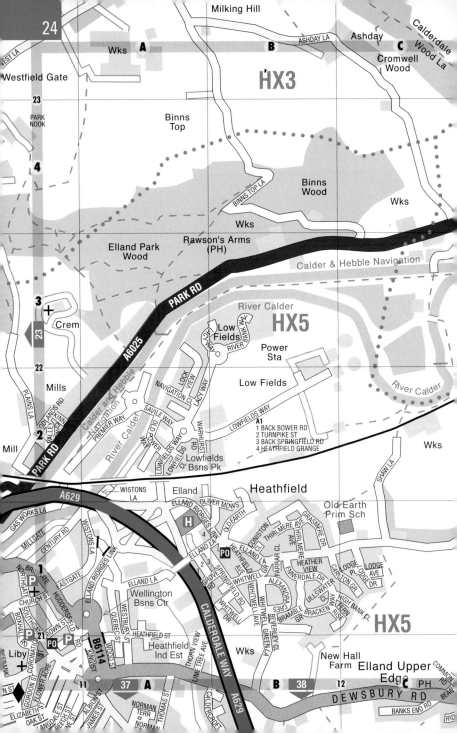

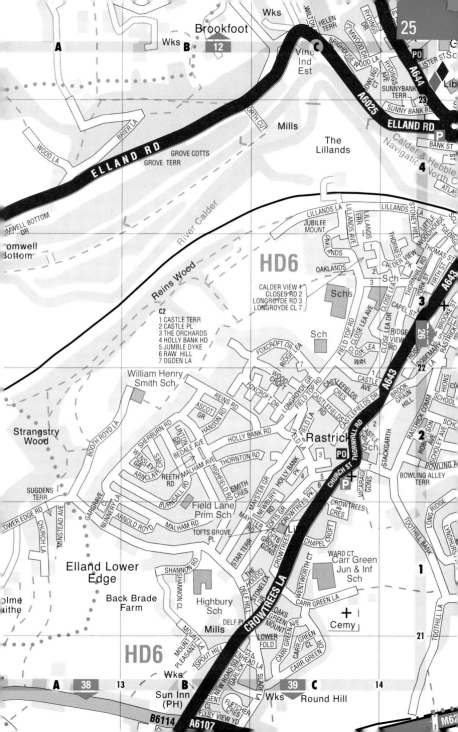

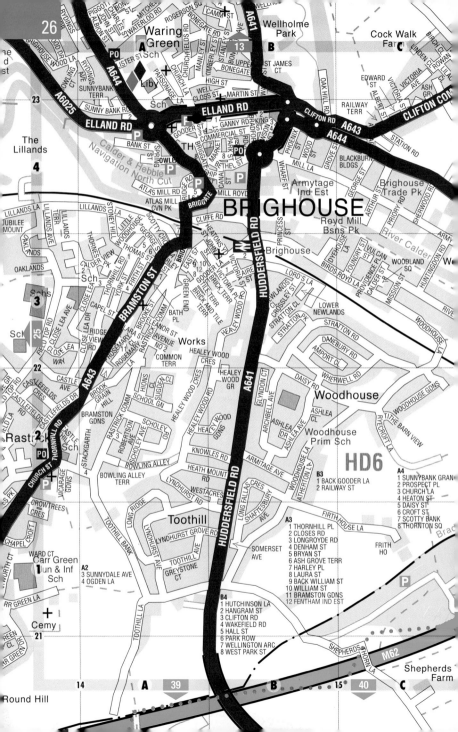

Church Farm

Church Field Farm

B6119

A

15

B

C

Church La

Beggerington

23

Grey Ox Inn (PH)

BLAKE LAW LA

FREAKFIELD LA

Kirklees Way

WF15

M62

Brontë Way

Hartshead Jun & Inf Sch

4

Lawn Wood

Hollin Wood

HARTSHEAD LA

Hartshe

CROSS HILL LA

Hartsh

3

Kirklees Hall

HD6

27

A644

22

Kirklees Park

Spen Valley Heritage Trail

HARTSHEAD HALL LA

Ha

Nun Brook

2

Bradley Hall Farm

Castle Hill

Robin Hood's Grave

Spen Valley Heritage Trail

Kirklees Way & Spen Valley Heritage Trail

Nun Brook House

WAKEFIELD RD

Park Bottom Wood

Three Nunns (PH)

A62

Mills

MA

1

LC

A644

21

Kirklees Way

LOWER QUARRY RD

River Calder

Sewage Wks

COOPER BRIDGE RD A62

HD5

CLIFTON SIDE

PARK LEA

STEEPLANDS

17

41

A

18

42

C

Sewage Wks

A6107

WOODLANDS CL

UPPER QUARRY RD

B

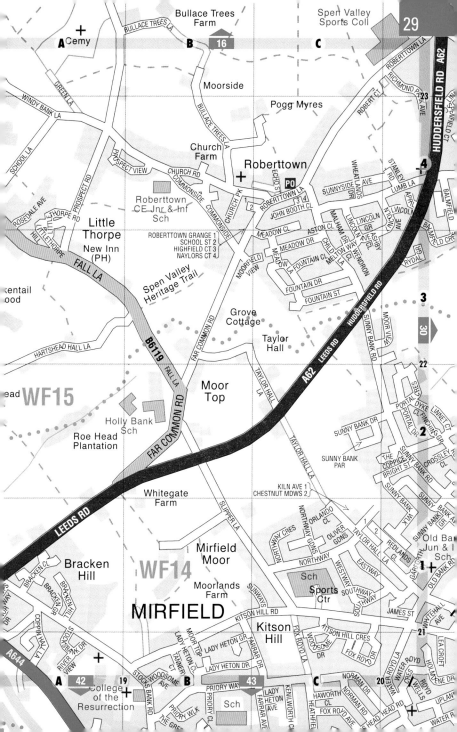

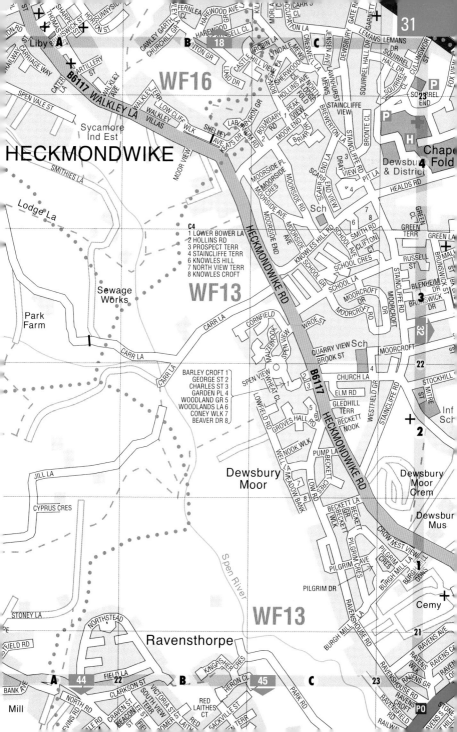

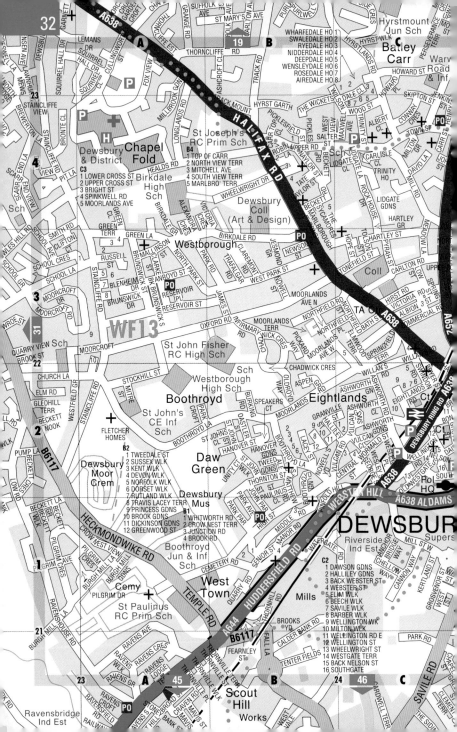

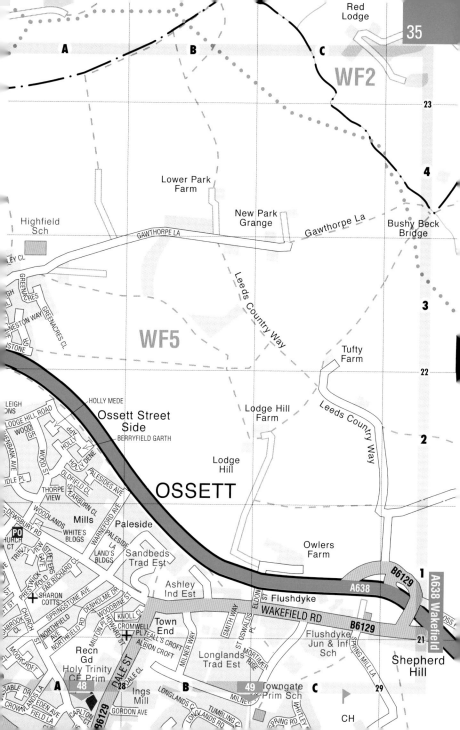

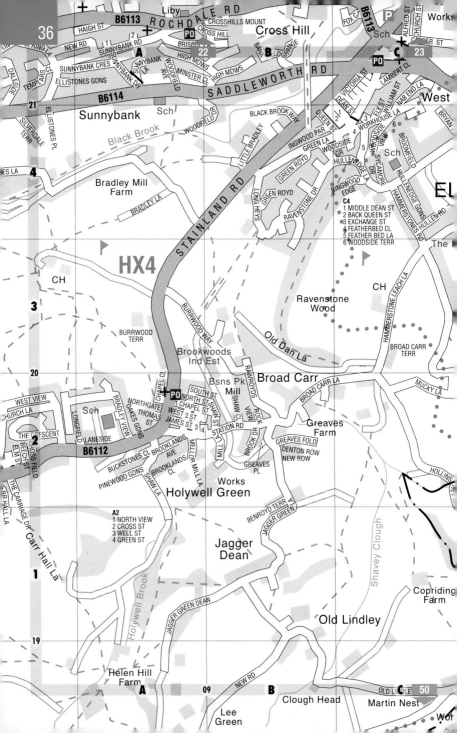

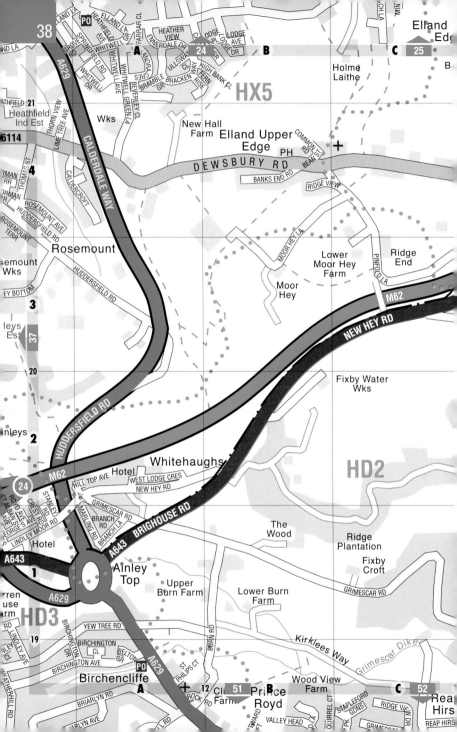

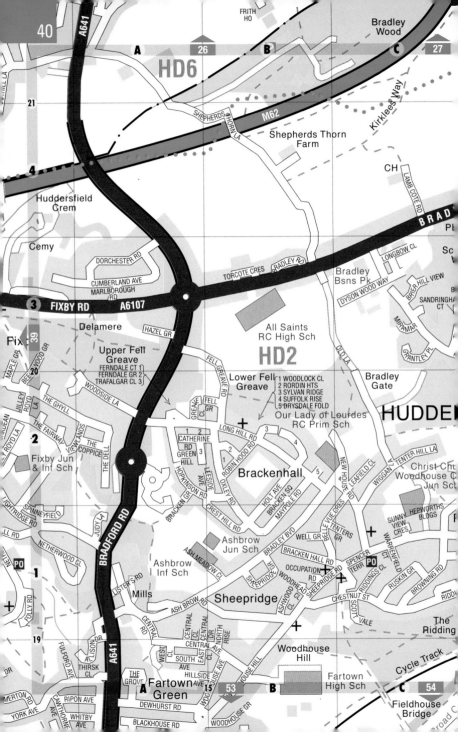

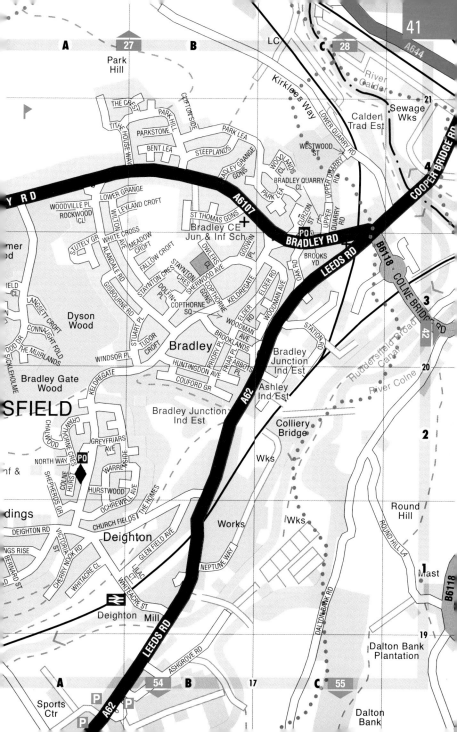

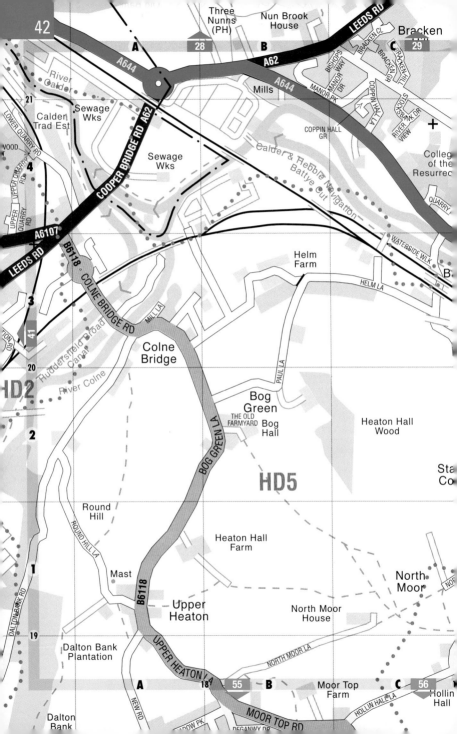

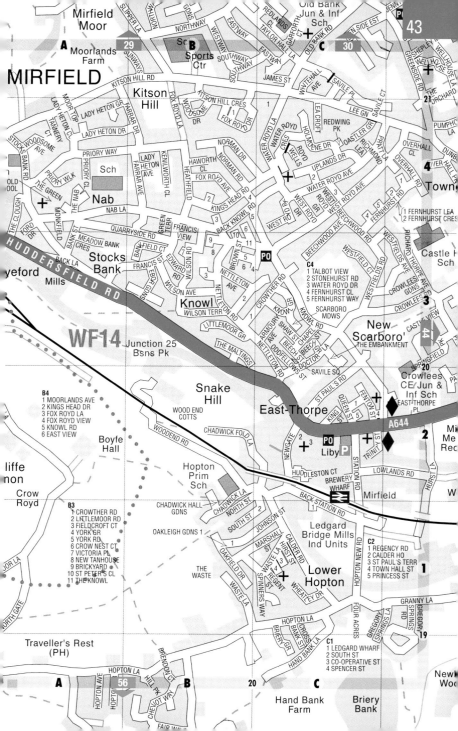

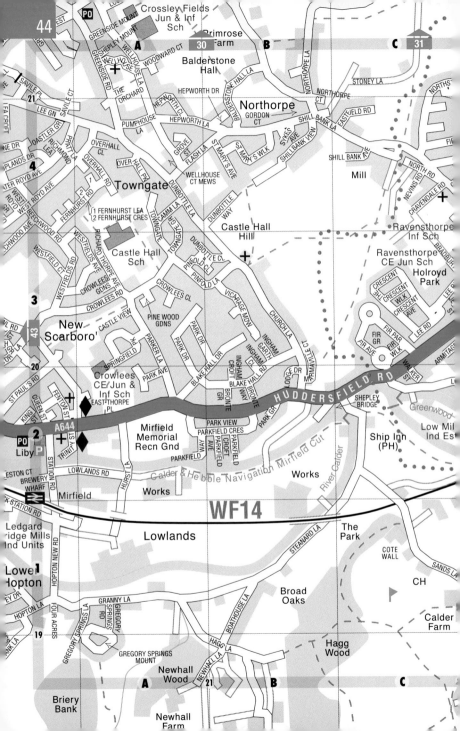

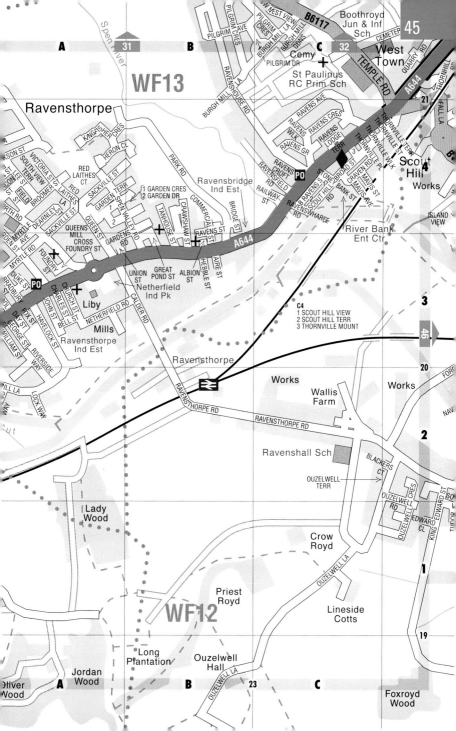

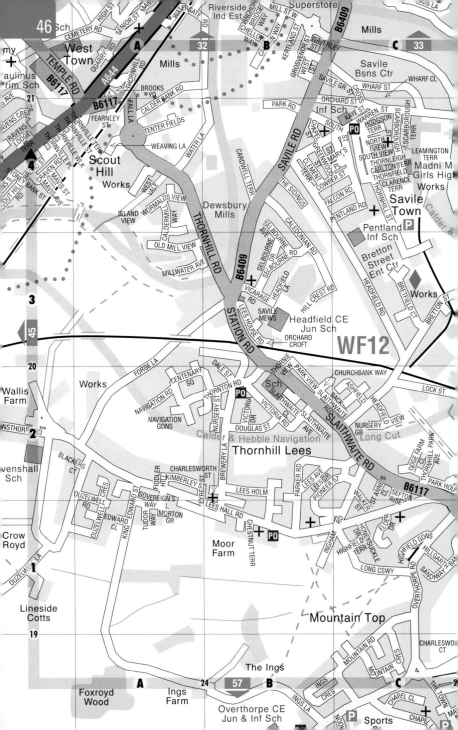

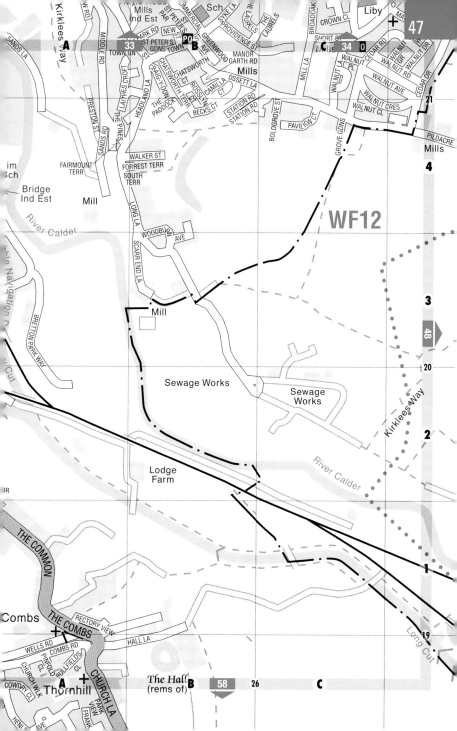

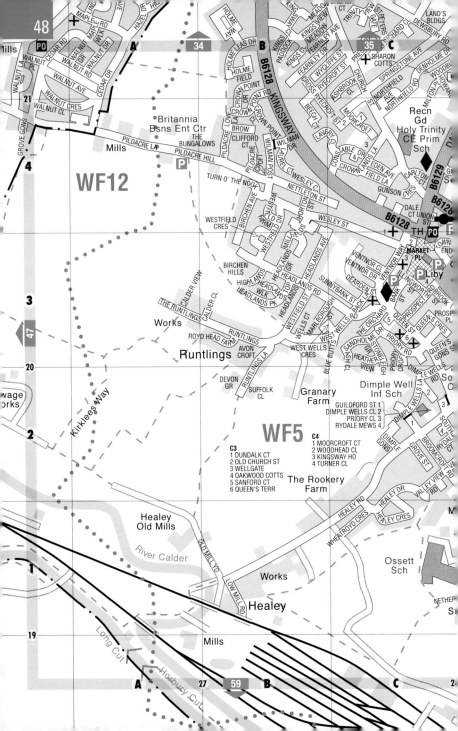

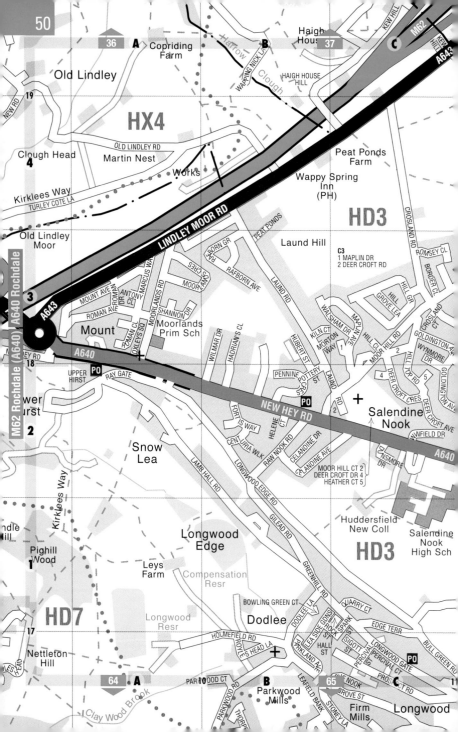

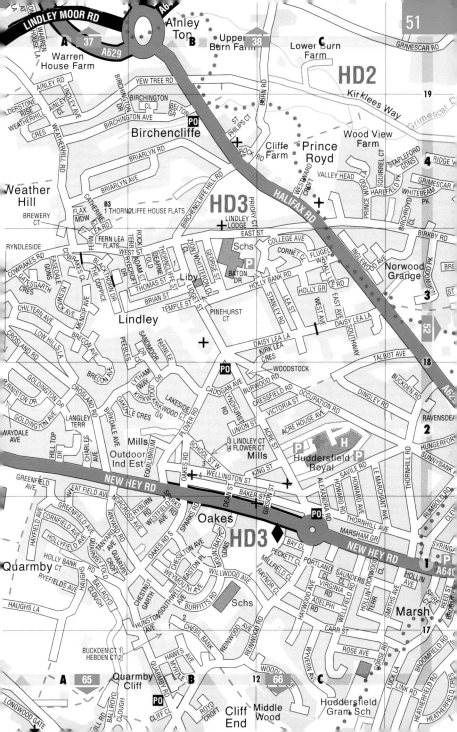

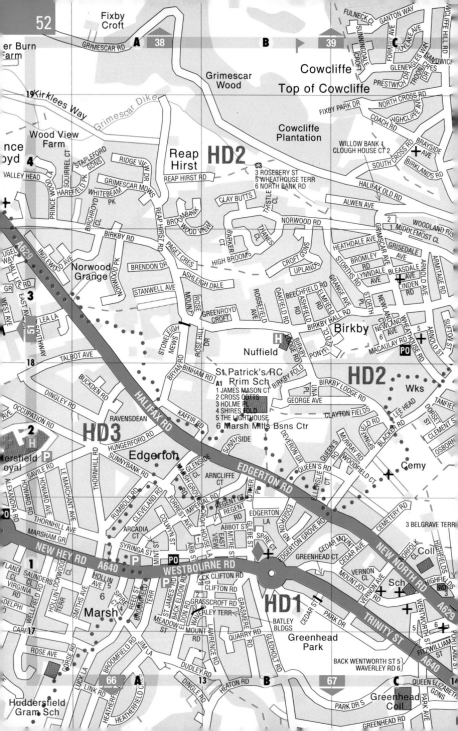

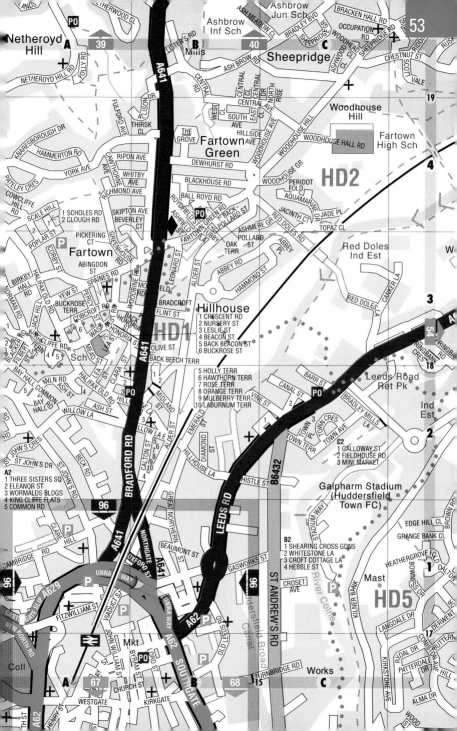

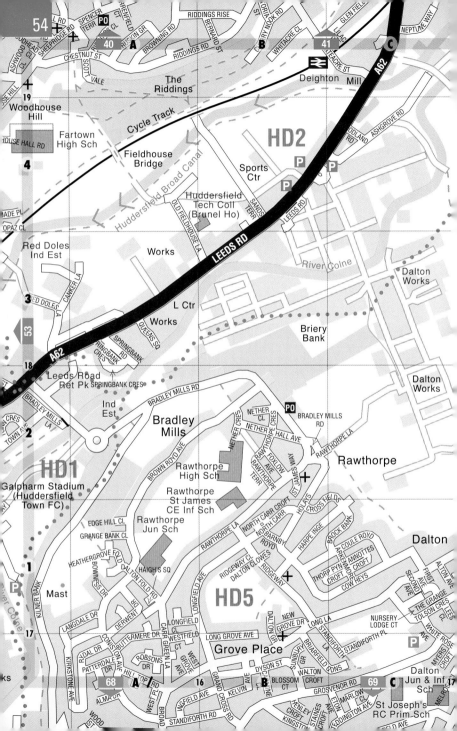

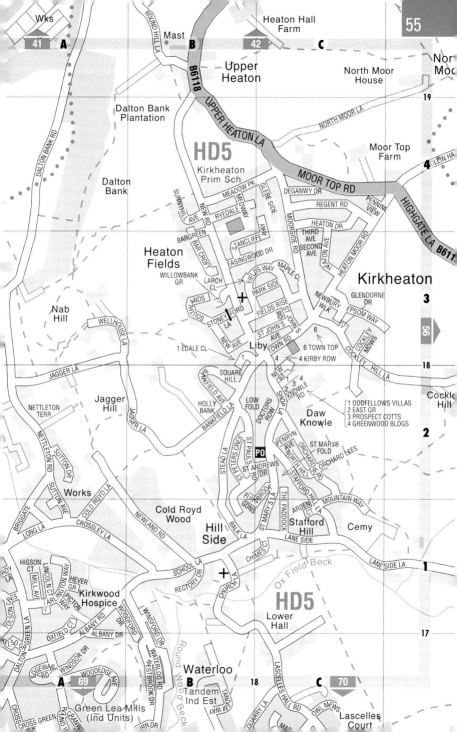

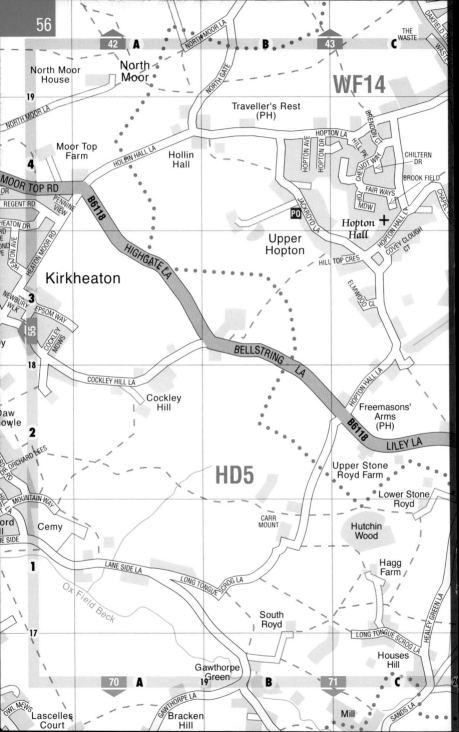

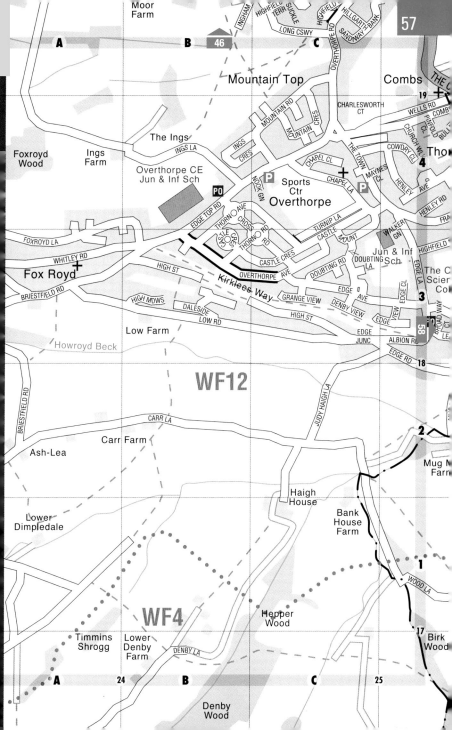

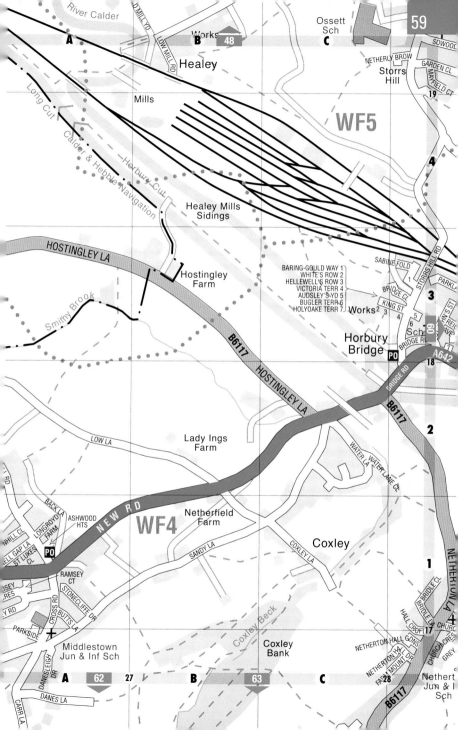

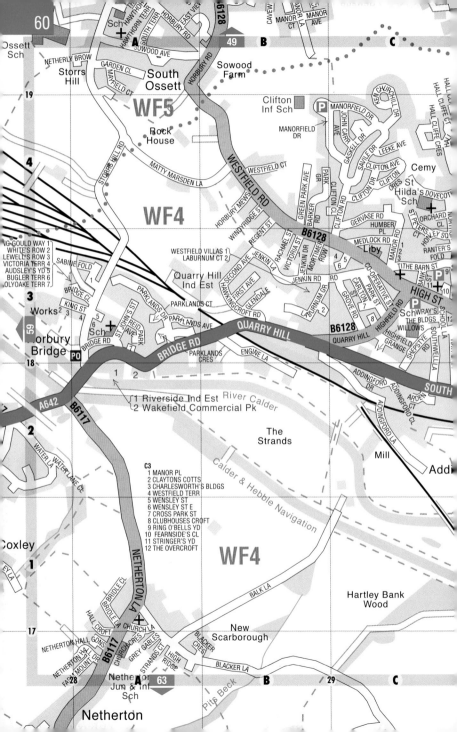

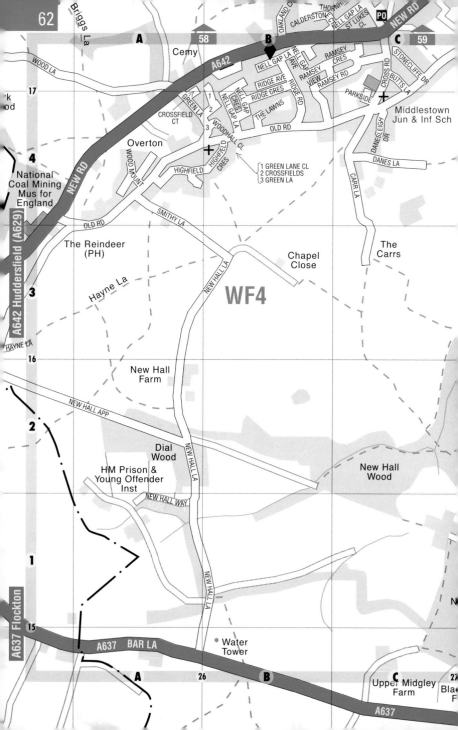

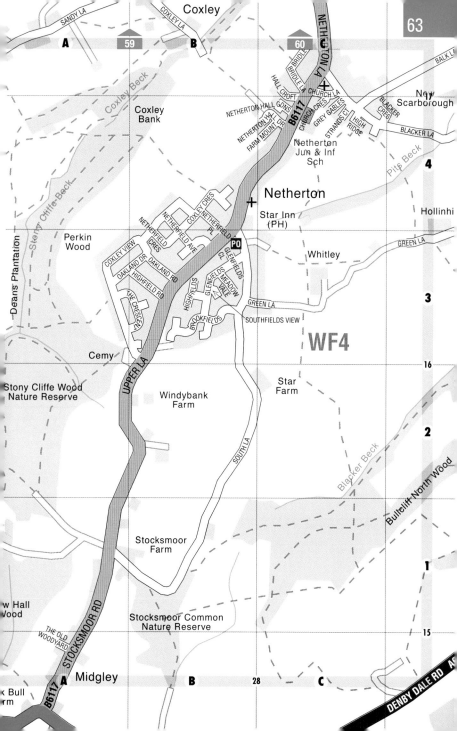

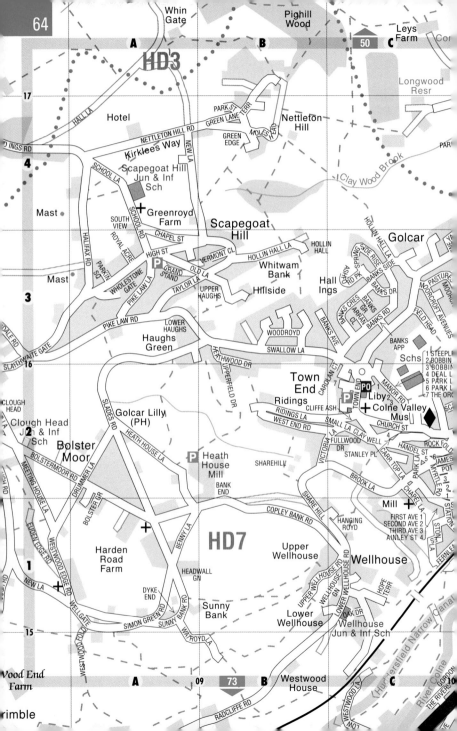

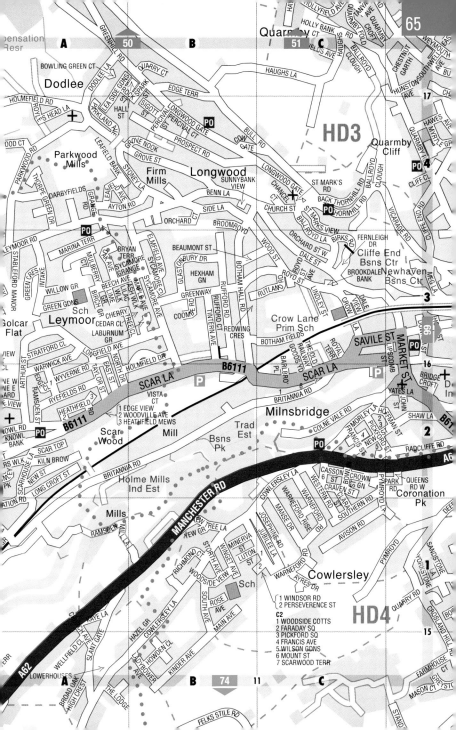

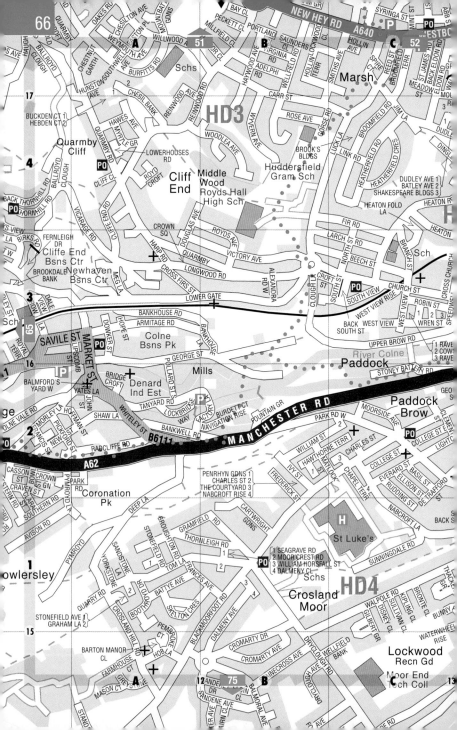

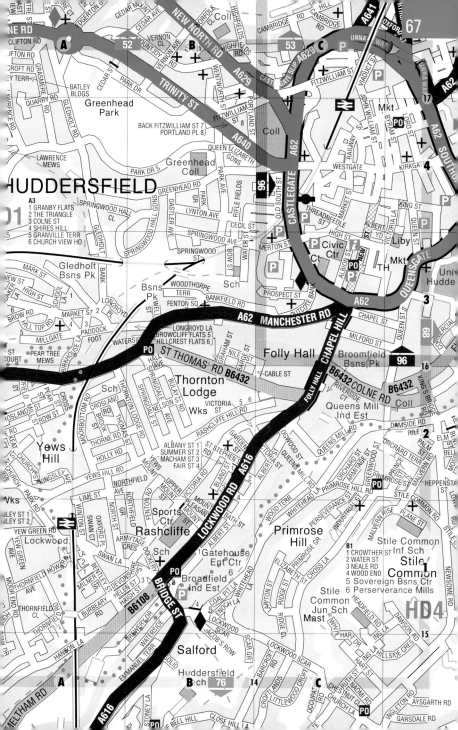

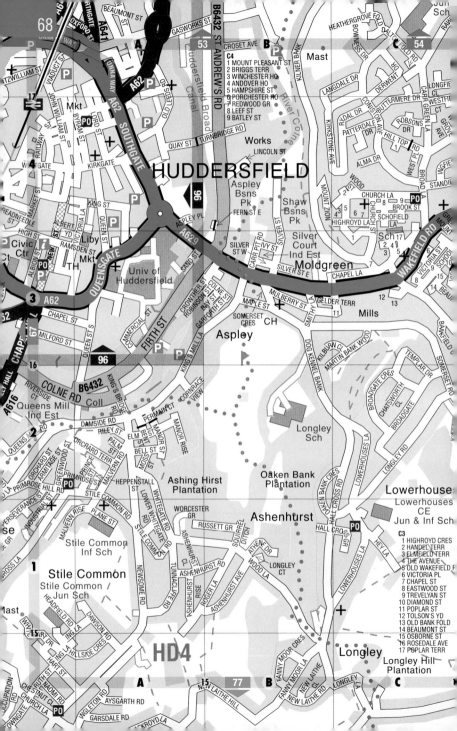

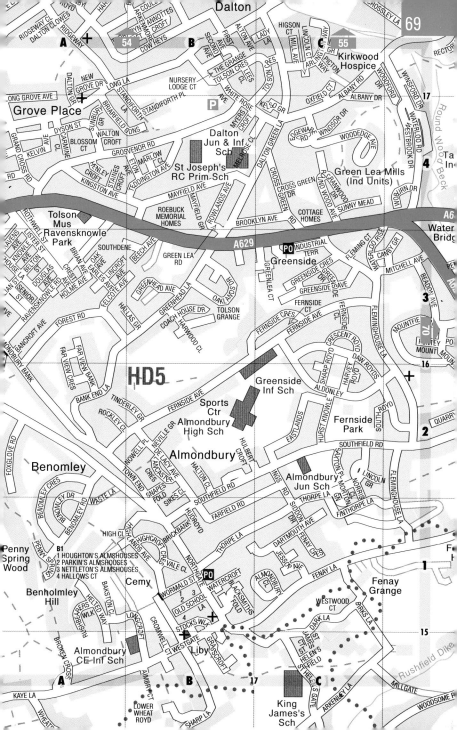

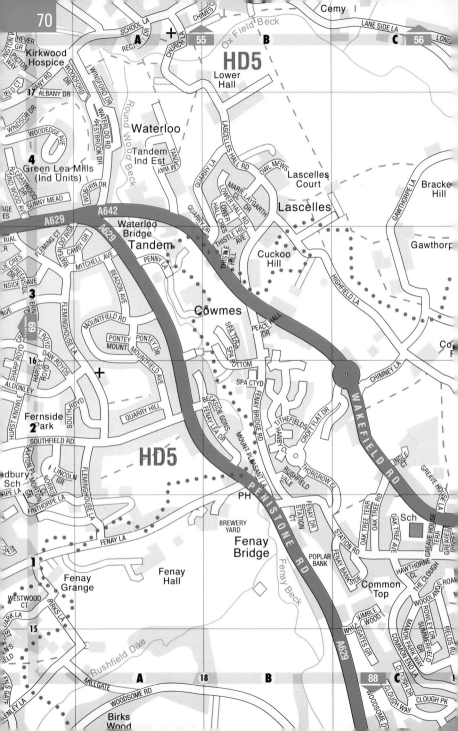

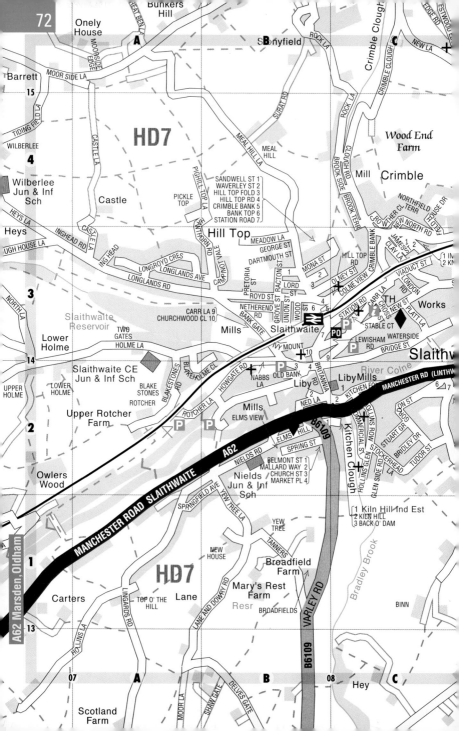

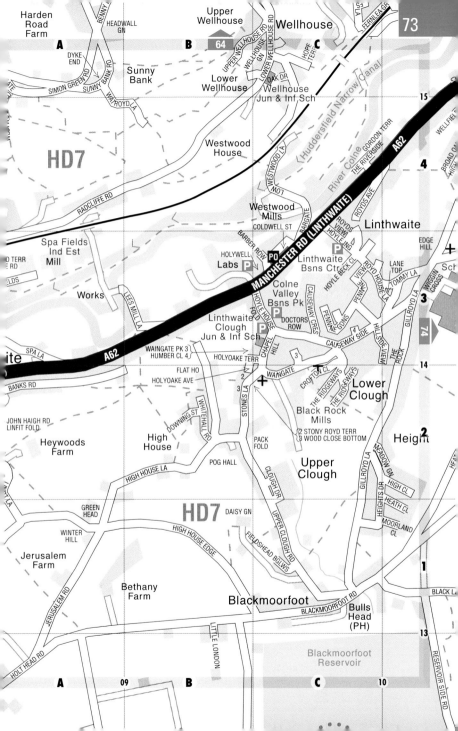

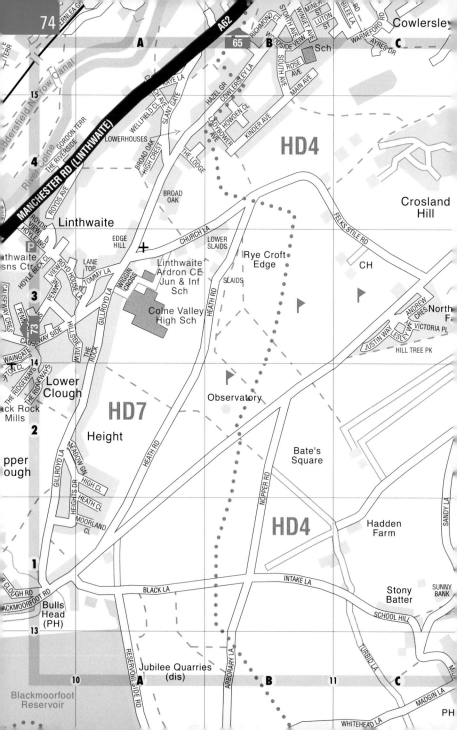

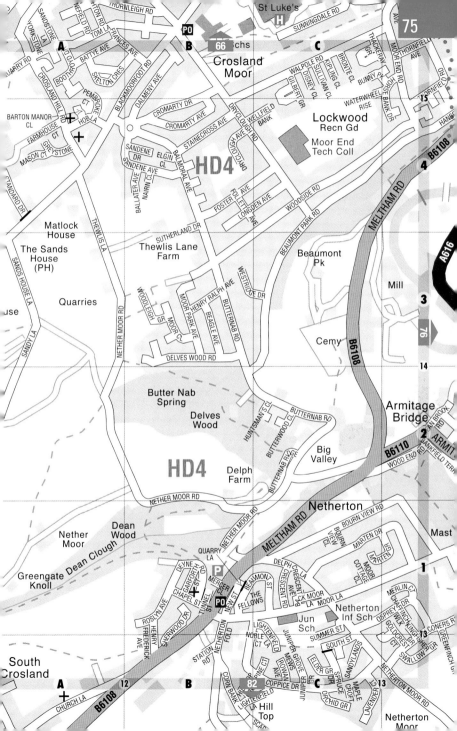

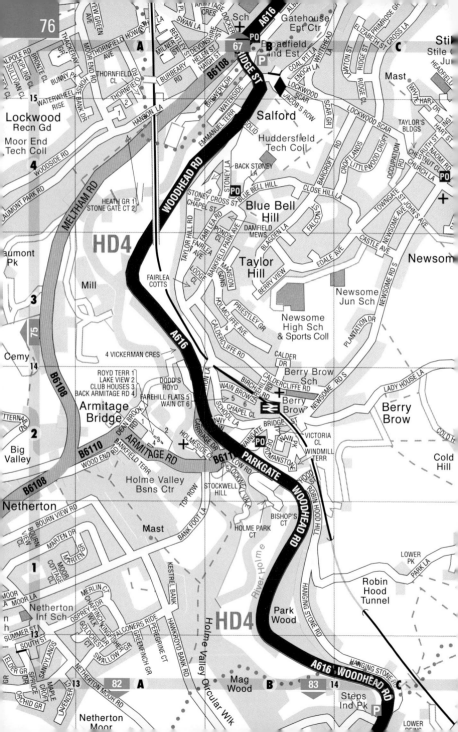

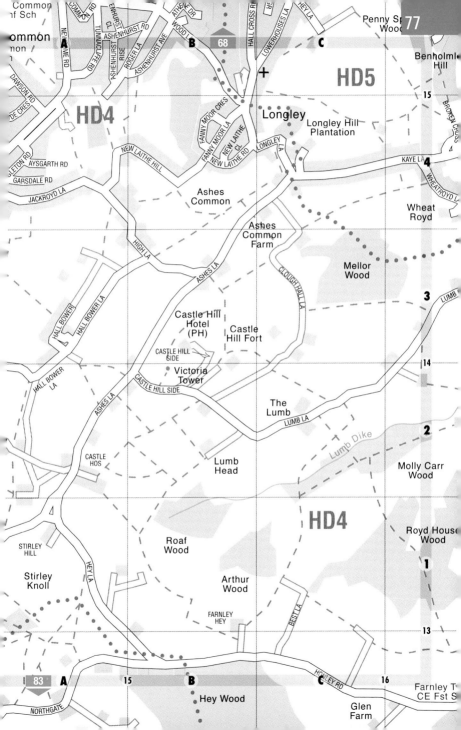

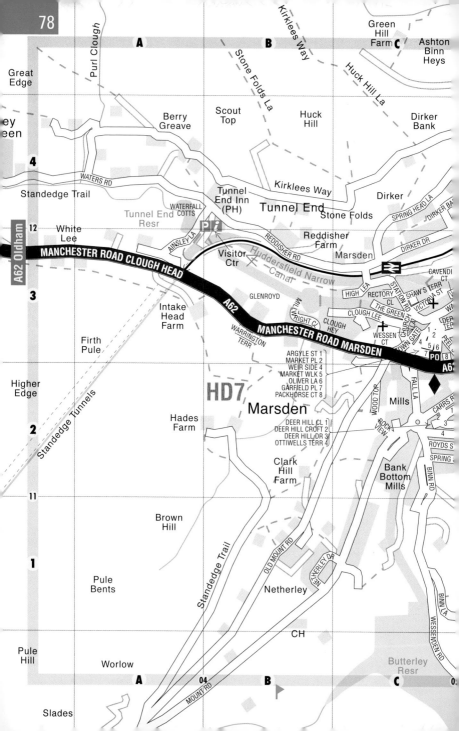

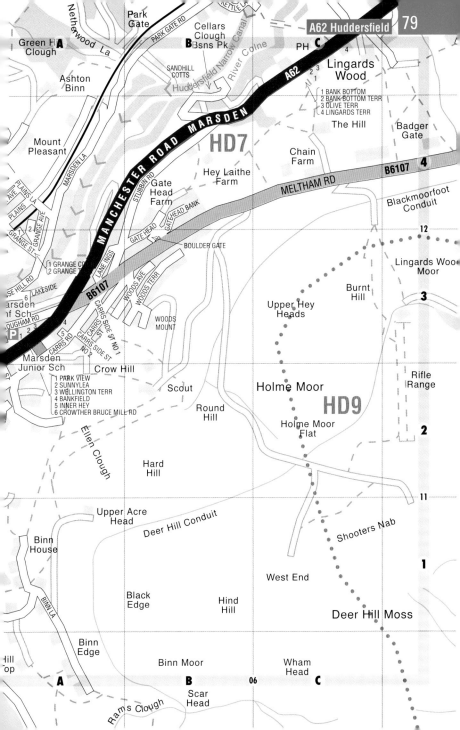

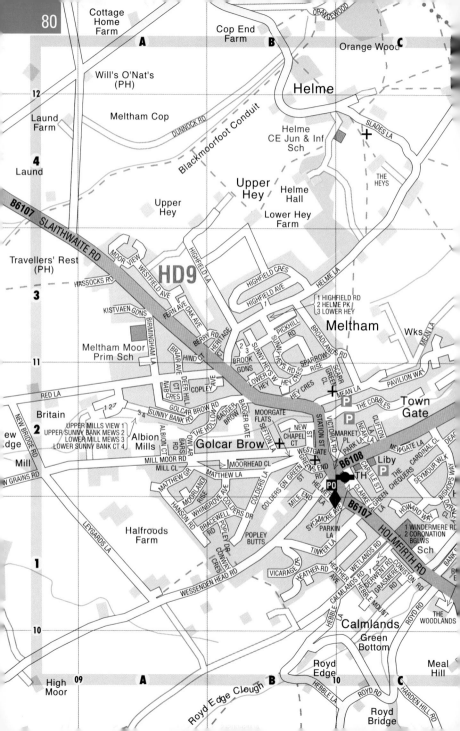

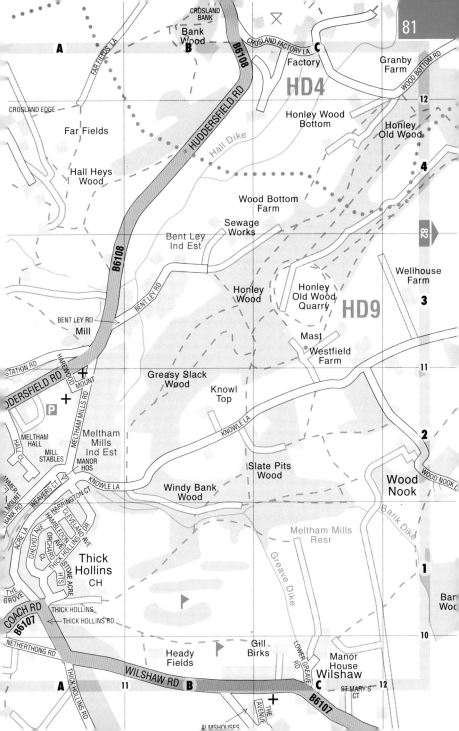

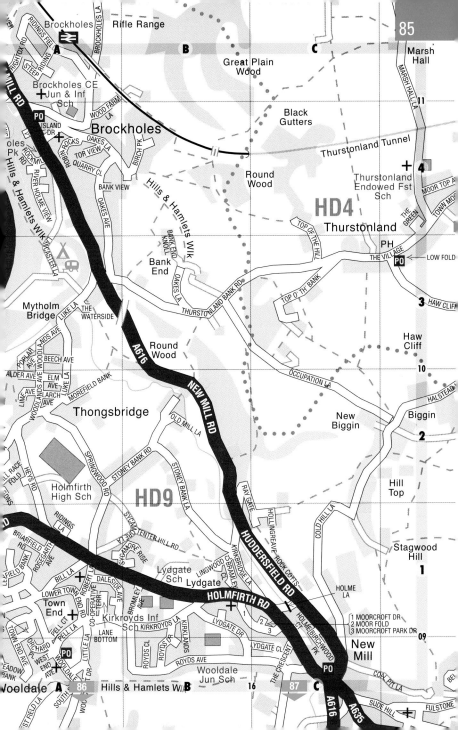

Brockholes
Rifle Range
Marsh Hall

RIDINGS FIELD
BROCKHOLES LA
Great Plain Wood
MARSH HALL LA
BRIGHTOX RD
STEEP RIDING
11
Brockholes CE Jun & Inf Sch
WOOD FARM LA
Black Gutters
PO
ISLAND DR
Brockholes
Thurstonland Tunnel
ROCKS
OAKES LA
BIRCH PK
TOR VIEW
ROBIN LA
QUARRY CL
4
LANCASTER LA
Thurstonland Endowed Fst Sch
MOOR TOP A
BANK VIEW
TOWN MO
OAKES AVE
THE GREEN
HD4
Hills & Hamlets Wik
Thurstonland
Hills & Hamlets Wik
BANK END KNOLL
PH
LOW FOLD
THE VILLAGE
PO
Bank End
OAKES LA
Mytholm Bridge
LUKE LA
THE WATERSIDE
THURSTONLAND BANK RD
3
HAW CLIFF
WOODLANDS AVE
TOP 0'TH' BANK
POPLAR AVE
BEECH AVE
Round Wood
TOP OF THE HILL
Haw Cliff
A616
LUKE LA
ALDER AVE
ELM AVE
LARCH AVE
10
WOODLANDS AVE
MOREFIELD BANK
OCCUPATION LA
LIME AVE
HALSTEAD
Thongsbridge
NEW MILL RD
Biggin
OLD MILL LA
New Biggin
2
SPRINGWOOD RD
STONEY BANK RD
Hill Top
HEY'S RD
Holmfirth High Sch
STONEY BANK LA
HD9
Stagwood Hill
RAY GATE
1
HUDDERSFIELD RD
COLD HILL LA
RIDINGS LA
SYCAMORE RISE
TENTER HILL RD
HOLLINGREAVE ROCK CROFTS
BRIARFIELD RD
ROSEGARTH AVE
Lydgate Sch
KIRKBRIDGE LA
Lydgate
HOLME LA
BILL LA
DALESIDE AVE
LINGWOOD CL
BRAMLEY LA
1 MOORCROFT DR
2 MOOR FOLD
3 MOORCROFT PARK DR
LOWER TOWN END RD
ROBERT LA
BROMLEY AVE
HOLMFIRTH RD
09
Town End
CO-OPERATIVE TERR
HOLME
LA
HOLME
BIRCHWOOD PK
PELL LA
Kirkroyds Inf Sch
KIRKROYDS LA
1
New Mill
PELL CT
LANE BOTTOM
KIRKLANDS
2
PO
ORCHARD
LITTLE LA
ROYDS CL
ROYDS DR
LYDGATE DR
3
COAL PIT LA
PO
WEST AVE
ROYDS AVE
LYDGATE CL
THE CRESCENT
SUDE HILL
MEADOW BANK
Wooldale Jun Sch
A616
FULSTONE
ST FIELD LA
Wooldale
A
86
Hills & Hamlets Wik
B
16
87
C
A635
BEL

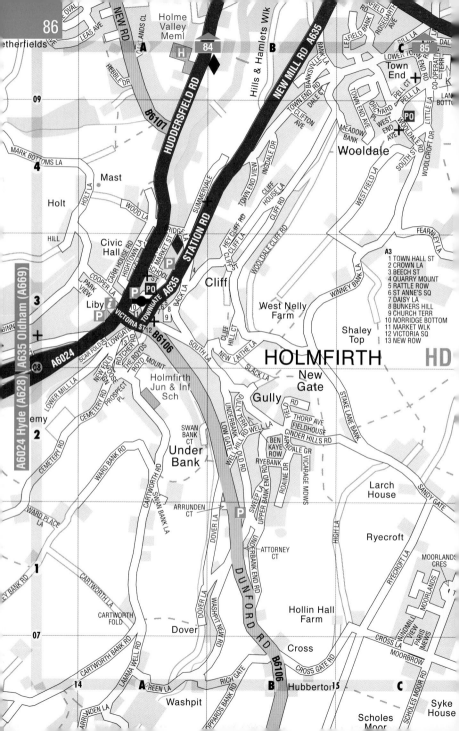

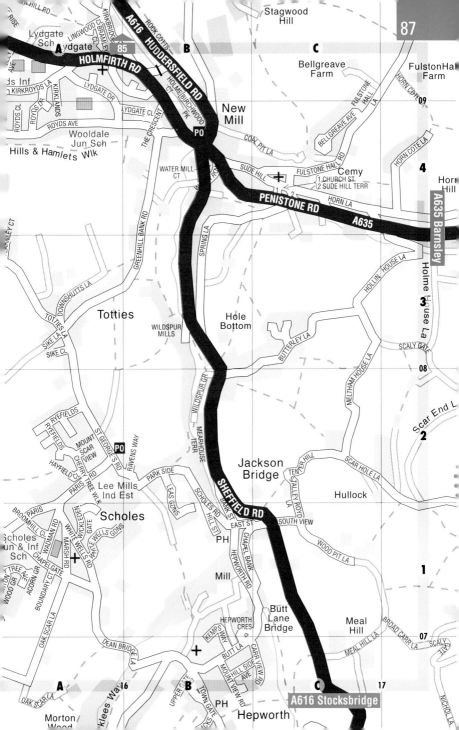

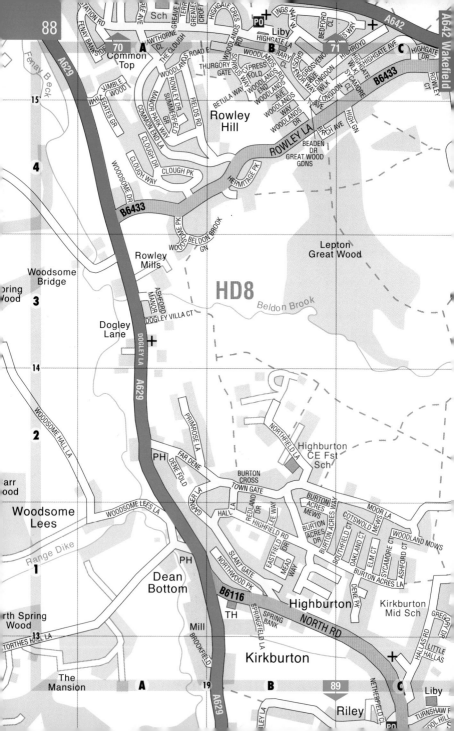

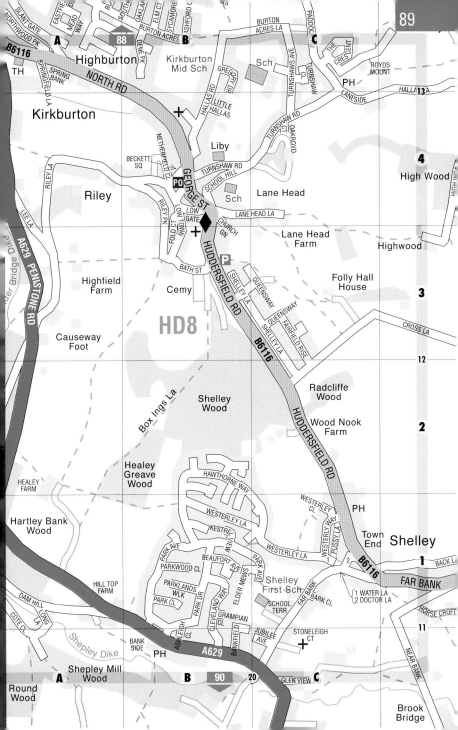

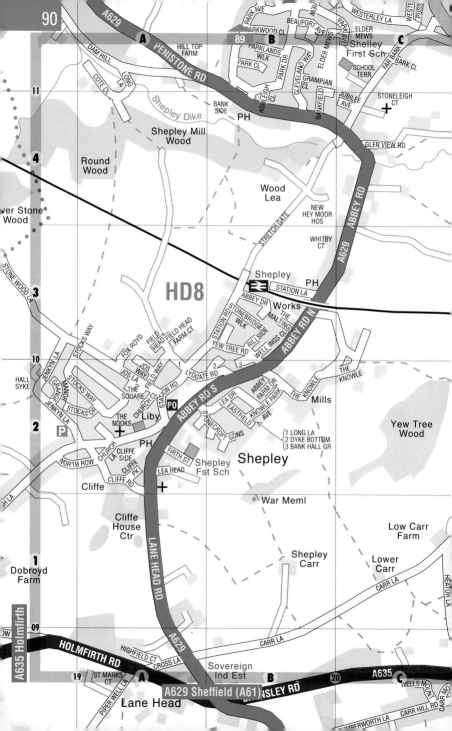

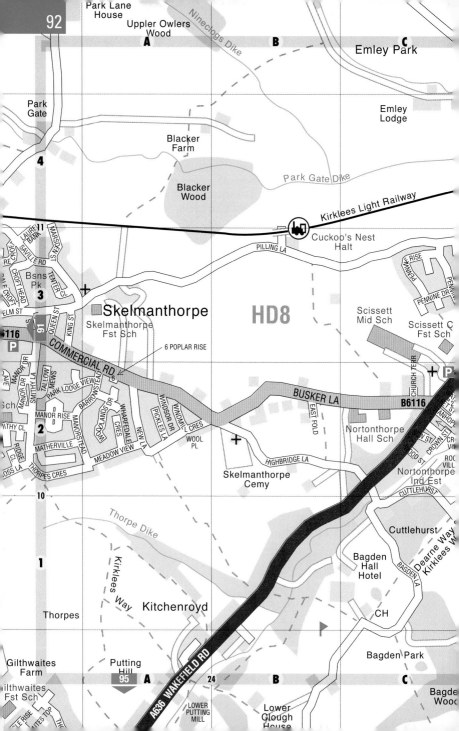

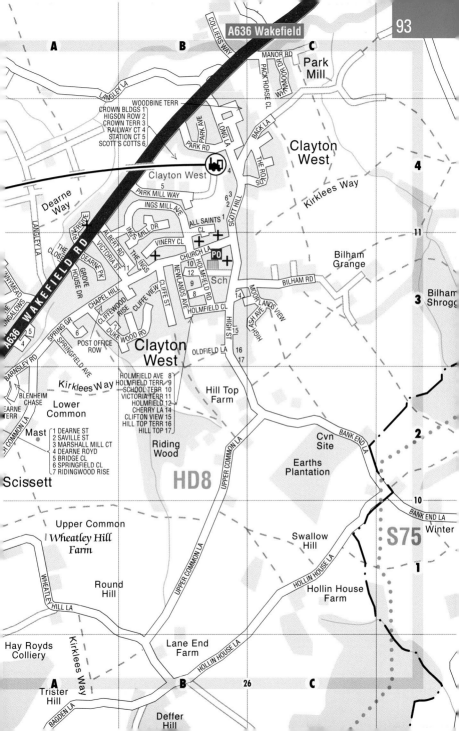

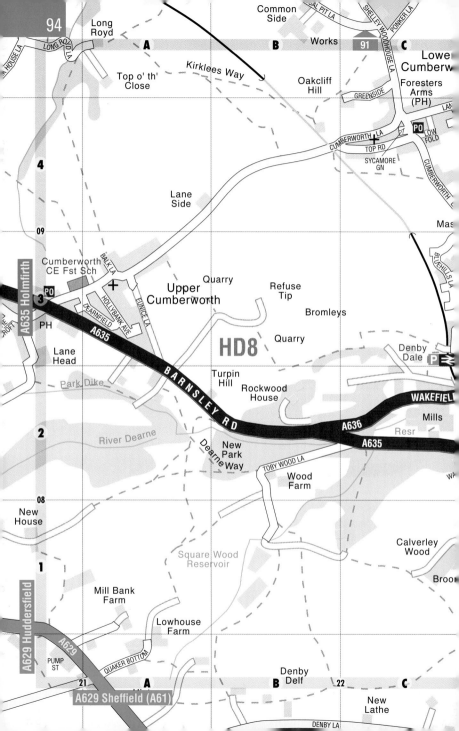

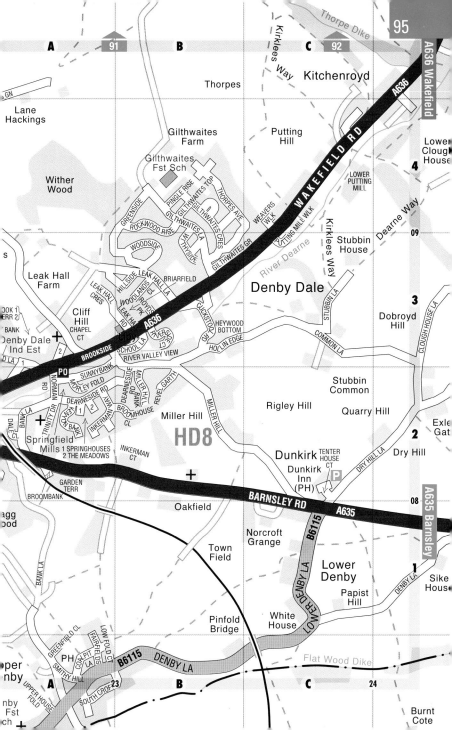

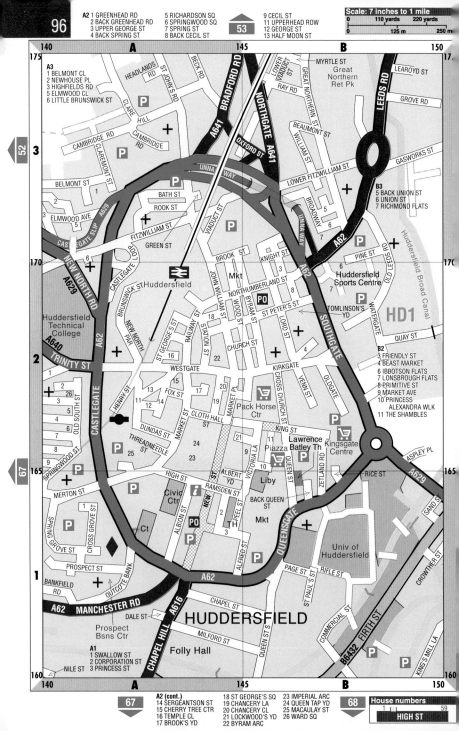

Index

Street names are listed alphabetically and show the locality, the Postcode district, the page number and a reference to the square in which the name falls on the map page

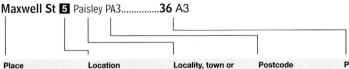

Maxwell St 5 Paisley PA3..............36 A3

Place name	Location number	Locality, town or village	Postcode district	Page and grid square
May be abbreviated on the map	Present when a number indicates the place's position in a crowded area of mapping	Shown when more than one place has the same name	District for the indexed place	Page number and grid reference for the standard mapping

Towns and villages are listed in CAPITAL LETTERS
Public and commercial buildings are highlighted in magenta. **Places of interest** are highlighted in blue with a star★

Abbreviations used in the index

Acad	**Academy**	Ct	**Court**	Hts	**Heights**	Pl	**Place**
App	**Approach**	Ctr	**Centre**	Ind	**Industrial**	Prec	**Precinct**
Arc	**Arcade**	Ctry	**Country**	Inst	**Institute**	Prom	**Promenade**
Ave	**Avenue**	Cty	**County**	Int	**International**	Rd	**Road**
Bglw	**Bungalow**	Dr	**Drive**	Intc	**Interchange**	Recn	**Recreation**
Bldg	**Building**	Dro	**Drove**	Junc	**Junction**	Ret	**Retail**
Bsns, Bus	**Business**	Ed	**Education**	L	**Leisure**	Sh	**Shopping**
Bvd	**Boulevard**	Emb	**Embankment**	La	**Lane**	Sq	**Square**
Cath	**Cathedral**	Est	**Estate**	Liby	**Library**	St	**Street**
Cir	**Circus**	Ex	**Exhibition**	Mdw	**Meadow**	Sta	**Station**
Cl	**Close**	Gd	**Ground**	Meml	**Memorial**	Terr	**Terrace**
Cnr	**Corner**	Gdn	**Garden**	Mkt	**Market**	TH	**Town Hall**
Coll	**College**	Gn	**Green**	Mus	**Museum**	Univ	**University**
Com	**Community**	Gr	**Grove**	Orch	**Orchard**	Wk, Wlk	**Walk**
Comm	**Common**	H	**Hall**	Pal	**Palace**	Wr	**Water**
Cott	**Cottage**	Ho	**House**	Par	**Parade**	Yd	**Yard**
Cres	**Crescent**	Hospl	**Hospital**	Pas	**Passage**		
Cswy	**Causeway**	HQ	**Headquarters**	Pk	**Park**		

Index of towns, villages, streets, hospitals, industrial estates, railway stations, schools, shopping centres, universities and places of interest

A

Abbey Dr HD8 . . . . **90** B3
Abbey Farm Dr HD8. . **90** B2
Abbey Pl HD2. . . . . **53** C3
Abbey Rd
 Batley WF17 . . . . **18** C2
 Huddersfield HD2. . . . **53** B3
 Shepley HD8. . . . . **90** C4
Abbey Rd N HD8 . . . . . **90** B3
Abbey Rd S HD8 . . . . . **90** A2
Abbots Pl HD2. . . . . . . **41** B3
Abbot St HD1. . . . . **52** B1
Abingdon St HD2 . . . . **53** A3
Acacia Dr HX3. . . . . **5** A1
Acer Way 8 BD19 . . . . . **6** C2
Acomb Terr BD12 . . . . . **5** C4
Acorn Gr HD9 . . . . . . **87** A1
Acre House Ave
 HD3. . . . . **51** C2
Acre La HD9 . . . . **81** A1
Acre St HD3 . . . . **51** C2
Acton Flat La HD3 . . **37** C1
Adam Ct HD3. . . . . . . **51** B3

Adams Ct HD6 . . . . . . **12** B3
ADDINGFORD **60** C2
Addingford Cl WF4 . . **60** C2
Addingford Dr WF4 . . **60** C2
Addingford La WF4 . . **60** C2
Addison Ct WF4 . . . . . **61** B4
Addle Croft La HD8 . . **71** B3
Adelphi Rd HD3 . . . . . **51** C1
Ainley St
Adwalton Cl BD11 . . . . **3** A3
Adwalton Gn BD11. . . . **3** A3
ADWALTON **4** A4
Ainley Bottom HX5 . . **37** C3
Ainley Cl HD3. . . . . . . **51** A4
Ainley Pk HD7 . . . . . . **65** A2
Ainley Rd HD3 . . . . . . **37** C1
Aimleys Ind Est HX5 . . **37** C3
Ainley St
 10 Elland HX5. . . . . . **37** B4
 Huddersfield HD7. . . . **64** C2
AINLEY TOP **38** A1
Ainsley La HD7 . . . . . **78** A3
Airedale Ho HX3. . . . . **32** C4
Aire St
 Brighouse HD6 . . . . . **26** B3
 Dewsbury WF13 . . . . **45** B3

Alandale Rd HD2 . . . . **41** A3
Albany Dr HD5. . . . . . **69** C4
Albany Rd HD5 . . . . . . **55** A1
Albany St HD1 . . . . . . **67** B2
Albert Cl WF17 . . . . . . **32** C4
Albert Cres BD11 . . . . . **2** B2
Albert Pl WF12 . . . . . **33** C4
Albert Rd HD8 . . . . . . **93** A3
Albert St
 Bradford, Wyke
  BD12 . . . . **5** C4
 Brighouse HD6 . . . . . **26** C4
 Cleckheaton BD19 . . . **8** A2
 Elland HX5 . . . . **37** B4
 Huddersfield HD1. . . . **67** B1
 Liversedge WF15 . . . . **17** C1
Albert Terr 5 BD12 . . . **6** A4
Albert Way BD11 . . . . . **2** B2
Albert Yd HD1 . . . . . . **96** A1
Albion Croft WF5 . . . . **49** A4
Albion Ct
 Batley WF16 . . . . **18** A2
 Meltham HD9 . . . . . . **80** A2
Albion Pl 18 HD6 . . . . **13** A1
Albion Rd WF12 . . . . . **58** A3

Albion St
 Batley, Heckmondwike
  WF16. . . . . **18** A2
 Batley WF17 . . . . **20** A2
 Brighouse HD6 . . . . . **13** A1
 Cleckheaton BD19 . . . . **8** B1
 Dewsbury, Ravensthorpe
  WF13. . . . . **45** B3
 Dewsbury WF13 . . . . **32** C3
 Elland HX5 . . . . **37** C4
 Huddersfield HD1. . . . **96** A1
 1 Liversedge WF15 . . **17** B2
Aldams Rd WF12 . . . . **32** C1
Alderney Rd WF12 . . . **33** C4
Alder St HD1, HD2. . . **53** B3
Alderstone Rise
 HD3. . . . . **51** A4
Aldersyde WF17 . . . . . **10** B3
Aldonley HD5. . . . . . . **69** C2
Alegar St HD5 . . . . . . **26** C4
Alexandra Ave 3
 WF17 . . . . **10** C3
Alexandra Cres
 Dewsbury WF13 . . . . **32** A4

Alexandra Rd
 continued
Alexandra Rd
 Batley WF17 . . . . **20** A2
 Huddersfield HD3. . . . **51** C1
Alexandra Rd W
 HD3. . . . . **66** B3
Alexandra St 4
 WF15 . . . . **17** A2
Alfred St
 4 Batley,
  Heckmondwike
  WF16. . . . . **18** A1
 Batley, Mount Pleasant
  WF17. . . . . **19** B2
 5 Brighouse HD6 . . . **13** B1
 1 Dewsbury WF13 . . **33** B3
 Elland HX4 . . . . **23** A1
 Huddersfield HD1. . . . **96** A1
 3 Liversedge WF15 . **17** B2

Alfreds Way WF17 ...19 C3
Alice St **2** BD19 .....8 A2
Allen Croft BD11.....2 A3
Allison Dr HD2 ......53 B4
All Saints' CE Jun & Inf
  Sch HX3............22 C4
All Saints Cl HD8 ....93 B4
All Saints RC High Sch
  HD2.................40 B3
Alma Dr HD5 .....68 C4
Alma La WF16 .....18 A4
Alma St **3** HX5...37 C4
ALMONDBURY.....69 B2
Almondbury Bank
  HD5.................69 A3
Almondbury Cl HD5..69 C1
Almondbury High Sch
  HD5.................69 B2
Almondbury Jun Sch
  HD5.................69 C2
Almondroyd WF16...17 C3
Almond Way WF17...10 C3
Almscliffe Ave
  WF12 ....33 B2
Almshouses HD9....84 B2
Alpine Cl WF17 ....19 B2
Alton Ave HD5.....54 C1
Alwen Ave HD2 ....52 C4
Amber St WF17....19 A4
Amberthorne BD11 ..2 B3
America La HD6.....26 C4
Amport Cl HD6....26 B3
Anchor Bridge Way
  WF12..............32 C1
Anchor Pl HD6 ....27 A2
Anchor St HD1.....96 B3
Andover Ho **4** HD5..68 C4
Andrew Cres HD4...74 C3
Angus Ave BD12 ...5 C3
Anne St WF17 .....11 A1
Annottes Croft HD5..54 C1
Anroyd St WF13....32 A3
Antony Cl HD3......50 A3
Anvil St HD6.......13 A1
Apple Cl WF17.....11 A4
April Ct WF15......30 A4
Aquamarine Dr HD2 .53 C4
Aquila Way WF15 ...16 A3
Arcade The **5**
  WF12..............33 A2
Arcadia Ct HD1.....52 A1
Archbell Ave HD6...26 B2
Archer Rd HD6.....27 A3
Arden Ct
  Horbury WF4 .....60 C2
  Kirkheaton HD5....55 C1
Argyle St HD7 .....78 C3
Arkenmore HD5 ....54 C1
Arkwright Ct **9**
  WF15..............17 A3
Arley Cl HD9........84 A2
Arlington Way HD5 ..55 A1
Armitage Ave HD6...26 B2
Armitage Bldgs
  WF12..............21 B4
ARMITAGE BRIDGE..76 A2
Armitage Cl HD8...91 C3
Armitage Rd
  Huddersfield, Armitage
    Bridge HD4.......76 A2
  Huddersfield, Birkby
    HD2..............21 A2
  Huddersfield HD3...66 A3
Armitage St
  Dewsbury WF13....44 C3
  Huddersfield HD4...67 C2
Armoury Ave WF14 ..43 C3

Armytage Cres HD1..67 B1
Armytage Ind Est
  HD6................26 B4
Armytage Rd HD6 ..27 A3
Armytage Way HD6 .27 A3
Arncliffe Cres HD6...25 B2
Arncliffe Ct HD1....52 B1
Arncliffe Gdns
  WF17...............19 B3
Arncliffe Rd WF17 ..19 B3
Arndale Gr HD9......86 B2
Arnold Ave HD2 ....52 C3
Arnold Royd HD6 ...25 B1
Arnold St
  Huddersfield HD2...52 C3
  Liversedge WF15 ...17 A2
Arran Cl HD7........64 C3
Arrunden Ct HD9 ...86 B1
Arthur Gr WF17.....10 C2
Arthur St
  Brighouse HD6 .....26 C4
  Huddersfield HD7...65 A2
Artillery St HD4.....18 A1
Arundel Cl WF17....11 B4
Arundel Wlk WF17...11 B3
Ascot Gr HD6.......25 B2
Ashbourne Ave
  BD19...............16 A4
Ashbourne Croft
  BD19...............16 A4
Ashbourne Dr BD19..16 A4
Ashbourne Gdns
  BD19...............16 A4
Ashbourne View
  BD19...............16 A4
Ashbourne Way
  BD19...............16 A4
Ashbrook Cl WF5....35 A1
Ashbrow Inf Sch
  HD2................40 A1
Ashbrow Jun Sch
  HD2................40 B1
Ash Brow Rd HD2...40 A1
Ashby Cl WF15......29 C3
Ash Cl WF5.........48 C3
Ashcroft Cl WF17 ...19 B1
Ash Ct BD19........6 C2
ASHENHURST.....68 B1
Ashenhurst Ave
  HD4................68 B1
Ashenhurst Cl HD4 .68 A1
Ashenhurst Rd HD4..68 A1
Ashenhurst Rise
  HD4................68 A1
Ashes La HD4.......77 B3
Ashfield Ave HD8 ...91 C3
Ashfield Rd
  Batley WF17.......11 A4
  Elland HX4........22 B1
  Huddersfield HD2...52 B3
Ashfield St HD2.....53 B4
Ashfield Terr
  10 Cleckheaton
    BD19.............8 B1
  Elland HX4........22 B2
Ashford Ct HD8.....88 C1
Ashford Manor HD8..88 A3
Ashford Pk HD7 ....64 C3
Ash Gr
  Birkenshaw BD11....2 A4
  Brighouse HD6......26 C4
  Cleckheaton BD19...15 B4
  Cleckheaton, Birdacre
    HD9.............9 A3
Ashgrove Rd HD2...54 C4
Ash Grove Terr **6**
  HD5................26 B2
Ashlea Ave HD6.....26 B2
Ashlea Cl HD6.......26 B2
Ashlea Dr HD6.......26 B2

Ashleigh Cl HD8 .....89 B1
Ashleigh Dale HD2...52 B3
Ashleigh Gdns WF5 ..34 C2
Ashley Cl BD19 .....9 A4
Ashley Ind Est
  Huddersfield HD2....41 C2
  Ossett WF5........35 B1
Ashley Rd BD12.....5 C4
Ashmead WF17 .....19 A1
Ash Meadow Cl HD2 .40 B1
Ashmere Gr HD2....53 C4
Ashmore Dr WF5 ...34 C3
Ash St
  Cleckheaton BD19 ....7 C1
  Huddersfield HD1...53 A2
Ashton Clough Rd
  WF15...............17 A2
Ash Wlk HD7 ....65 A3
Ashwood Cl HD2....40 B1
Ashwood Ct WF5 ...34 C3
Ashwood Gr WF4 ...65 A3
Ashwood Hts WF4...59 A1
Ashworth Cl WF13 ..32 C2
Ashworth Gdns
  WF13...............32 C2
Ashworth Gn WF13..32 C2
Ashworth Rd WF13 .32 C2
Aspen Gr WF13......32 B2
ASPLEY...............68 B3
Aspley Bsns Pk HD1 .68 B4
Aspley Pl HD1......96 B2
Asquith St WF17 ....11 B4
Aston Cl WF15.......29 C4
Aston Ct WF5.......49 C2
Athene Dr HD4 .....68 B1
Atherton La HD6....26 B2
Athlone Dr WF12 ...33 B4
Athold Dr WF5.....49 B3
Athold St WF5......49 B3
Atlas Mill Cvn Pk
  HD6................26 A4
Atlas Mill Rd HD6...26 A4
Attorney Ct HD9.....86 B1
Audrey St WF17.....49 A2
Audsley's Yd WF4...60 A1
Austin Ave HD6......12 C2
Avenue No 2 HD6...26 A3
Avenue The
  Batley, Birstall
    WF17.............10 B3
  Batley, Carlinghow
    WF17.............11 A1
  Batley WF17.......68 C3
  4 Huddersfield HD5.68 C3
  Meltham HD9......84 C2
Avison Rd HD4......65 C1
Avon Croft WF5.....48 B3
Axminster Dr BD19 ...5 B1
Ayres Dr HD4........65 C1
Aysgarth Av HX3....13 A4
Aysgarth Cl BD12 ...5 C4
Aysgarth Rd
  Batley WF17.......19 A3
  Huddersfield HD4...77 A4
Ayton Rd HD3.......65 A4

B

Back Armitage Rd
  HD4................76 A2
Back Beacon St
  HD2................53 A3
Back Beaumont St
  WF17 ....19 C1
Back Beech Terr
  HD1................53 B3
Back Bower Rd **1**
  HX5................24 A1
Back Bradshaw Rd
  HD9................83 A1

Back Brunswick St
  WF13 ....32 A3
Back Carlinghow La
  WF17 ....10 B1
Back Cecil St **8**
  HD1................96 A2
Back Charles St **10**
  HD6................13 A1
Back Clifton Rd HD1 .52 B1
Back Cross La HX5...37 A4
Back Dudwell Terr
  HX3................22 C4
Back Eldon Rd HD1 .52 A1
Back Fitzwilliam St
  HD1................67 B4
Back Gladstone St **5**
  WF13 ....32 A3
Back Gooder La **1**
  HD6................26 B3
Back Greenhead Rd **2**
  HD1................96 A2
Back Henrietta St **3**
  WF17 ....19 C3
Backhold Av HX3....23 B4
Backhold Dr HX3....23 B4
Backhold La HX3....23 B4
Backhold Rd HX3....23 B4
Back Honoria St
  HD1................53 A3
Back Knowl Rd
  WF14 ....43 B4
Back La Batley WF16 .18 A2
  Clayton West HD8...93 C4
  Holmfirth HD9......86 A3
  Middlestown WF4...59 A1
  Mirfield WF14......43 A3
  Ossett WF5........48 C3
Back Leatham St **3**
  WF13 ....32 A3
Back Marriot St **4**
  WF13 ....33 A3
Back Moor La HD4...75 C3
Back Mount Ave **4**
  WF17 ....20 A1
Back Nelson St **15**
  WF13 ....32 C2
Back New St **8**
  HD6................13 A1
Back Norfolk St
  WF17 ....19 B2
Back O' Dam HD7...72 C2
Back Pollard St HD2 .53 B4
Back Providence St **6**
  WF17 ....19 C3
Back Purlwell Hall Rd
  WF17 ....19 C1
Back Purlwell La
  WF17 ....19 C2
Back Queen St
  2 Elland HX4......36 C4
  Huddersfield HD1...96 B1
Back Ravens St
  WF13 ....45 C4
Back Slaithwaite Rd
  WF12 ....46 B2
Back South St HD1 ..66 C3
Back Springfield Rd **3**
  HX5................24 A1
Back Spring St **4**
  HD1................96 A2
Back Stanley St
  HD1................67 A1
Back Station Rd
  Batley WF17.......20 A2
  Mirfield WF14......43 C1
Back Stoney La HD4 .76 B4
Back Thornhill Rd
  HD3................65 C4
Back Union St **5**
  HD1................96 B3

Back Warwick Terr **1**
  WF17 ....20 A1
Back Webster St **3**
  WF13 ....32 C2
Back Wentworth St
  HD1................52 C1
Back William St **9**
  HD6................26 A3
Baden Terr **4** BD19 ..8 A1
Badger Brow HD9 ...80 B1
Badger Gate HD9 ...80 B2
Badger Hill HD6 .....39 A4
Badgers Wlk WF16...18 B1
Bagden La HD8......92 C1
Bagshaw Mus ★
  WF17 ....11 A2
BAILIFF BRIDGE 5 B1
Bailiff Bridge Jun & Inf
  Sch HD6...........5 B1
Baines St WF17.....19 B2
Baker St HD3........51 B2
Bakston Cl HD5......69 A1
Balderstone Hall La
  WF14 ....30 C1
Balk La
  Denby Dale HD8....94 A3
  Kirkheaton HD5.....55 B1
  Netherton WF4.....60 B1
Balks WF15..........16 C2
Balk St WF17........19 B3
Balk The WF17......11 C1
Ballater Ave HD4 ...75 B4
Ballroyd Clough
  Huddersfield HD5...65 C4
  Huddersfield, Quarmby
    HD3.............51 A1
Ballroyd La HD3.....65 C3
Ball Royd Rd HD2...53 B4
Balme Rd BD19......8 A2
Balmfield WF15......30 A4
Balmfield Cres
  WF15..............30 A3
Balmfrey's Yard W
  HD3................66 A2
Balmoral Ave HD4 ..75 B4
Bancroft Ave HD5...69 A3
Bank Bldgs HD9.....80 C1
Bank End HD7.......64 B2
Bank End La
  Clayton West HD8...93 C2
  Huddersfield HD5...69 A2
Bank End Rd HD7...64 B1
Bankfield
  Marsden HD7......79 A3
  Shelley HD8.......90 B4
Bankfield Ave HD5...55 B2
Bankfield Cl WF5....49 B2
Bankfield Ct
  Huddersfield HD5...68 C3
  Mirfield WF14......43 B3
Bank Field Grange
  HX4................22 C1
Bankfield La HD5....55 C1
Bankfield Park Ave
  HD4................76 B3
Bankfield Rd HD1...67 B3
Bank Field Rd WF17..19 C3
Bankfield Terr HD4...76 B2
BANK FOOT.........20 A3
Bank Foot La HD4 ..76 A1
Bank Foot Pl WF17...19 C3
Bank Foot St WF17...19 C3
Bank Gate HD7......72 B3
Bank Gr WF12.......34 A1
Bank Hall Gr HD8...90 B2
Bankhouse La
  Halifax HX3........23 A4
  Huddersfield HX3...66 B3
Bankhouse Rd HD3 .66 B3
Bank La HD8........95 A1
Banks HD9...........83 B2

Banks App HD7 . . . . . .**64** C3
Banks Ave HD7 . . . .**64** C3
Banks Cres HD7 . . . . . .**64** C3
Banks Dr HD7 . . . .**64** C3
Banks End La HD9 . . .**85** B3
Banks Gr HD7 . . . .**64** C3
Bank Side HD8 . . . .**90** B4
Banks Rd
 Honley HD9. . . . .**83** C1
 Huddersfield HD7 . . . . .**64** C3
 Slaithwaite HD7 . . . . .**73** A2
Banks Side HD7 . . . . .**64** C3
Banks St WF17. . . . . . .**19** C2
Bank St
 Brighouse HD6 . . . .**26** A4
 Cleckheaton BD19 . . . . .**7** C1
 Dewsbury WF12 . . . . . .**33** A2
 Holmfirth HD9. . . . .**87** B2
 Horbury WF4 . . . .**60** C3
 Liversedge WF15 . . . . .**17** B2
 Mirfield WF14. . . . .**43** A3
 Ossett WF5. . . . .**48** C3
Bank Top Elland HX4 . .**22** C2
 Slaithwaite HD7 . . . . .**72** B3
Bank View
 Birkenshaw BD11. . . . . .**2** A4
 Dewsbury WF12. . . . . .**34** A2
 Honley HD9. . . . .**85** A4
Bankwell Rd HD3 . . . .**66** A2
Bankwood WF17. . . . . .**4** B2
Bankwood Way WF17 .**4** B1
Baptist St WF17. . . . . .**19** A1
Barber Row HD7. . . . .**73** C3
Barber Sq WF16 . . . . .**17** C2
Barber St ■ HD6 . . . .**13** B1
Barber Wlk ■
 WF13 . . . .**32** C2
Bar Croft HD5 . . . .**55** B3
Barcroft Rd HD4 . . . . .**76** C4
Barden Cl WF17 . . . . .**19** B3
Bargate HD7 . . . .**73** C3
Barge St HD1. . . . .**67** B2
Bargreen HD5 . . . .**55** B3
Baring-Gould Way
 WF4 . . . .**60** A3
Bark Cl HD8 . . . .**89** C1
Barker Ct HD2 . . . .**52** B3
Barker Rd WF4 . . . . . .**60** B4
Barker St WF15 . . . . . .**17** B2
Barlbro' Pl HD4. . . . . .**65** C2
Barley Croft WF13 . . .**31** C2
Barmby Cl WF5 . . . . . .**49** B2
Barmby Cres WF5. . . .**49** C2
Barmby Fold WF5. . . .**49** B2
Barnby Royd HD5. . . .**54** B1
Barnsley Rd
 Clayton West HD8. . . .**93** A2
 Denby Dale HD8 . . . . . .**94** A2
Barracks St WF16. . . .**17** C2
Barrington Par BD19 . .**9** A2
Barrowstead HD8. . . . .**92** A2
Barr St HD1 . . . .**53** C2
Bar St WF17 . . . .**20** A2
Barton Manor Cl
 HD4. . . . .**75** A4
Barton Pl WF17. . . . . .**19** C2
Barton St ■ HD6 . . . .**13** A1
Basil St HD4 . . . .**66** C2
Bath Ct WF16 . . . .**18** A2
Bath Pl
 Brighouse HD6 . . . .**26** A3
 Cleckheaton BD19 . . . . .**8** A1
Bath Rd Batley WF16. .**18** A2
 Cleckheaton BD19 . . . . .**8** A1
Bath St Batley WF17 . .**20** A3
 Dewsbury WF13 . . . . . .**32** C3
 Elland HX5 . . . .**37** B4
 Huddersfield HD1. . . . . .**96** A3
 Huddersfield, Rashcliffe
 HD1. . . . .**67** B1

Bath St continued
 Kirkburton HD8. . . . . . .**89** B3
BATLEY **19** C2
Batley Ave HD1 . . . . .**66** C4
Batley Bldgs HD1 . . . .**52** B1
Batley Bsns Ctr
 WF17 . . . .**19** B4
Batley Bsns & Ent Coll
 WF17 . . . .**11** C1
Batley Bsns & Tech Ctr
 WF17 . . . .**20** B2
BATLEY CARR **19** C1
Batley Ent Ctr WF17 .**19** B4
Batley Field Hill
 WF17 . . . .**19** C4
Batley Girls' High Sch
 WF17 . . . .**11** B3
Batley Gram Sch
 WF17 . . . .**11** B1
**Batley Parish CE Jun &
 Inf Sch** WF17 . . . . .**19** C4
Batley Rd WF16. . . . . .**18** C2
Batley St ■ HD5. . . . .**68** C4
Batley Sta WF17 . . . . .**20** A2
Baton Dr HD3 . . . .**51** C3
Battye Ave HD4 . . . . . .**66** A1
BATTYEFORD **43** A3
Battyeford CE Prim Sch
 WF14 . . . .**43** A4
Battye St
 Batley WF16 . . . .**18** A2
 Dewsbury WF13 . . . . . .**33** A2
Bawson Ct BD19 . . . . . .**9** A3
Bay Cl HD3 . . . .**51** C1
Bay Hall HD1 . . . .**53** A2
Bay Hall Common Rd
 HD1. . . . .**53** A2
Bayldons Pl ■
 WF17 . . . .**19** C3
Beacon St
 Dewsbury WF13 . . . . . .**45** A4
 Huddersfield HD2. . . . .**53** A3
Beaden Dr HD8 . . . . . .**71** A1
Beadon Ave HD5. . . . .**70** A3
Beagle Ave HD4 . . . . .**75** B3
Bean St HX5. . . . .**38** B4
Beast Market ■
 HD1. . . . .**96** B2
Beatrice St ■ BD19. . .**8** A2
Beaufort Ave HD8. . . .**89** B1
Beaumont Ave HD5. . .**68** C3
Beaumont Park Rd
 HD4. . . . .**75** C4
Beaumont Pl WF17 . .**18** C1
Beaumont St
 Batley WF17 . . . .**19** C1
 Huddersfield HD1. . . . . .**96** B3
 Huddersfield, Longwood
 HD3 . . . .**65** B3
 ■ Huddersfield,
 Moldgreen HD5. . . . . . .**68** C3
 Huddersfield, Netherton
 HD4. . . . .**75** C1
Beaver Dr WF13 . . . . .**31** C1
Becker's Ave WF17. . .**11** B4
Beckett Cl WF4 . . . . . .**61** B4
Beckett Cres WF13. . .**31** C2
Beckett Gr WF13 . . . . .**31** C1
Beckett La WF13 . . . . .**31** C1
Beckett Nook WF13. . .**31** C2
Beckett Rd WF13 . . . . .**32** B4
Beckett Sq HD8. . . . . .**89** B4
Beckett St WF17 . . . . .**20** A1
Beckett Wlk WF13 . . .**31** C1
Beckfield Cl BD19. . . .**13** B4
Beck La WF16 . . . .**17** C1
Beck Rd HD1 . . . .**53** A2
Becks Ct WF12. . . . . . .**46** A2
Beckside Gdns HD5. .**70** B2
Beckside Works
 WF17 . . . .**20** A1

Bedale Ave
 Brighouse HD6 . . . .**25** B2
 Skelmanthorpe HD8 . . .**91** B2
Bedale Cl HD8. . . . . . .**91** B2
Bedale Dr HD8 . . . . . .**91** B2
Bedford Cl HD8. . . . . .**71** A1
Bedford St
 Cleckheaton BD19 . . . . .**7** C1
 ■ Elland HX5. . . . .**37** B4
Beech Ave
 Holmfirth HD9. . . . .**85** A3
 Huddersfield HD5. . . . .**69** B3
 Huddersfield, Leymoor
 HD7. . . . .**65** A3
Beech Ct WF5 . . . .**48** B4
Beechdale Ave
 WF17 . . . .**11** A1
Beeches The BD11. . . .**2** A3
Beechfield Ave HD8. .**91** C2
Beechfield Rd HD2 . .**52** B3
Beechfield Terr ■
 BD19. . . . .**8** B1
Beech Gr
 Brighouse HX3 . . . .**5** A1
 Cleckheaton BD19 . . . . .**9** A3
 Liversedge WF16 . . . . .**17** C3
 Mirfield WF14. . . . .**43** C3
Beech Inf & Jun Sch
 HD7. . . . .**65** A3
Beech St Elland HX5 . .**37** B4
 ■ Holmfirth HD9. . . . .**86** A3
 Huddersfield HD1. . . . . .**66** C3
 Mirfield WF14. . . . .**43** C3
Beech Way WF17 . . . .**11** A4
Beech Wlk
 Birkenshaw BD11. . . . . .**2** B2
 ■ Dewsbury WF13 . . .**32** C2
Beechwood Ave
 WF14 . . . .**43** C3
Beechwood Gr
 Horbury WF4 . . . .**61** B3
 Huddersfield HD2. . . . .**39** C2
Beechwood Pk
 BD19. . . . .**13** B4
Beechwood Rd
 WF14 . . . .**43** C4
Beehive Ct WF15. . . . .**30** C4
Beldon Brook Gn
 HD8. . . . .**88** A3
Belgrave Ave WF5 . . .**49** A2
Belgrave St WF5. . . . .**49** A2
Belgrave Terr HD1 . . .**52** C1
Belle Vue Cres HD2 . .**40** B1
Belle Vue St WF17. . .**18** C3
Bellgreave Ave HD9. .**87** C4
Bell St
 Dewsbury WF13 . . . . . .**45** A3
 Huddersfield HD5. . . . .**68** A2
Bellstring La WF14. . .**56** B3
Belmont Cl ■ HD1. . .**96** A3
Belmont Grange
 WF15 . . . .**30** A4
Belmont St
 Huddersfield HD1. . . . . .**96** A3
 Slaithwaite HD7 . . . . . .**72** B2
Belton Gr HD3 . . . .**51** B4
Belton St HD5 . . . .**69** A3
Belvedere Rd WF17 . .**19** B2
Bempton Gr WF17 . . .**10** C4
Bendigo Rd WF12. . . .**33** C3
Benjamin St WF17. . . .**11** B3
Ben Kaye Row HD9 . .**86** B2
Bennett Ave WF4 . . . .**61** B4
Bennett La WF12 . . . . .**33** C4
Bennett St ■ WF15 . .**17** B2
Benn La HD3 . . . .**65** B4
Benny La HD7 . . . .**64** A1
Benny Parr Cl WF17. .**20** B3
BENOMLEY. **69** A2
Benomley Cres HD5 .**69** A2
Benomley Dr HD5 . . .**69** A1

Benomley Rd HD5 . . .**69** A1
Benroyd Terr HX4 . . . .**36** B2
Bent Lea HD2. . . . .**41** B4
Bentley Ave HX3 . . . . . .**5** A1
Bent Ley Ind Est
 HD9. . . . .**81** B3
Bent Ley Rd HD9. . . . .**81** B3
Bentley St HD1 . . . . . .**67** A1
Benton Cres WF4 . . . .**61** B4
Benton Mews WF4. . .**61** B4
Bent St HD4 . . . .**68** A2
Bernard St HD2 . . . . . .**41** A1
BERRY BROW. **76** C2
Berry Brow Inf Sch
 HD4. . . . .**76** B2
Berry Brow Sta HD4 .**76** B2
Berry Croft HD9 . . . . .**83** A3
Berryfield Garth
 WF5 . . . .**35** A2
Berry La WF4 . . . .**61** A3
Berry Rd HD9. . . . .**80** A3
Berry's Yd WF4 . . . . . .**61** A4
Berry View HD4 . . . . .**76** B3
Berwick Ave WF16 . . .**18** A4
Best La HD4 . . . .**77** C1
Bethel St HD6 . . . .**26** B4
Betula Way HD8 . . . . .**71** A1
Beverley Ave BD12. . . .**6** A4
Beverley Cl HX5 . . . . .**24** B1
Beverley Ct HD2 . . . . .**53** B4
Beverley Dr
 Bradford BD12 . . . .**6** A4
 Dewsbury WF12 . . . . . .**33** C2
Beverley Gdns WF17 .**11** B4
Bevor Cres WF16 . . . .**18** A4
Bilham Rd HD8 . . . . . .**93** C3
Binham Rd HD2 . . . . . .**52** A2
Binks Fold ■ BD12 . . .**6** A4
Binn HD7 . . . .**72** C1
Binn La HD7 . . . .**79** A1
Binn Rd HD7 . . . .**78** C2
Binns Top La HX3 . . . .**24** B4
Birch Ave HD8 . . . .**88** B4
Birch Cl HD6 . . . .**13** C1
Birch Ct BD11. . . . .**2** B4
Birchen Ave WF5 . . . .**48** B4
BIRCHENCLIFFE **51** B4
Birchencliffe Hill Rd
 HD3. . . . .**51** B4
Birchen Hills WF5 . . .**48** B3
Birchfield Ave LS27 . . .**4** C4
Birchfield Gr HD8. . . .**91** C2
Birchfield Prim Sch
 LS27 . . . .**4** C4
Birch Gr Batley WF17 .**11** A2
 Huddersfield HD7. . . . .**65** A3
Birchington Ave
 HD3. . . . .**51** B4
Birchington Cl HD3 . .**51** B4
Birchington Dr HD3. .**51** A4
Birch Pk HD9 . . . .**85** B4
Birch Rd HD4 . . . .**76** B2
Birchroyd Cl HD2 . . . .**52** A4
Birchwood Ave
 WF17 . . . .**10** C4
Birchwood Ct ■
 WF15 . . . .**17** B1
Birchwood Pk HD9 . .**87** B4
BIRDACRE **9** B3
Birds Royd La HD6 . . .**26** C3
Birdswell Ave HD6. . .**14** A1
BIRKBY. **52** C3
Birkby Brow Cres
 WF17 . . . .**11** B4
Birkby Fold HD2 . . . . .**52** B2
Birkby Hall Rd HD2 . .**52** B3
Birkby Jun Sch HD1 .**53** A3
Birkby La HD6 . . . .**6** A1
Birkby Lodge Rd
 HD2. . . . .**52** C2
Birkby Rd HD2. . . . . . .**52** A3

Birkdale Ave HD3 . . .**51** A2
Birkdale Gr WF13 . . . .**32** A3
Birkdale High Sch
 WF13 . . . .**32** A4
Birkdale Rd WF13. . . .**32** B3
BIRKENSHAW **2** B3
**BIRKENSHAW
 BOTTOMS** **2** C2
Birkenshaw CE Fst Sch
 BD11. . . . .**2** B4
Birkenshaw La BD11 . .**2** C2
Birkenshaw Mid Sch
 BD11. . . . .**2** B2
Birkett St BD19 . . . . . .**8** A2
Birkhead St WF16. . . .**18** B1
Birk Hey Cl BD19. . . . .**13** B4
Birkhill Cres BD11 . . . .**2** B3
Birkhouse La
 Brighouse HD6 . . . .**14** A4
 Huddersfield HD5. . . . .**69** A3
 Huddersfield, Yews Hill
 HD1, HD4 . . . .**67** A3
Birkhouse Rd HD6 . . .**13** C4
Birklands Rd HD2. . . .**52** C4
Birks La HD4, HD5,
 HD8. . . . .**69** C1
Birksland Moor BD11 .**2** B1
Birks Rd HD3 . . . .**65** C3
Birmingham La HD9 .**80** A3
BIRSTALL. **10** C4
Birstall La BD11 . . . . . .**3** B3
Birstall Park Ct ■
 WF17 . . . .**3** C1
Birstall Prim Sch
 WF17 . . . .**10** C3
**BIRSTALL
 SMITHIES** **10** B2
Bishop's Ct HD4 . . . . .**76** B1
Bishops Way
 Meltham HD9 . . . .**80** C2
 Mirfield WF14. . . . .**29** A1
Black Brook Way
 HX4. . . . .**36** B4
Blackburn Bldgs
 HD6. . . . .**26** C4
Blackburn Pl WF17 . .**20** A3
Blackburn Rd
 Batley WF17 . . . .**19** C1
 Brighouse HD6 . . . .**13** A2
Blacker Cres WF4. . . .**63** C4
Blacker Rd HD1, HD2 .**52** C2
Blackers Ct WF12. . . .**46** A2
Blackhouse Rd HD2. .**53** B4
Black La HD7 . . . .**74** A1
BLACKLEY. **37** A2
Blackley Rd HX5 . . . . .**37** A2
BLACKMOORFOOT. .**73** C1
Blackmoorfoot Rd
 Huddersfield HD4. . . . .**67** A2
 Linthwaite HD7 . . . . . .**73** C1
Black Rock Mills
 HD7. . . . .**73** C2
Blacksmiths Fold
 HD5. . . . .**69** B2
Blackstone Ave BD12 .**5** C4
Blackthorn Dr HD3 . .**51** A3
Blacup Moor View
 BD19. . . . .**8** A1
Blagden La HD4 . . . . .**76** B3
Blake Hall Dr WF14 . .**44** B2
Blake Hall Rd WF14 . .**44** B2
Blakeholme Cl HD7 . .**72** A2
Blakelaw Dr HD6 . . . . .**14** A1
Blake Law La
 Brighouse WF15 . . . . . .**27** C4
 Liversedge HD6 . . . . . .**28** A4
Blakeridge La WF17. .**19** B3
Blake Stones HD7 . . .**72** A4

Blakestones Rd HD7 .**72** A2
Bland St HD1 . . . .**67** B2
Blanket Hall St
WF16 . . . .**18** A1
Bleak St Lower BD19 . .**9** C2
Bleak St BD19 . . . .**9** C2
Bleasdale Ave HD2. .**52** C3
Blenheim Chase
HD8 . . . .**93** A2
Blenheim Dr
Batley WF17 . . . .**19** C4
Dewsbury WF13 . . . . .**32** A3
Blenheim Sq WF17 . .**19** C4
Blenheim Terr
WF17 . . . .**19** C4
Blossom Ct HD5 . . . . .**69** A4
Bluebell Ct WF17 . . . .**10** B4
BLUE BELL HILL. **76** B4
Blue Bell Hill HD4 . . .**76** B4
Blue Butts WF5 . . . . .**48** C3
Bluehills La HD8 . . . .**94** C3
BMK Ind Est WF15 . . .**17** B2
Boathouse La WF14 . .**44** B1
Bobbin Cl HD7 . . . . . .**64** C2
Bobbin Ct HD7 . . . . . .**64** C2
Boggart La HD8 . . . . .**91** C4
BOG GREEN **42** B2
Bog Green La HD5 . . .**42** B2
Boldgrove St WF12 . .**47** C4
Bolehill Pk HD6 . . . . .**12** B4
Bolster Gr HD7 . . . . . .**64** A1
BOLSTER MOOR **64** A2
Bonaccord Sq WF17 .**19** C2
Bonaccord Terr
WF17 . . . .**19** C2
Bond St
6 Batley, Birstall
WF17 . . . .**10** B3
Batley WF17 . . . .**19** C4
Brighouse HD6 . . . . . .**13** A1
Dewsbury WF13 . . . . .**32** C2
Bonegate Ave HD6 . .**13** B1
Bonegate Rd HD6 . . .**13** B1
Bookers Field BD19 . .**9** C1
BOOTHROYD **32** A2
Boothroyd Dr HD4 . .**66** A1
Boothroyd Gn WF13 .**32** B2
Boothroyd Jun & Inf
Sch WF13 . . . .**32** A1
Boothroyd La WF13 .**32** A2
Booth Royd La HD6 . .**25** A2
Booth's Bldgs HD6 . . .**5** B1
Booth St BD19 . . . .**8** A2
Border Cl HD3 . . . . . .**50** C3
Borrowdale Rd
WF12 . . . .**33** B4
Botany La HD8 . . . . . .**71** B2
Botham Fields HD3 . .**65** C3
Botham Hall Rd
HD3 . . . .**65** B3
Bottomley St **2**
HD6 . . . .**13** B2
Bottoms La BD11 . . . .**2** B2
Boulder Gate HD7 . . .**79** B3
Boundary Cl HD9 . . . .**87** A1
Boundary Rd WF13 . .**31** C4
Boundary St WF16 . . .**17** C2
Bourn View Cl HD4. .**75** C1
Bourn View Rd HD4 . .**75** C1
Bower La WF13 . . . . . .**18** C1
Bower The **1** WF17 . .**10** C1
Bowling Alley HD6. . .**26** A2
Bowling Alley Terr
HD6 . . . .**26** A2
Bowling Ct HD6 . . . . .**12** C1
Bowling Green Ct
HD3 . . . .**50** B1

Bowling Green View
BD11 . . . .**3** B4
Bowling St HD4 . . . . .**65** C2
Bowness Dr HD5 . . . .**54** A1
Bowood Rd HX5 . . . . .**37** B3
Bow St HD1 . . . .**67** B3
Boxhall Rd HX5 . . . . .**23** C1
Box's Bldgs WF17 . . .**18** C4
Bracewell Rd HD9 . . .**80** B1
Bracken Ave HD6 . . .**13** A3
Bracken Cl
Brighouse HD6 . . . . . .**13** A3
Mirfield WF14 . . . . . .**29** A1
Bracken Gr
Huddersfield HD2. . . .**40** A2
Mirfield WF14 . . . . . .**29** A1
BRACKENHALL **40** B2
Bracken Hall Rd
HD2. . . . .**40** B1
BRACKEN HILL **29** A1
Bracken Hill WF14 . . .**29** A1
Bracken Pk LS27 . . . . . .**4** C3
Bracken Rd HD6 . . . .**13** A3
Bracken Sq HD2 . . . .**40** B2
Bracken Way HX5 . . .**24** B1
Bradbury St WF13 . . .**45** A3
Bradcroft HD1. . . . . .**53** B3
Bradd Cl WF15 . . . . . .**17** B3
Bradfield Cl HD2 . . . .**41** A3
Bradford Rd
Batley WF17 . . . .**20** A3
Birkenshaw BD11 . . . . .**2** A3
Brighouse HD6 . . . . . .**13** B3
Brighouse HD6 . . . . . .**26** B4
Cleckheaton BD19 . . . .**8** B2
Cleckheaton, Birstall
BD19, WF17 . . . .**9** C4
Gildersome BD11,
LS27 . . . .**4** B3
Huddersfield HD1,
HD2. . . . .**40** A1
Liversedge WF15 . . . .**17** B2
Bradford St WF13 . . .**33** A3
BRADLEY. **41** B3
Bradley Bsns Pk
HD2. . . . .**40** C3
Bradley Bvd HD2. . . .**40** B1
Bradley CE Jun & Inf
Sch HD2. . . . .**41** B3
Bradley Grange Gdns
HD2. . . . .**41** B4
Bradley Junction Ind
Est HD2 . . . .**41** B2
Bradley La HX4 . . . . .**36** A4
BRADLEY MILLS **54** C2
Bradley Mills La
HD1. . . . .**53** C2
Bradley Mills Rd
HD5. . . . .**54** A2
Bradley Quarry Cl
HD2. . . . .**41** C4
Bradley Rd HD2. . . . .**40** C4
Bradley View HX4 . . .**36** A2
Bradshaw Ave HD9 . .**82** C1
Bradshaw Cl HD9 . . .**82** C1
Bradshaw Cres HD9 .**82** C1
Bradshaw Dr HD9. . .**82** C1
Bradshaw Rd HD9 . . .**84** C1
Bradwell La WF5 . . . .**49** A3
Bramble Gr HX5 . . . . .**24** B1
Bramble Wlk WF17 . .**10** C3
Bramhope Rd BD19 . .**7** C2
Bramston Gdns **11**
HD6. . . . .**26** A3
Bramston St HD6 . . .**26** A3
Branch La HD2 . . . . .**38** A1
Branch Rd
Batley WF17 . . . .**19** C3
Brighouse BD19 . . . . . .**6** C3
Dewsbury WF13 . . . . .**32** C2
Huddersfield HD2. . . .**38** A2

Branch St HD1. . . . . .**66** C3
Branstone Gr WF5 . . .**35** A3
Branwell Ave WF17 . .**3** C1
Branwell Wlk WF17 . .**3** C1
Branxholme Ind Est
HD6. . . . .**5** B1
Brayside Ave HD2. . .**52** C4
Bream Ave BD19 . . . . .**7** C1
Brearley Gdns WF15 .**17** A1
Brearley Pl WF17 . . . .**19** C2
Brearley St WF17 . . . .**19** B2
Brecon Ave HD3 . . . .**51** A3
Brendon Ct WF14 . . .**56** C4
Brendon Dr HD2 . . . .**52** A3
Brentwood Cl WF17 . .**20** B3
Bretfield Ct WF12 . . .**46** C3
Bretton Park Way
WF12 . . . .**47** A3
Bretton St WF12 . . . .**46** C3
Bretton Street Ent Ctr
WF12 . . . .**46** C3
Brewerton La WF13 . .**31** C4
Brewery Ct HD3 . . . . .**51** A3
Brewery Dr HD4 . . . .**76** B3
Brewery La WF12 . . . .**46** B2
Brewery St **5** WF16. .**18** A1
Brewery Wharf
WF14 . . . .**43** C2
Brewery Yard HD8 . .**70** B1
Brian Ave HD5 . . . . . .**69** A3
Brian St HD3 . . . .**51** B3
Briar Ave HD9 . . . . . .**80** A3
Briar Cl Batley WF16 . .**18** A3
Elland HX5 . . . .**37** A3
Briar Dr WF13 . . . . . .**31** C4
Briarfield HD8 . . . . . .**95** B3
Briarfield Gdns
Gildersome LS27 . . . . . .**4** C4
Huddersfield HD5. . . .**69** A4
Briarlyn Ave HD3 . . .**51** A4
Briarlyn Rd HD3 . . . .**51** B4
Briarmains Rd
WF17 . . . .**10** C4
Brickbank HD5 . . . . . .**69** B1
Brick Terr HD6 . . . . . .**26** B3
Brick & Tile Terr
HD6. . . . .**26** A3
Brickyard **9** WF14 . .**43** B3
Bridge Cl
Clayton West HD8. . . .**93** A3
Horbury WF4 . . . .**60** A3
Bridge Croft HD3 . . .**66** A2
Bridge End HD6 . . . . .**26** A3
Bridge Ind Est WF12 **47** A4
Bridge La HD9 . . . . . .**86** A4
Bridge Rd
Brighouse HD6 . . . . . .**26** A4
Horbury WF4 . . . .**60** A3
Bridge St
Batley, Bank Foot
WF17 . . . .**20** A3
Batley, Birstall Smithies
WF17 . . . .**10** B3
Dewsbury WF13 . . . . .**45** B4
Huddersfield HD4. . . .**76** B2
Huddersfield, Rashcliffe
HD4 . . . .**67** B1
Liversedge WF16 . . . .**17** C2
Slaithwaite HD7 . . . . .**72** C1
Bridge Works Bsns Pk
HD9. . . . .**83** B2
Bridle Ave WF5 . . . . .**34** C2
Bridle Cl WF4. . . . . . .**60** A1
Bridle La
Netherton WF4 . . . . . .**60** A1
Ossett WF5 . . . .**34** C2
Bridle Pl WF5 . . . .**35** A2
Bridle St WF17 . . . . . .**20** B3
Bridley Dr HD7 . . . . . .**72** C2
Bridon Way BD19 . . .**16** B4

Brier Hill Cl BD19 . . . .**15** A4
Brier Hill View HD2 . .**40** C3
Brier La HD6 . . . .**25** B2
Briggate
Brighouse HD6 . . . . . .**26** A4
Elland HX5 . . . .**23** C1
Huddersfield HD5. . . .**55** A1
Briggs Terr **2** HD5. .**68** C4
BRIGHOUSE **26** B4
Brighouse High Sch
Brighouse HD6 . . . . . .**26** A4
Brighouse, Hove Edge
HD6. . . . .**12** C3
Brighouse Rd HD6 . . .**38** A1
Brighouse Sta HD6 . .**26** B3
Brighouse Trade Pk
HD6. . . . .**26** C4
Brighouse Wood La
HD6. . . . .**12** C1
Brighouse Wood Row
HD6. . . . .**12** C1
Brighton Cl WF17 . . .**18** B4
Brighton St WF16 . . .**18** A2
Brighton Terr BD19 . .**6** C3
Bright's Bldgs HD9 . .**83** C2
Bright St
3 Dewsbury
WF13. . . . .**32** C3
Mirfield WF14 . . . . . .**29** A1
Briscoe La HX4 . . . . . .**22** B1
Britannia Bsns Ent Ctr
WF5 . . . .**48** A4
Britannia Mills Trad Est
HD3. . . . .**65** B2
Britannia Rd
Huddersfield HD3,
HD7. . . . .**65** B2
Slaithwaite HD7 . . . . .**72** B2
Britannia Terr BD19 . .**8** A2
Britton St BD19 . . . . .**16** C4
Broadacre Rd WF5 . .**49** B3
Broadacres HD9 . . . .**83** A1
Broadbent Croft
HD9. . . . .**83** B2
BROAD CARR **36** B2
Broad Carr La HX4 . .**36** B2
Broad Carr Terr
HX4 . . . .**36** C3
Broad Cut Rd WF4 . .**61** C1
Broadfield Ind Est
HD1. . . . .**67** B1
Broadfields HD7 . . . .**72** B1
Broadgate
Huddersfield HD5. . . .**68** C2
Ossett WF5 . . . .**49** A3
Broadgate Cres
HD5. . . . .**68** C2
Broad La HD5 . . . .**68** C2
Broadlands Rd HD9 . .**80** B3
Broad Oak HD7 . . . . .**74** A4
Broad Oak La HX3 . . .**12** A4
Broad Oak Pl HX3. . .**12** A4
Broadoaks Cl WF12 . .**34** A1
Broad Oak St HX3. . .**12** A4
Broadowler La WF5 . .**49** B3
Broad St WF13 . . . . . .**45** C4
Broad View WF5 . . . . .**49** B3
Broadway HD1 . . . . . .**96** B3
Broad Way Ct WF12 .**58** A3
Broadwell Rd WF5 . . .**49** B3
Brock Bank HD5 . . . .**54** C1
BROCKHOLES **85** A4
Brockholes Bsns Pk
HD9. . . . .**85** A4
Brockholes CE Jun &
Inf Sch HD9 . . . .**85** A4
Bromley Bank HD8. .**94** C3
Bromley Rd
Batley WF17 . . . .**20** B1
Huddersfield HD2. . . .**52** C2
Bromley St WF17 . . . .**20** A1

Bronte Cl
Batley WF13 . . . .**31** C2
Cleckheaton BD19 . . . .**9** B3
Huddersfield HD4. . . .**66** C1
Bronte Gr WF14. . . . .**44** B2
Bronte Rd WF17 . . . .**10** B3
Bronte Way WF14 . . .**44** B2
Brook Cl WF5. . . . .**49** B1
Brookdale Ave WF5 . .**35** A3
Brookdale Bank
HD3. . . . .**65** C3
Brook Dr HX4. . . . . . .**36** B2
Brooke Fold HD9 . . . .**83** A2
Brooke St
8 Batley WF16 . . . . .**18** A1
Brighouse HD6 . . . . . .**26** A3
Cleckheaton BD19 . . . .**8** B1
Brookfield HD8 . . . . . .**89** A4
Brook Field WF14 . . .**56** C4
Brookfield Ave BD19 . .**8** B3
Brookfields WF4 . . . . .**63** B3
Brookfields Ave BD12 .**6** B3
Brookfields Rd BD12. .**6** B3
Brookfield Terr BD19 . .**8** B3
Brookfield View
BD19. . . . .**8** B3
BROOKFOOT **12** B1
Brookfoot Ave BD11 . .**2** A3
Brookfoot Bsns Pk
HD6. . . . .**12** C1
Brookfoot Ind Est
HD6. . . . .**12** B1
Brookfoot La HD6. . .**12** B1
Brook Gdns
10 Dewsbury
WF13. . . . .**32** B2
Meltham HD9 . . . .**80** B3
Brook Grain Hill
HD6. . . . .**26** A2
Brook La
Cleckheaton WF15 . . .**15** C2
Huddersfield HD7. . . .**64** C2
Brooklands HD2 . . . .**41** B3
Brooklands Ave
HX4 . . . .**36** A2
Brooklands Cl HX4 . .**36** A2
Brooklands Ct WF5 . .**49** C2
Brooklyn Ave HD5 . .**69** C4
Brooklyn Cl WF13. . .**18** C2
Brooklyn Ct BD19 . . .**8** A2
Brooklyn Dr BD19. . . .**8** A2
Brooklyn Grange
BD19. . . . .**8** A2
Brooklyn Rd BD19 . . .**8** A2
Brooklyn Terr HD6 . .**12** B3
Brook Rd **4** WF12 . . .**32** B1
BROOKROYD **11** A2
Brookroyd Ave HD6 . .**13** B4
Brookroyd Gdns **3**
WF17 . . . .**10** C2
Brookroyd La WF17 . .**11** C2
Brooksbank Gdns
HX5 . . . .**37** B4
Brooksbank Sch The
HX5 . . . .**37** A4
Brook's Bldgs HD1. . .**66** C4
Brookside HD8 . . . . . .**95** B4
Brook Side HD7 . . . . .**72** C4
Brook St
Dewsbury WF13 . . . . .**31** C3
1 Elland HX5. . . . . . .**37** C4
Huddersfield HD1. . . .**96** A3
Huddersfield, Moldgreen
HD5. . . . .**68** C4
Huddersfield, Yews Hill
HD1. . . . .**67** A2
Ossett WF5 . . . .**48** C3
Brooks Yd
Dewsbury WF13 . . . . .**32** B1
Huddersfield HD2. . . .**41** C3
Brook's Yd **17** HD1 . .**96** A3

Brook Terr HD7 . . . . . . **72** C4
Brookwoods Ind Est
HX4 . . . . **36** A3
Broombank
Denby Dale HD8 . . . . . **95** A2
Huddersfield HD2 . . . . **52** A4
Broomcroft Rd WF5 . . **48** C2
Broomer St WF13 . . . . **45** A4
Broomfield HX5 . . . . . **36** C4
Broomfield Bsns Pk
HD1 . . . . **67** C2
Broomfield Rd
Huddersfield HD2 . . . . **39** C3
Huddersfield, Marsh
HD1 . . . . **66** C4
Broomfield Terr
Cleckheaton BD19 . . . . . **7** B1
Huddersfield HD1 . . . . **52** A1
Broomhill Cl HD9 . . . . **87** A1
Broomhill Terr
WF17 . . . . **20** A2
Broomhouse Cl HD8 . **95** B2
Broomroyd HD3 . . . . . **95** A2
Broomsdale Rd
WF17 . . . . **20** B3
Broom St BD19 . . . . . **15** B4
Broom Wlk WF17 . . . . **20** B3
Broomy Lea La HD9 . . **84** A1
Brougham Rd HD2 . . . **79** A3
Broughton Rd HD4 . . . **66** A1
Browcliff Flats HD1 . . **67** B2
Brow Cotts HD6 . . . . . **12** A3
Brow Mills Ind Est
HX3 . . . . **12** A4
BROWN HILL **10** C3
Brownhill Cl WF17 . . . **10** C3
Brown Hill Dr BD11 . . . **10** C3
Brownhill Garth
WF17 . . . . **10** C3
Brownhill Inf Sch
WF17 . . . . **11** A3
Brownhill Rd WF17 . . . **10** C3
Browning Rd HD2 . . . . **40** C1
Brown Royd Ave
HD5 . . . . **54** A2
Brownroyd Rd HD9 . . **82** C2
Brown's Pl WF17 . . . . . **19** B2
Brown St WF14 . . . . . **43** B3
Brow Rd HD1 . . . . **67** A3
Brow Wood Rd
WF17 . . . . **11** B3
Brunswick Dr WF13 . . **32** A3
Brunswick St
Batley, Heckmondwike
WF16 . . . . **18** A1
7 Batley WF17 . . . . . **19** C3
Dewsbury WF13 . . . . . **32** A3
Huddersfield HD1 . . . . **52** A1
Bryan Rd Elland HX5 . **36** C4
Huddersfield HD2 . . . . **52** A3
Bryan St 5 HD6 . . . . . **26** A3
Bryan Terr HD3 . . . . . **65** A4
Bryer St WF13 . . . . . . **32** C2
Buckden Ct HD3 . . . . **51** B1
Buckden Rd HD3 . . . . **52** A2
Buckrose St HD1 . . . . **53** A3
Buckrose Terr HD1 . . **53** A3
Buckstones Cl HX4 . . **36** A3
Bugler Terr WF4 . . . . . **60** A3
Bulay Rd HD1 . . . . **67** B2
Bullace Trees La
WF15 . . . . **16** B1
Bullfields Cl WF12 . . . **58** A4
Bull Green Rd HD3 . . **65** B4
Bulrush Bsns Pk
WF17 . . . . **11** B1
Bungalows The
Clayton West HD8 . . . . **93** A3

Bungalows The
continued
Halifax, Salterhebble
HX3 . . . . **23** B4
Ossett WF5 . . . . **48** B4
Bunkers Hill 8 HD9 . **86** A3
Bunkers La WF17 . . . . **18** C2
Bunny Pk HD4 . . . . . . **66** C1
Burbeary Rd HD1 . . . . **67** A1
Burdett Ct HD3 . . . . . **66** B2
Burfitts Rd HD3 . . . . . **51** B1
Burgh Mill Gdns
WF13 . . . . **32** A1
Burgh Mill La WF13 . . **32** A1
Burhouse Ct HD9 . . . . **83** A2
Burking Rd WF13 . . . . **32** B2
Burley Bsns Ctr 8
HX5 . . . . **37** B4
Burley St 11 HX5 . . . . **37** B4
Burley Wlk WF17 . . . . **19** B3
Burniston Dr HD3 . . . . **51** A2
Burnleyville BD19 . . . . . **9** A3
Burn Rd HD2, HD3 . . . **38** B1
Burnsall Ave WF17 . . . **19** A3
Burnsall Rd
Batley WF17 . . . . **19** A3
Brighouse HD6 . . . . . . **25** B2
Liversedge WF15 . . . . . **16** C2
Burns Ct WF17 . . . . . . **10** A4
Burnside Cl WF17 . . . . **11** A3
Burnup Gr BD19 . . . . . . **7** C1
Burrows The WF17 . . . **10** C1
Burrwood Terr HX4 . . **36** A3
Burrwood Way HX4 . . **36** A3
Burton Acres Dr
HD8 . . . . **88** B1
Burton Acres La
HD8 . . . . **88** C1
Burton Acres Mews
HD8 . . . . **88** B1
Burton Acres Way
HD8 . . . . **88** B1
Burton Cross HD8 . . . **88** B2
Burwood Rd HD3 . . . . **51** C2
Busker La HD8 . . . . . . **92** B2
Bute Ave HD6 . . . . **13** A3
Buttercup Way BD11 . . . **4** B3
Butterley La HD9 . . . . **87** C3
Buttermere Dr HD5 . . **68** C4
Butternab Rd HD4 . . . **75** C2
Butternab Ridge
HD4 . . . . **75** C2
Buttershaw La
WF15 . . . . **15** B3
Butterwood Cl HD4 . . **75** C2
Butts Hill BD19 . . . . **9** B2
Butts La WF4 . . . . **59** A1
Butts Yd 8 BD19 . . . . . **8** A1
Byram Arc 22 HD1 . . **96** A2
Byram St HD1 . . . . . . **96** A2
Byron Gr WF13 . . . . . . **31** B4
Bywater Row BD11 . . . . **2** B3
Bywell CE Jun Sch
WF12 . . . . **33** C3
Bywell Cl WF12 . . . . . **34** A2
Bywell Rd WF12 . . . . . **33** C3

C

Cable St HD1 . . . . **67** C2
Cadogan Ave HD1 . . . **51** B2
Caenarvon Cl WF17 . . **11** A3
Caister Cl WF17 . . . . . **11** A4
Calder Bank Rd
WF13 . . . . **32** B1
Calder Cl Elland HX4 . **23** A1
Ossett WF5 . . . . **48** B3
Caldercliffe Rd HD4 . . **76** B3
Caldercroft HX5 . . . . . **38** A4
Calderdale Way
HX5 . . . . **38** A4

Calder Dr HD4 . . . . . . **76** B2
Calder Ho
10 Elland HX5 . . . . . **23** C1
2 Mirfield WF14 . . . **43** C2
Caldermill Way
WF12 . . . . **46** A4
Calder Rd
Dewsbury WF13 . . . . . **45** B3
Mirfield WF14 . . . . **43** C1
Calder St
Brighouse HD6 . . . . . . **26** C3
Elland HX4 . . . . **23** A1
Calderstone Ct WF4 . **58** C1
Calder Terr
Elland HX3 . . . . **22** A3
Horbury WF4 . . . . **61** B2
Calder Trad Est
HD5 . . . . **41** C4
Calder Vale Rd WF4 . **61** B2
Calder View
Brighouse HD6 . . . . . . **26** A3
Ossett WF5 . . . . **48** A3
Caledonian Rd
WF12 . . . . **46** B3
Caledonia Rd WF12 . . **20** A3
Calf Hill Rd HD9 . . . . . **84** C3
California Dr WF4 . . . . **61** B3
California La DB19 . . . . **9** B1
CALMLANDS **80** C1
Calmlands Rd HD9 . . **80** B1
Calton St HD1 . . . . **53** B2
Calverts Wlk WF5 . . . . **49** A2
Camborne Dr HD2 . . . **39** B1
Cambridge Chase
BD19 . . . . **9** B4
Cambridge Rd
Batley WF17 . . . . **10** A4
Huddersfield HD1 . . . . **96** A3
Cambridge St
Batley, Heckmondwike
WF16 . . . . **18** B2
Batley WF17 . . . . **19** C3
Cameron Ave 1
BD12 . . . . **5** C3
Camilla Ct WF12 . . . . **33** C1
Cam La HD6 . . . . **14** A1
Camm La WF14 . . . . . **44** A4
Campinot Vale HD7 . . **72** B3
Camroyd St WF13 . . . **33** A3
Canal St
Brighouse HD6 . . . . . . **26** B4
Huddersfield HD1 . . . . **53** C2
Canary St 4 BD19 . . . . **8** A2
Canby Gr HD5 . . . . **70** A3
Canker La HD2 . . . . . . **54** A3
Cannon Gr WF16 . . . . **18** B3
Cannon Hall Cl HD6 . . **27** A4
Cannon Hall Dr HD6 . . **27** A4
Cannon Way WF13 . . . **32** C1
Canterbury Rd
WF12 . . . . **33** C3
Capas Heights Way
WF16 . . . . **18** B1
Capel St HD6 . . . . **26** A3
Cardigan Cl WF17 . . . **20** B3
Cardigan La WF5 . . . . **49** C1
Cardinal Cl HD9 . . . . . **80** C2
Cardwell Terr WF12 . . **46** B4
Carlile St HD9 . . . . . . **80** C2
CARLINGHOW **19** A4
Carlinghow Ct
WF13 . . . . **18** C1
Carlinghow Hill
WF17 . . . . **11** B1
Carlinghow La
WF17 . . . . **18** C2
Carlinghow Mills
WF17 . . . . **18** C1

Carlinghow Princess
Royal Jun & Inf Sch
WF17 . . . . **11** A1
Carlisle Cl WF13 . . . . **32** C4
Carlton Ave WF17 . . . **19** B1
Carlton Cl 1 BD19 . . . . **8** A1
Carlton Ct
Cleckheaton BD19 . . . . . **8** A2
Ossett WF5 . . . . **48** C4
Carlton Gr HX5 . . . . . . **24** C1
Carlton Jun & Inf Sch
WF13 . . . . **32** B4
Carlton Rd
Batley WF16 . . . . **17** C4
Dewsbury WF13 . . . . . **32** C3
Liversedge WF15 . . . . . **17** A1
Carlton St WF4 . . . . . . **60** C3
Carlton Terr WF12 . . . **46** C4
Carlton Way 2 BD19,
OL2 . . . . **8** A1
Carmine Cl HD5 . . . . . **69** A4
Carolan St HD7 . . . . . **64** C3
Caroline St 11 BD19 . . **8** A2
Carr Green Ave HD6 . . **39** B4
Carr Green Cl HD6 . . . **39** B4
Carr Green Dr HD6 . . . **39** B4
Carr Green Jun & Inf
Sch HD6 . . . . **25** C1
Carr Green La
Brighouse HD6 . . . . . . **25** C1
Huddersfield HD6 . . . . **39** B4
Carr House Rd HD9 . . **86** A3
Carriage Dr
Cleckheaton BD19 . . . . . **9** B4
Huddersfield HD4 . . . . **76** B2
Carriage Dr The
HX4 . . . . **22** C2
Carriage Way WF16 . . **18** A1
Carr La
Dewsbury,
Heckmondwike
WF16 . . . . **31** B3
Dewsbury WF12 . . . . . **57** B2
Middlestown WF4 . . . . **62** C4
Slaithwaite HD7 . . . . . **72** C3
Carr Mills WF17 . . . . . **10** B2
Carr Mount HD5 . . . . . **56** B1
Carr Pit Rd HD5 . . . . . **68** B3
Carr's Cl WF13 . . . . . . **18** C1
Carr Side Cres
WF17 . . . . **19** C1
Carrs Rd HD7 . . . . **79** A3
Carrs Side St No 1
HD7 . . . . **79** A3
Carrs Side St No 2
HD7 . . . . **79** A3
Carrs St HD7 . . . . **79** A3
Carr St
Batley, Batley Carr
WF17 . . . . **32** C4
Batley, Birstall WF17 . . **10** B3
Brighouse HD6 . . . . . . **13** A2
Cleckheaton BD19 . . . . . **8** A1
Huddersfield HD3 . . . . **51** C1
Liversedge WF15 . . . . . **17** A3
Carr Top Cl WF17 . . . . **32** B4
Carr Top La HD7 . . . . . **64** C2
Cartworth Fold HD9 . . **86** A1
Cartworth La HD9 . . . . **86** A1
Cartworth Rd HD9 . . . **86** A2
Cartwright Gdns
HD4 . . . . **66** B1
Cartwright House 7
WF15 . . . . **17** A3
Cartwright St BD19 . . **16** C4
Carver St BD19 . . . . . . **8** A2
Casson St HD4 . . . . . . **65** C2
Castle Ave
Brighouse HD6 . . . . . . **25** C2
Huddersfield HD4 . . . . **76** C3

Castle Cl WF17 . . . . . . **11** A3
Castle Cres WF12 . . . **57** C3
Castlefields Cres
HD6 . . . . **25** C2
Castlefields Dr HD6 . . **25** C2
Castlefields Inf Sch
HD6 . . . . **25** C3
Castlefields Rd HD6 . **25** C2
Castlegate HD1 . . . . . **96** A2
Castlegate Ho 17
HX5 . . . . **23** C1
Castlegate Loop
HD1 . . . . **96** A2
Castlegate Slip HD1 . **96** A3
Castle Gr WF4 . . . . **61** B2
Castle Hall Sch
WF14 . . . . **44** A3
Castle Hill Rd HD5 . . . **25** C2
Castle Hill Fort★
HD4 . . . . **77** B3
Castle Hill Rd HD3 . . **17** B4
Castle Hill Side HD4 . **77** B2
Castle Hill View
WF16 . . . . **18** C1
Castle Hos HD4 . . . . . **77** A2
Castle La HD7 . . . . **72** A4
Castle Mount HD7 . . . **57** C3
Castle Pl 2 HD6 . . . . . **25** C2
Castle Terr 1 HD6 . . . **25** C2
Castle View
Honley HD9 . . . . **83** A1
Horbury WF4 . . . . **61** B2
Mirfield WF14 . . . . **44** A3
Cater La WF16 . . . . . . **18** A1
Catherine Cl HD3 . . . . **51** A4
Catherine Cres 16
HX5 . . . . **37** B4
Catherine Rd HD2 . . . **40** A2
Catherine Slack
HD6 . . . . **12** C4
Catherine St
Brighouse HD6 . . . . . . **13** A1
Elland HX5 . . . . **37** B4
Caulms Wood Rd
WF13 . . . . **33** A3
Causeway Cl HD7 . . . **73** C3
Causeway Side HD7 . **73** C3
Cavendish App BD11 . . **3** B4
Cavendish Cl
Birkenshaw,
Drighlington BD11 . . . . **3** B3
Marsden HD7 . . . . **78** C3
Cavendish Mews
BD11 . . . . **3** B4
Cavewell Cl WF5 . . . . **49** B1
Cavewell Gdns WF5 . **49** B1
Cawcliffe Dr HD6 . . . . **13** A3
Cawcliffe Rd HD6 . . . . **13** A3
Cawley Garth WF16 . . **18** B1
Cawley La WF16 . . . . . **18** B1
Cawley Lane Jun & Inf
Sch WF16 . . . . **18** B2
Cawthorne Ave HD2 . **53** A4
Cecil St 9 HD1 . . . . . . **96** A2
Cedar Ave
Huddersfield HD1 . . . . **52** C4
Ossett WF5 . . . . **49** A2
Cedar Cl HD7 . . . . **65** B3
Cedar Dr WF12 . . . . . . **34** B2
Cedar Gr
2 Batley WF17 . . . . . **20** A1
Brighouse BD19 . . . . . **13** B4
Elland HX4 . . . . **22** C1
Cedar Mount HD1 . . . **52** C4
Cedar Rd WF12 . . . . . **34** A1
Cedar St HD1 . . . . **52** B1
Cedar Way BD19 . . . . . **9** A2
Celandine Ave HD3 . . **50** B2

Celandine Dr HD3 . . . . **50** B2
Celete Ind Pk BD19 . . . . **7** C1
Cemetery Rd
  Batley, Heckmondwike
    WF16 . . . . **18** A2
  Batley WF17 . . . . **19** B3
  Dewsbury WF13 . . . . **32** B1
  Huddersfield HD1 . . . . **52** C1
Centenary Sq WF12 . . **46** A2
Centenary Way
  WF17 . . . . **19** B4
Central Arc 5 BD19 . . **8** B1
Central Ave
  Cleckheaton WF15 . . . . **15** B3
  Huddersfield WF2 . . . . **53** B4
Central Cl HD2 . . . . **40** A1
Central Dr HD2 . . . . **40** A1
Central Par 6 BD19 . . **8** B1
Central Rd HD2 . . . . **40** A1
Central St WF13 . . . . . **32** C2
Centre 27 Bsns Pk
  WF17 . . . . **4** B1
Centre St 1 WF16 . . **17** C2
Centuria Wlk HD3 . . **50** B2
Centurion Way BD19 . . **7** C4
Century Rd HX5 . . . . **23** C1
Chadwick Cres
  WF13 . . . . **32** B3
Chadwick Fold La
  WF14 . . . . **43** B2
Chadwick Hall Gdns
  WF14 . . . . **43** B1
Chadwick La WF14 . . **43** B2
Chaffinch Wlk HD4 . . **76** A1
Chain Bar Rd BD19 . . . . **8** A3
Chalcroft Cl WF16 . . **18** B3
Challenge Way WF12,
  WF17 . . . . **21** A1
Chalwood HD2 . . . . **41** A2
Chancel Ct HD3 . . . . . . **65** C4
Chancery Cl 20 HD1 . . **96** A2
Chancery La
  19 Huddersfield
    HD1 . . . . **96** A2
  Ossett WF5 . . . . **34** C2
Chancery Rd WF5 . . **34** B2
Chandler Cl WF17 . . **10** B3
Chandler La HD9 . . . . **82** B2
Change La HX3 . . . . . . **23** B4
Chapel Ave WF16 . . . . **18** B3
Chapel Bank HD9 . . . . **87** B1
Chapel Cl
  Dewsbury WF12 . . . . **57** C4
  Elland HX4 . . . . **36** A2
  Huddersfield HD4 . . . . **76** B2
  Skelmanthorpe HD8 . . **91** C3
Chapel Croft HD6 . . **25** C1
Chapel Ct
  Denby Dale HD8 . . . . **95** A3
  Meltham HD9 . . . . . . **80** B2
CHAPEL FOLD **32** A4
Chapel Fold
  Batley WF17 . . . . **19** A1
  Brighouse BD12 . . . . . . **5** C2
Chapelgate HD9 . . . . **87** A1
Chapel Hill
  Clayton West HD8 . . **93** A3
  Huddersfield HD1 . . . . **96** A1
  Mirfield WF14 . . . . . . **56** C4
  Slaithwaite HD7 . . . . **73** C3
Chapel La
  6 Batley, Birstall
    WF17 . . . . **10** C3
  Batley WF16 . . . . **18** B2
  Dewsbury WF12 . . . . **57** C4
  Huddersfield, Moldgreen
    HD5 . . . . **68** C3

Chapel La continued
  Huddersfield, Wellhouse
    HD7 . . . . **64** C2
Chapel St
  Brighouse, Hove Edge
    HD6 . . . . **12** B3
  Cleckheaton BD19 . . . . **8** B2
  Cleckheaton, Hightown
    WF15 . . . . **15** C3
  Dewsbury WF12 . . . . **46** B4
  Elland HX4 . . . . **36** A2
  Huddersfield, Blue Bell
    Hill HD4 . . . . **76** A4
  Huddersfield HD1 . . . . **96** A1
  Huddersfield,
    Moldgreen HD5 . . . . **68** C3
  Huddersfield, Netherton
    HD4 . . . . **75** B1
  Liversedge WF15 . . . . **17** C2
  Mirfield WF14 . . . . . . **43** C3
  Ossett WF5 . . . . **49** C2
  Slaithwaite HD7 . . . . **64** A3
Chapel Terr
  Honley HD9 . . . . **83** A2
  Huddersfield HD4 . . . . **66** C2
Charles Ave HD3 . . . . **51** A2
Charles Jones Ct
  WF17 . . . . **19** A3
Charles St
  Batley WF17 . . . . **19** C2
  Brighouse HD6 . . . . . . **13** A1
  Cleckheaton BD19 . . . . **9** B2
  Dewsbury, Dewsbury
    Moor WF13 . . . . **31** C2
  Dewsbury, Ravensthorpe
    WF13 . . . . **45** A3
  Dewsbury WF12 . . . . **33** B2
  Elland HX5 . . . . **37** B4
  Horbury WF4 . . . . **61** C1
  Huddersfield HD4 . . . . **66** C2
  Ossett WF5 . . . . **49** B1
Charlesworth Ct
  WF12 . . . . **57** C4
Charlesworth's Bldgs
  3 WF4 . . . . **60** C3
Charlesworth Sq
  BD19 . . . . **9** A2
Charlesworth St
  WF12 . . . . **46** B2
Charlotte Cl WF17 . . **3** C1
Charlotte Gr WF5 . . **49** B2
Charnwood Bank
  WF16 . . . . **18** B2
Chaster St WF17 . . . . **19** A4
Chatsworth Cl HD5 . . **68** C2
Chatsworth Ct
  WF12 . . . . **33** C1
Chatsworth Terr
  WF12 . . . . **33** C1
Chaucer Cl HD9 . . . . . **83** A1
Cheapside
  Batley WF17 . . . . **20** B1
  Cleckheaton BD19 . . . . **8** B1
Chellow Way WF12 . . **32** C1
Chequers The HD9 . . **80** C2
Cherry La HD8 . . . . . . **93** B3
Cherry Nook Rd
  HD2 . . . . **41** A1
Cherry Tree Cl HD7 . . **65** B3
Cherry Tree Ctr 15
  HD1 . . . . **96** A2
Cherry Tree Dr HX4 . . **22** C1
Cherry Tree Wlk
  HD9 . . . . **87** A2
Chesil Bank HD3 . . **66** A4
Chesilton Ave HD3 . . **51** B1
Chesterton Ct WF4 . . **61** B4
Chesterton Dr HD9 . . **83** A1
Chestnut Ave WF17 . . **19** A2
Chestnut Cl
  Elland HX4 . . . . **22** B1

Chestnut Cl continued
  Huddersfield HD4 . . . . **76** C4
Chestnut Garth HD3 . **51** B1
Chestnut Mdws
  WF14 . . . . **29** C2
Chestnut St HD2 . . . . **40** C1
Chestnut Terr WF12 . . **34** B1
Chevinedge Cres
  HX3 . . . . **23** A3
Chevins Cl WF17 . . . . **10** C2
Cheviot Ave HD9 . . . . **81** A1
Cheviot Way WF14 . . **56** C4
CHICKENLEY **34** B2
Chickenley La WF12 . . **34** B1
Chickenly Com Jun &
  Inf Sch WF12 . . . . . . **34** A1
CHIDSWELL **21** B1
Chidswell Gdns
  WF12 . . . . **21** B1
Chidswell La
  Batley WF12 . . . . **21** A1
  Ossett WF5, WF12 . . **34** B4
Child La WF15 . . . . . . **29** C3
Chiltern Ave HD3 . . . . **51** A3
Chiltern Dr WF14 . . . . **56** C4
Chiltern Rd WF12 . . **33** C3
Chiltern Way WF15 . . **16** A3
Chimes Ct HD5 . . . . . . **55** C1
Chimney La HD8 . . . . **70** C2
Chinewood Ave
  WF17 . . . . **19** B4
Christ Church
  Woodhouse CE Inf &
  Jun Sch HD2 . . . . . . **40** C2
Church Ave
  Huddersfield,
    Linthwaite HD7 . . . . **74** A4
  Huddersfield, Yews Hill
    HD4 . . . . **67** A2
Churchbank Way
  WF12 . . . . **46** B2
Church Cl HD8 . . . . . . **90** C2
Church Cres WF4 . . **63** C4
Church Ct WF5 . . . . . . **35** A1
Churchfield Cl 5
  WF15 . . . . **17** A2
Churchfields HD2 . . **41** B1
Church Fields HD2 . . **41** B1
Churchfields Rd
  HD6 . . . . **13** A1
Churchfield St 1
  WF17 . . . . **19** C3
Churchfield Terr 6
  WF15 . . . . **17** A2
Church Gn HD8 . . . . . **89** B4
Church Grange 4
  BD19 . . . . **8** B1
Church Ho 13 HX5 . . **23** C1
Churchill Gr WF16 . . **18** B1
Church La
  Batley WF16 . . . . **18** A1
  Brighouse, Elland Lower
    Edge HD6 . . . . **25** A1
  3 Brighouse HD6 . . **26** A4
  Brighouse, Waring Green
    HD6 . . . . **13** A1
  Clayton West HD8 . . **93** B3
  Cleckheaton BD19 . . . . **9** C2
  Dewsbury, Dewsbury
    Moor WF13 . . . . **31** C2
  Dewsbury, Thornhill
    WF12 . . . . **58** A4
  Huddersfield, Moldgreen
    HD5 . . . . **68** C4
  Huddersfield, Newsome
    HD4 . . . . **76** C4
  Kirkheaton HD5 . . . . **55** B1
  Liversedge, Knowler Hill
    WF15 . . . . **17** A3
  Liversedge WF15 . . . . **15** B1
  Marsden HD7 . . . . . . **78** C3

Church La continued
  Mirfield WF14 . . . . . . **44** B3
  Netherton WF4 . . . . . . **60** A1
  Shepley HD8 . . . . **90** A2
  Slaithwaite HD7 . . . . **74** A3
Church Mdws WF17 . . **10** A3
Church Paddocks
  HD6 . . . . **27** B3
Church Pk WF15 . . . . **29** B4
Church Rd
  Batley WF17 . . . . **10** C2
  Liversedge FW15 . . . . **29** B4
Church St
  Batley, Birstall
    WF17 . . . . **10** B3
  Batley, Heckmondwike
    WF16 . . . . **18** A1
  Brighouse HD6 . . . . . . **25** C2
  Cleckheaton BD19 . . . . **8** B1
  Cleckheaton, Hightown
    WF15 . . . . **15** C3
  Dewsbury, Ravensthorpe
    WF13 . . . . **45** A3
  Dewsbury WF13 . . . . **33** A2
  Elland HX5 . . . . **23** C1
  Elland, West Vale
    HX4 . . . . **23** A1
  Holmfirth, Netherthong
    HD9 . . . . **84** A2
  Holmfirth, New Mill
    HD9 . . . . **87** C4
  Honley HD9 . . . . **83** B4
  Horbury WF4 . . . . **61** A3
  Huddersfield HD1 . . . . **96** B1
  Huddersfield, Longwood
    HD3 . . . . **65** C4
  Huddersfield, Moldgreen
    HD5 . . . . **68** C4
  Huddersfield, Paddock
    HD1 . . . . **66** C3
  Huddersfield, Town End
    HD7 . . . . **64** C2
  Huddersfield, Yews Hill
    HD4 . . . . **67** A2
  Liversedge WF15 . . . . **17** A3
  Ossett WF5 . . . . **35** A1
  Slaithwaite HD7 . . . . **72** B2
Church Terr
  Clayton West HD8 . . **92** C2
  9 Holmfirth HD9 . . **86** A3
Church View BD19 . . . . **7** B2
Church Wlk
  Batley WF17 . . . . **19** A1
  Dewsbury WF12 . . . . **58** A4
Churchwood Cl HD7 . . **72** B3
Churwell Ave 3
  WF13 . . . . **18** C1
Churwell Vale WF12 . . **34** A4
Cinder Hills Rd HD9 . . **86** B2
Clara St
  Brighouse HD6 . . . . . . **26** A3
  Huddersfield, Cowlersley
    HD4 . . . . **65** C1
  Huddersfield, Fartown
    HD1 . . . . **53** A3
  Huddersfield HD1 . . . . **53** A2
Clare Cres BD12 . . . . . . **5** C4
Clare Hill HD1 . . . . . . **96** A3
Claremont WF16 . . . . **18** A2
Claremont Rd WF13 . . **32** B3
Claremont St
  8 Cleckheaton
    BD19 . . . . **8** A2
  5 Elland HX5 . . . . . . **37** C4
  Huddersfield HD1 . . . . **96** A3
Clarence St
  Batley WF17 . . . . **20** A3
  Cleckheaton BD19 . . . . **8** A1
Clarence Terr WF12 . . **46** C4
Clarendon Cotts
  WF5 . . . . **49** A1

Clare Rd
  Bradford BD12 . . . . **5** C4
  Cleckheaton BD19 . . . . **8** A1
Clarke La HD9 . . . . . . **80** C2
Clarke St WF13 . . . . . **32** A3
Clarkson Ave WF16 . . **18** B2
Clarkson Cl WF16 . . **18** B2
Clarkson St WF13 . . **45** A4
Claydon Pl 4
  WF16 . . . . **18** A2
Clayborn View BD19 . **16** B4
Clay Butts HD2 . . . . **52** B4
Clay House La HX4 . . **23** A1
Clay La HD7 . . . . **72** C3
Clayton Fields HD2 . **52** C2
Claytons Cotts 2
  WF4 . . . . **60** C3
CLAYTON WEST **93** B3
Clayton West Sta*
  HD8 . . . . **93** B4
Clay Well HD7 . . . . . **64** C2
CLECKHEATON **15** C4
Clement St
  Huddersfield HD1 . . . . **52** C2
  Huddersfield, Paddock
    Brow HD4 . . . . **66** C2
Clement Terr WF12 . . **46** B4
Clerk Green St
  WF17 . . . . **19** B2
Cleveland Ave
  Horbury WF2 . . . . **61** C4
  Meltham HD9 . . . . . . **81** A1
Cleveland Garth
  WF2 . . . . **61** C4
Cleveland Gr WF2 . . **61** C4
Cleveland Rd HD1 . . **52** A1
Cleveland Way HD8 . . **89** B1
CLIFF **86** B3
Cliff Cl HD3 . . . . **66** A4
Cliff Ct WF15 . . . . . . **17** A1
Cliffe Ash HD7 . . . . . **64** C2
Cliffe Ave HX3 . . . . **5** A1
Cliffe Com Bsns Pk
  HD1 . . . . **67** B3
Cliffe Crest WF4 . . . . **61** A4
Cliffe End Bsns Ctr
  HD3 . . . . **65** C3
Cliffe End Rd HD3 . . **66** A4
Cliffe Hill Com Prim
  Sch HX3 . . . . **13** A4
Cliffe La BD19 . . . . **8** C3
Cliffe Mount BD19 . . **9** A3
CLIFF END **66** A4
Cliffe Pk HD8 . . . . . . **90** A2
Cliffe Rd
  Brighouse HD6 . . . . . . **26** B4
  Shepley HD8 . . . . **90** A2
Cliffe Side HD8 . . . . **90** A2
Cliffe St Batley WF17 . **18** C2
  Clayton West HD8 . . **93** B3
  Dewsbury WF13 . . . . **33** A3
Cliffe Terr HX3 . . . . . . **22** C4
Cliffe View HD8 . . . . **93** B3
Cliffewood Rise
  HD8 . . . . **93** A3
Cliff Hill Ct HD9 . . . **86** B3
Cliff House La HD9 . . **86** B4
Cliff La HD9 . . . . **86** B3
Clifford Ct WF5 . . . . **48** B4
Cliff Rd HD9 . . . . **86** B4
Cliff St HD9 . . . . **86** B3
CLIFTON **27** A4
Clifton Ave
  Holmfirth HD9 . . . . . . **86** B4
  Horbury WF4 . . . . **60** C4
Clifton Cl WF4 . . . . . . **60** C4
Clifton Comm HD6 . . **13** C1
Clifton Cres WF4 . . **60** C4
Clifton Ct WF16 . . . . **31** B4
Clifton Dr WF4 . . . . . **60** C4
Clifton Inf Sch WF4 . . **60** B4

Clifton La HD9 . . . . . . .80 C2
Clifton Rd
3 Brighouse HD6 . . .26 B4
Horbury WF4 . . . . . . .60 C4
Huddersfield HD1 . . . .52 B1
Clifton Side HD2. . . . .41 B4
Clifton Terr
Batley WF17 . . . . .20 A3
Ossett WF5 . . . . .34 C2
Clifton View HD8 . . . . .93 B3
Clog Sole Rd HD6 . . . . .12 C2
Close Hill La HD4 . . . .76 B4
Close Lea HD6 . . . . .5 A2
Close Lea Ave HD6 . . .25 C3
Close Lea Dr HD6 . . . .25 C3
Close Lea Way HD6 . .25 C3
Closes Rd **2** HD6 . . . .26 A3
Close The HD8 . . . . . . .93 A3
Cloth Hall St
Dewsbury WF13 . . . . . .33 A2
Huddersfield HD1 . . . .96 A2
Clough Dr
Batley WF17 . . . . .11 A4
Lepton HD8 . . . . .88 A4
Linthwaite HD7 . . . . . .73 C2
Clough Hall La HD4 . .77 C3
Clough Hey HD7 . . . . . .78 B3
Clough House Ct
HD2 . . . . .52 C4
Clough La
Brighouse, Bailiff
    Bridge HD6 . . . . . . .14 A4
Brighouse, Elland Lower
    Edge HD6 . . . . .39 B4
Huddersfield, Paddock
    HD1, HD2 . . . . .66 B3
Liversedge WF15 . . . .16 A1
Clough Lee HD7 . . . . .78 C3
Clough Pk HD8 . . . . . .88 A4
Clough Rd
Huddersfield HD2 . . . .53 A4
Slaithwaite, Crimble
    HD7 . . . . .72 C4
Clough The
Lepton HD8 . . . . .70 C1
Mirfield WF14 . . . . . . .43 A4
Clough Way HD8 . . . . .88 A4
Clover Hill WF15 . . . . .16 A3
Club Houses HD4 . . . .76 A2
Clubhouses Croft **8**
WF4 . . . . .60 C3
Clumber Dr BD19 . . . . .9 B1
Cluntergate WF4 . . . . .61 A3
Clutton St WF17 . . . . .20 B3
Coach House Dr
HD5 . . . . .69 B3
Coach La **1** BD19 . . . . .8 B2
Coach Rd
Brighouse HD6 . . . . . .12 C4
Huddersfield HD2 . . . .52 C4
Meltham HD9 . . . . . . .81 A1
Coal Pit La
Batley WF17 . . . . .19 A4
Brighouse HD6 . . . . . .27 B4
Holmfirth HD9 . . . . . . .87 C4
Huddersfield HD4 . . . .67 B1
Coal Pit Mews
WF17 . . . . .19 A4
Coates Cl WF12 . . . . . .33 C3
Cobbles The HD9 . . . .80 C2
Cobcroft Rd HD1,
HD2 . . . . .53 A3
Cobden Cl **9** WF17 . .19 C3
Cobden Terr HX5 . . . . .37 B3
Cocking Steps La
HD4 . . . . .82 B3
Cockley Hill La HD5 . .56 A2
Cockley Meadows
HD5 . . . . .55 C3
Colbeck Ave WF17 . . .19 A3
Colbeck Row WF17 . .10 B3

Colbeck Terr WF17 . . .19 A3
Colders Dr HD9 . . . . . .80 B1
Colders Gn HD9 . . . . . .80 B2
Colders La HD9 . . . . . .80 B1
Cold Hill La HD4 . . . . .76 C2
Cold Royd La HD5 . . . .55 A1
Coldwell St HD7 . . . . .73 C3
College Ave HD3 . . . . .51 C3
College St E HD4 . . . . .66 C2
College St
1 Batley WF17 . . . . . . .10 B3
Huddersfield HD5 . . . . .66 C2
Collin Moor La HX4 . .22 C2
Collinson St BD19 . . . .8 A2
Coll of the
Resurrection
WF14 . . . . .43 A4
COLNE BRIDGE 42 A3
Colne Bridge Rd
HD2 . . . . .42 A3
Colne Bsns Pk HD3 . .66 A3
Colne Hurst HD2 . . . .41 A2
Colne Rd HD1 . . . . . . .67 C2
Colne St
Huddersfield, Aspley
    HD1 . . . . .68 B3
3 Huddersfield HD1 . .67 A3
Colne Vale Rd HD3 . . .65 C2
Colne Valley Bsns Pk
HD7 . . . . .73 C3
Colne Valley High Sch
HD7 . . . . .74 A3
Colne Valley Mus★
HD7 . . . . .64 C2
Colne View HD7 . . . . .72 C3
Colwyn St HD1 . . . . . .52 A1
COMBS. 47 A1
Combs Rd WF12 . . . . .58 A4
Combs The WF12 . . . . .47 A1
Commercial Rd
Dewsbury WF13 . . . . .32 C3
Skelmanthorpe HD8 . .92 A3
Commercial St
Batley, Heckmondwike
    WF16. . . . . .18 B2
Batley WF17 . . . . .19 C3
Brighouse HD6 . . . . . .26 B4
Cleckheaton BD19 . . . . .8 B1
Dewsbury, Earlsheaton
    WF12. . . . . .33 C1
Dewsbury, Ravensthorpe
    WF13. . . . . .45 B3
Huddersfield HD1 . . . .96 B1
Slaithwaite HD7 . . . . .72 C2
Common End La
HD8. . . . . .88 A4
Common La HD8 . . . .95 C3
Common Rd
Batley WF17 . . . . .18 C2
Elland HX5 . . . . .38 B4
5 Huddersfield HD1 . .53 A2
Commonside
Batley WF17 . . . . .20 A1
Liversedge FW15 . . . .29 B4
Common Terr HD6 . . .26 A3
Common The WF12 . . .47 A1
Com Science Coll The
WF12 . . . . .58 A3
Concord St HD9 . . . . .83 A2
Coney Wlk WF13 . . . . .31 C2
Coniston Ave HD5 . . . .68 C4
Coniston Cl HX5 . . . . .24 B1
Coniston Ho **15** HX5 .23 C1
Coniston Rd
Batley WF12 . . . . .33 C4
Meltham HD9 . . . . . . .80 C1
Connaught Fold
HD2 . . . . .41 A3
Constable Dr WF5 . . .48 C4

Conway Cres
Batley WF17 . . . . .32 C4
Meltham HD9 . . . . . . .80 B1
Cooke Cres BD19 . . . . .9 A2
Cook La WF16 . . . . . . .17 C2
Cookson St HD6 . . . . .12 C1
Coombe Rd HD3 . . . . .65 B3
Co-operative Bldgs
HD6 . . . . .5 B1
Co-operative St
Dewsbury WF12 . . . . . .34 B2
Horbury WF4 . . . . . . .60 C3
3 Mirfield WF14 . . . . . .43 C1
Cooper Bridge Rd HD5,
WF14 . . . . .42 A4
Cooper La HD9 . . . . . .86 A3
COPLEY 22 A4
Copley Ave HD9 . . . . .80 B2
Copley Bank Rd
HD7 . . . . .64 B1
Copley Cl HX3 . . . . . . .22 B3
Copley Glen HX3 . . . . .22 B4
Copley Gr HX3 . . . . . . .22 B4
Copley Hall St HX3 . . .22 B4
Copley Hall Terr
HX3 . . . . .22 B4
COPLEY HILL 11 A3
Copley Hill WF17 . . . .10 C3
Copley La HX3 . . . . . . .22 B4
Copley Mill House
HX3 . . . . .22 A4
Copley Mount HX3. . .22 B4
Copley Prim Sch
HX3 . . . . .22 B4
Copley St WF17 . . . . . .11 A1
Copley Terr HX3 . . . . .22 B4
Copley View HX3 . . . . .22 B4
Coppice Dr HD4 . . . . .82 B4
Coppice The
Batley WF17 . . . . .10 A3
Huddersfield, Fixby
    HD2 . . . . .40 A2
Huddersfield, Lindley
    HD3 . . . . .51 A3
Mirfield WF14 . . . . . . .30 A2
Coppin Hall Gr
WF14 . . . . .42 C4
Coppin Hall La
WF14 . . . . .42 C4
Copse The
Brighouse, Hartshead
    Moor Top BD19 . . . . . .6 C1
Brighouse, Hove Edge
    HD6 . . . . .12 C2
Copthorne Gdns
HD2 . . . . .41 B3
Copthorne Sq HD2 . . .41 B3
Corby St HD7 . . . . .53 A3
Corfe Cl WF17 . . . . . . .11 B4
Corn Bank HD4 . . . . . .82 A4
Cornet Cl HD3 . . . . . . .51 C3
Cornfield WF13 . . . . . .31 C3
Cornfield Ave HD3 . . .51 A1
Cornmill Ave WF15 . .17 C1
Cornmill Cres WF15 . .30 B4
Cornmill Dr WF15 . . . .17 B1
Cornmill La WF15 . . . .17 B1
Cornrace View HD4 . .68 A2
Cornwall Cres HD6 . .13 B4
Cornwall Ho **16** HX5 .23 C1
Coronation Bglws
HD9 . . . . .80 C1
Coronation St
Elland HX5 . . . . .37 B4
Elland, Lindwell HX4 . .22 C1
Coronation Terr **2**
WF17 . . . . .10 C3
Corporation St
Dewsbury WF13 . . . . . .33 A2
2 Huddersfield HD1 . .96 A1

Corrance Rd BD12 . . . .6 A3
Cote Cl HD8 . . . . .89 A1
Cote La HD2 . . . . .39 A3
Cote Wall WF14 . . . . . .44 C1
Cotswold Dr WF15 . . .16 A3
Cotswold Mews
HD8 . . . . .88 C1
Cottage Homes
Huddersfield, Dalton
    HD5 . . . . .69 C4
Huddersfield, Netherton
    HD4 . . . . .75 C1
Couford Gr HD2 . . . . .41 B2
Coule Royd HD5 . . . . .54 C1
Council Terr HD9 . . . .83 B3
County Cl WF17 . . . . . .19 C4
Court No 6 WF17 . . . . .19 C2
Court The WF15 . . . . . .16 B2
Courtyard The
Batley WF17 . . . . .10 C4
Huddersfield HD4 . . . .66 C2
Covert The WF17 . . . . .10 C1
Covey Clough Ct
WF14 . . . . .56 C3
COWCLIFFE 39 A1
Cowcliffe Hill Rd
HD2 . . . . .39 B1
Cow Close La BD12 . . .6 B4
Cowdray Dr **9** BD19 . .6 C2
Cowdry Cl WF12 . . . . .58 A4
Cow Gate HD3 . . . . . . .65 B4
Cow Heys HD5 . . . . . . .54 C1
Cow La
Brighouse HX3 . . . . . .12 A2
Halifax HX3 . . . . .22 C4
COWLERSLEY 65 C1
Cowlersley La HD4,
HD7 . . . . .65 B1
Cowlersley Prim Sch
HD4 . . . . .65 B1
COWMES 70 B3
Cowper St WF12 . . . . .46 B4
Cowrakes Cl HD3 . . . .51 A3
Cowrakes Rd HD3 . . .51 A3
Cowslip St HD1 . . . . . .66 C3
COXLEY 59 C1
Coxley Cres WF4 . . . . .63 B4
Coxley La WF4 . . . . . . .59 C1
Coxley View WF4 . . . .63 A3
Crabtree Ave WF16 . .18 B3
CRACKENEDGE 33 A3
Crackenedge La
WF13 . . . . .33 A3
Crackenedge Terr
WF13 . . . . .33 A3
Craig Cl WF17 . . . . . . .19 C4
Craiglea Dr BD12 . . . . .6 A4
Craig-y-don WF12 . . .33 C1
Cranmer Gdns HD9 . .81 A2
Cranwood Dr HD5 . . .69 C4
Craven Cl BD19 . . . . . . .9 C2
Cravendale Rd
WF13 . . . . .44 C4
Craven Dr BD19 . . . . . .9 C2
Craven La BD19 . . . . . . .9 C2
Craven Rd WF13 . . . . .45 C4
Craven St
Dewsbury WF13 . . . . . .45 A4
Huddersfield HD4 . . . .65 C2
Crawshaw St WF13 . .45 B4
Crawthorne Cres
HD2 . . . . .41 A2
Crescent Ave
Dewsbury WF13 . . . . . .44 C3
Huddersfield HD4 . . . .75 C1
Crescent Rd
Huddersfield, Fartown
    HD2 . . . . .53 A2
Huddersfield, Netherton
    HD4 . . . . .75 C1

Crescent Royd HD5 . .69 C3
Crescent The
3 Brighouse, Waring
    Green HD6 . . . . .13 B1
Cleckheaton WF15 . . .16 A3
Dewsbury WF13 . . . . . .44 C3
Elland HX5 . . . . .37 B3
Holmfirth HD9 . . . . . . .87 B4
Netherton WF4 . . . . . .63 B3
Crescent Wlk WF13 . .44 C3
Cressfield Rd HD3 . . .51 C2
Crest Ave
Bradford BD12 . . . . . . .5 C3
Huddersfield HD5 . . . .69 C3
Crestfield Ave HX5 . .37 A3
Crestfield Cres HX5 . .37 A3
Crestfield Dr HX5 . . . .37 A3
Crestfield Rd HX5 . . . .37 A3
Crest Hill Rd HD2 . . . .40 B1
Crest Pl HD6 . . . . .12 B3
Crest Rd HD3 . . . . .37 C1
Crest The HD2 . . . . . . .41 A4
Crest View HD6 . . . . . .12 B3
Creswell La WF13 . . . .18 C1
Cricketers Fold HX3 .23 A4
CRIMBLE 72 C4
Crimble Bank HD7 . . .72 C3
Croft Bank BD11 . . . . . .2 A3
Croft Cottage La **3**
HD1 . . . . .53 B2
Croft Ct HD9 . . . . .83 A1
Croft Dr HD9 . . . . .82 C2
Croft Flat Dr HD8 . . . .70 B2
Croft Gdns HD2 . . . . . .52 B3
Croft Head HD8 . . . . . .91 C3
Croft Ho **11** HD2 . . . .23 C1
Croft House La HD1 . .52 B1
Croftlands
Batley WF12 . . . . .33 C4
Huddersfield HD4 . . . .76 C4
Ossett WF5 . . . . .49 A3
Crofton Cl HD7 . . . . . .73 C2
Croft Pl **1** HD6 . . . . . .13 B2
Croft St
Birkenshaw BD11 . . . . .2 A3
6 Brighouse HD6 . . .26 A4
Dewsbury WF13 . . . . . .32 C2
Huddersfield HD1 . . . .66 B3
Liversedge WF16 . . . .18 A1
Crofts The WF17 . . . . .18 C2
Croft The BD11 . . . . . . .3 B3
Croisdale Cl WF15 . . .16 B2
Cromarty Ave HD4 . . .75 B4
Cromarty Dr HD4 . . . .75 B4
Cromwell Bottom Dr
HD6 . . . . .25 A4
Cromwell Ct BD11 . . . .3 A3
Cromwell Pl WF5 . . . .35 B1
Croset Ave HD1 . . . . . .53 C1
Crosland Ct HD3 . . . . .50 C3
Crosland Edge HD9 . .81 A4
CROSLAND HILL 74 C4
Crosland Hill Rd
HD4 . . . . .66 A1
CROSLAND MOOR . .66 B1
Crosland Moor Jun Sch
HD4 . . . . .66 B1
Crosland Rd
Huddersfield, Lidley
    HD3 . . . . .51 A3
Huddersfield, Yews Hill
    HD1 . . . . .67 A3
Crosland St HD4 . . . . .67 A2
Cross Bank Rd
WF17 . . . . .19 B4

Cross Church St
🔟 Cleckheaton
BD19...........8 B1
Huddersfield HD1...96 B2
Huddersfield, Paddock
HD1.............66 C3
Cross Cotts 🔟 HD1...52 A1
Cross Crown St 🔟
BD19.............8 A1
Crossfield Ct WF4....62 A4
Crossfields WF4......62 B4
Cross Fields HD5....54 B1
Firs Frs St HD3......66 A3
Cross Foundry St
WF13............45 A3
Cross Green Dr HD5..69 C4
Cross Green Rd
HD5...............69 C4
Cross Grove St HD1..96 A1
Cross Hill HX4........22 C1
Cross Hill La HX5....28 C3
Crosshills Mount
HX4..............22 C1
Crossings The WF17..10 C2
Cross Keys Ct WF4....61 A3
Cross La
Brighouse HD6.......27 C3
Elland HX5..........37 A4
Honley HD9..........84 A4
Huddersfield HD4....67 C1
Skelmanthorpe HD8...91 C2
Cross Lane Bsns Pk
WF15.............17 B2
Crosslane Ind Est
WF15.............17 A2
Cross Lane Prim Sch
HX5...............37 A3
Crossley Cl WF14....30 A2
Crossley Fields Jun &
Inf Sch WF14......30 B1
Crossley Gr WF14....30 A2
Crossley La
Huddersfield HD5....55 A1
Mirfield WF14.......30 B2
Crossley St
Batley WF15.........30 C4
Brighouse HD6.......26 B3
Crossley St WF17....19 C1
Cross View WF14....30 B2
Crossmount St
WF17.............19 C1
Cross Normanton St
WF4..............61 B2
Cross Park St
Batley WF17.........20 A3
Dewsbury WF12......33 C2
🔟 Horbury WF4.......60 C3
Cross Rd
Dewsbury WF12......57 C3
Middlestown WF4....59 A1
Cross Rink St 🔟
WF17.............20 A1
Cross Ryecroft St
WF5..............34 C1
Cross St Batley WF17..19 C3
Brighouse HD6......13 B2
Dewsbury, Savile Town
WF12.............33 A1
Dewsbury WF12......33 B2
🔟 Elland, Holywell Green
HX4..............36 A2
🔟 Elland, West Vale
HX4..............23 A1
Honley HD9.........83 A2
🔟 Horbury WF4......61 A3
Huddersfield HD4...67 A2
Liversedge WF15...30 A4
Ossett WF5.........34 C3

D

Dacre Cl WF15.......16 C3
Daisy Bank HX3......5 A4
Daisy Cl WF17.......10 B4

Cross St continued
Slaithwaite HD7......72 C3
Crow La HD3.........65 C3
Crow Lane Prim &
Foundation Scheme
Sch HD3...........65 C3
Crowlees CE Jun & Inf
Sch WF14..........44 A2
Crowlees Cl WF14....44 A3
Crowlees Gdns
WF14............44 A3
Crowlees Rd WF14...44 A3
Crown Bldgs HD8....93 B4
Crown Cl WF12.......34 A1
Crow nest Ct 🔟
WF14............43 B3
Crow Nest Terr 🔟
WF13............32 B1
Crow Nest View
WF13............32 A1
Crown Flatt Way
WF12............33 B3
Crown Gn HD4.......65 C2
Crown La 🔟 HD8.....65 C2
Crownlands La WF5..48 C4
Crown Point CI WF5..48 B4
Crown Point Dr
WF5.............34 C1
Crown Point Rd
WF5.............48 B4
Crown Sq HD3.......66 A3
Crown St
Brighouse HD6......13 A1
Clayton West HD8....92 C2
Cleckheaton BD19....8 A1
Elland HX5.........23 C1
Honley HD9.........83 A3
Ossett WF5.........49 A1
Crown Terr HD8......93 B4
Crown Villas HD8....92 C2
Crowther Bruce Mill Rd
HD7..............79 A3
Crowther Cl HD7.....72 C4
Crowther Rd
Batley WF16.........18 B3
Mirfield WF14.......43 C3
Crowther St
Batley WF17.........18 C3
🔟 Cleckheaton BD19...8 A2
Huddersfield, Aspley
HD1..............96 B1
🔟 Huddersfield,
Rashcliffe HD1.....67 B1
Crowtrees Cres HD6..25 C1
Crowtrees La HD6....25 C1
Crowtrees Pk HD6....25 C2
Cuckoo La HD9......83 A2
Cuckoo's Nest Halt ★
HD8..............92 B3
Cuckstool Rd HD8....95 B3
Cullingworth St
WF13............19 A1
Cumberland Ave
HD2..............40 A3
Cumberworth La
HD8..............94 C4
Cumberworth Rd
HD8..............91 B2
Cuniver Ct WF15.....15 C3
Curwen Cres WF16...18 B4
Curzon St HD2.......41 C4
Cuttlehurst HD8......92 C2
Cypress Fold HD8....71 A1
Cyprus Cres WF14...31 A1
Cyprus St WF5.......34 C2

Daisy Gn HD7........73 B1
Daisy Hill HD3.......32 C2
Daisy La 🔟 HD9.....86 A3
Daisy Lea La HD3....51 C3
Daisy Rd HD6........26 B2
Daisy Royd HD4.....76 C4
Daisy St 🔟 HD6.....26 A4
Dalby Ct BD19........9 B1
Dale Cl Batley WF17..19 C1
Denby Dale HD8......95 A2
Ossett WF5.........49 A4
Dale Croft HD8.......91 C3
Dale Ct WF5.........48 C4
Dale House Ind Sch
WF17............19 A4
Dale La WF16........18 B3
Daleside
Dewsbury WF12.....57 B3
Elland HX4.........22 A1
Dale St
Dewsbury WF12......46 B2
Huddersfield, Folly Hall
HD1..............96 A1
Huddersfield HD3...65 C3
Ossett WF5.........48 C4
Skelmanthorpe HD8..91 C3
Dale View
Birkenshaw,
Drighlington BD11...3 C4
Huddersfield HD3...65 C3
Dalmeny Ave HD4....66 B1
Dalmeny Cl HD4......66 B1
DALTON...........54 C1
Dalton Bank Rd HD2,
HD5..............41 C1
Dalton Clowes HD5...54 B1
Dalton Fold Rd HD5..54 A1
Dalton Gr HD5.......54 B1
Dalton Green La
HD5..............69 C4
Dalton Jun & Inf Sch
HD5..............69 B4
Dalton Works HD5...54 C3
Damfield Mews HD4..76 B4
Dam Head La HD8....71 B4
Dam Hill HD8........89 A1
Damside Rd HD4.....68 A2
Danebury Rd HD6....26 B3
Danes La WF4.......62 C4
Danesleigh Dr WF4..62 C4
Darbyfields HD7......65 A4
Dark La
Batley, Birstall
WF17..............3 C1
Batley, Mount Pleasant
WF17.............19 B2
Huddersfield HD4...69 C1
Darley Rd WF15.....16 C3
Darley St WF16......18 A2
Darnley Cl HD9......80 C1
Dartmouth Ave HD5..59 C1
Dartmouth St HD7...72 B3
David La WF13.......32 C4
DAW GREEN........32 B2
Daw La WF4.........61 B2
Daw Royds HD5......69 C2
Dawson Gdns 🔟
WF13............32 C2
Dawson Hill Yd 🔟
WF4.............61 A3
Dawson Rd HD4.....68 A1
Day St
Dewsbury WF13.....45 A3
Huddersfield HD1...68 B3
Deacon Cl HD9......80 C2
Deacons Wlk WF16..18 B2
Deadmanstone HD4..76 B2
Deal La HD7.........64 C2
Dean Ave HD9.......84 A2
DEAN BOTTOM.....88 A1

Dean Brook Rd
Holmfirth HD9........84 B3
Huddersfield HD4....76 A2
Dean Ct HX3........22 C4
Dean End HX4.......22 C2
Deanhouse HD9......84 A2
Dean Park Dr BD11..3 B4
Dean St
🔟 Elland HX5.......37 B4
Elland, West Vale
HX4..............23 A1
Huddersfield HD5...51 B2
Dean View WF17.....10 C4
Dean Wood View
HX3..............22 C4
Dearden St WF5.....51 B3
Dearne Fold HD3....51 B3
Dearne Pk HD8......93 A3
Dearne Royd HD8....93 A3
Dearneside Rd HD8..95 A3
Dearne St HD8.......92 C2
Dearne Terr HD8....93 A2
Dearnfield HD8......94 A3
Dearnley St WF13...45 A4
Deepdale Ho WF13..32 C4
Deep La
Brighouse HD6......27 C4
Huddersfield HD4...66 A1
Deer Croft Ave HD3..50 C2
Deer Croft Cres
HD3..............50 C2
Deer Croft Dr HD3...50 C2
Deer Croft Rd 🔟
HD3..............50 C3
Deer Hill Cl HD7.....78 C2
Deer Hill Croft HD7..78 C2
Deer Hill Ct HD9....80 A2
Deer Hill Dr HD7....78 C2
Deganwy Dr HD5....55 C4
DEIGHTON..........41 A1
Deighton La WF17...19 A2
Deighton Rd HD2....41 A1
Deighton Sta HD2...41 A1
De Lacy Ave HD5....69 B2
Delf Hill HD6........25 B1
Delf Pl HD6.........25 B1
Dell The HD2........40 A2
Delmont St WF17....18 B4
Delph La HD4.......75 C1
Delves Wood Rd
HD4..............75 B3
Denard Ind Est HD4..66 A2
Denby Cl
Batley WF15.........10 A3
Liversedge WF15....16 C3
DENBY DALE.......95 C3
Denby Dale Ind Est
HD8..............95 A3
Denby Dale Sta HD8..94 C3
Denby View WF12...57 C3
Dene Cl HX5........37 A3
Dene Fold HD8.......88 A2
Dene Pk HD8........88 C1
Dene Rd HD8........91 B2
Deneside WF5.......34 C1
Denham Cl WF13....32 C4
Denham Dr HD9.....84 A2
Denham St
Batley WF17.........11 A1
🔟 Brighouse HD6...26 A3
Denholme Dr WF5...35 A1
Denison St WF17....19 C2
Denton Row HX4....36 B2
Derby Terr HD7.....78 C3
Derwent Dr HD5....54 A1
Derwent Rd
Batley WF12.........33 C4
Honley HD9.........82 C1
Meltham HD9........80 C1
De Trafford St HD4..66 C2
Deveron Gr HD2.....52 B2

Devon Gr WF5.......48 B2
Devonshire St HD1..67 A1
Devon Way HD6.....13 B4
Devon Wlk 🔟 WF13..32 B2
Dewhirst Rd HD6....13 A2
Dewhurst Rd HD2...53 B4
DEWSBURY.........32 C1
Dewsbury Coll
WF13............18 C3
Dewsbury Coll (Art &
Design) WF13.....32 B4
Dewsbury District Golf
Course WF14.....44 C1
Dewsbury & District
Hospl WF13.......32 A4
Dewsbury Gate Rd
WF13............18 C3
Dewsbury Mills
WF12............46 B4
DEWSBURY MOOR..31 C1
Dewsbury Mus ★
WF13............32 A1
Dewsbury Rd
Cleckheaton BD19...9 B4
Cleckheaton, Marsh
BD19..............8 B1
Elland HD6, HX5...38 B4
Ossett WF5.........35 A1
Dewsbury Sta WF13..32 C2
Deyne Rd WF13......75 B1
Diamond St
Batley WF17.........19 B4
Huddersfield HD1...53 B2
🔟 Huddersfield,
Moldgreen HD5....68 C3
Dickinson Gdns 🔟
WF13............32 B2
Dickson Fold WF15..16 C2
Dimple Gdns WF5...48 C2
Dimple Well Inf Sch
WF5.............48 C2
Dimple Wells Cl
WF5.............48 C2
Dimple Wells La
WF5.............48 C2
Dimple Wells Rd
WF5.............48 C2
Dingle Rd HD1......66 C4
Dingley Rd HD3.....66 C4
Dirker Ave HD7.....79 A4
Dirker Bank Rd HD7..78 C4
Dirker Dr HD7.......78 C3
Disney Cl HD4.......66 C1
Dixon Cl HX4........22 B2
Dockery HD1........67 B1
Doctor Fold HD9....83 A3
Doctor La
Mirfield WF14......43 C3
Shelley HD8........89 C1
Doctors Row
Huddersfield HD7...73 C3
Kirkheaton HD5....55 C2
Dodd's Royd HD4...76 A2
Dodgson St HX5....37 B3
DODLEE............50 B1
Dodlee La HD3......50 B1
Dog Kennel Bank
HD5..............68 B2
Dogley La HD8......88 A3
Dogley Villa Ct HD8..88 A3
Dolfin Pl HD2........41 B3
Dorchester Rd HD2..40 A3
Dorset St HD1.......52 C2
Dorset Wlk 🔟 WF13..32 B2
Doubting La WF12...57 C3
Doubting Rd WF12...57 C3
Douglas Ave
Batley WF17.........20 C3
Huddersfield, Cliff End
HD3..............66 A4
Huddersfield HD5...69 C3

Douglas St WF12 ....46 B2
Dovecote Cl WF4 ....61 A4
Dovecote La WF4 ....60 C4
Dover La HD9........86 B1
Dowker St HD3 .....24 B3
Downing St HD7....73 B2
Drake La BD11.......3 B3
Dray View WF13 .....31 C4
DRIGHLINGTON 3 B3
Drighlington Prim Sch
  BD11..............3 B4
Drive The WF17....19 A4
DRUB 8 C4
Drub La BD19........8 C4
Drummer La HD7....64 A2
Dryclough Ave HD4 .75 B4
Dryclough CE Inf Sch
  HD4..............66 B1
Dryclough Rd HD4..75 B4
Dry Hill La HD8 .....95 C2
Drysdale Fold HD2...40 B2
Dudfleet La WF4.....61 A2
Dudley Ave
  Batley WF17 ......11 A4
  Huddersfield HD1...66 C4
Dudley Rd HD1.....66 C4
Dudwell Ave HX3 ....22 C4
Dudwell Gr HX3 .....22 C4
Dudwell La HX3 .....22 C4
Duke St
  Dewsbury, Chickenley
  WF12.............34 B1
  Dewsbury, Ravensthorpe
  WF13.............45 A3
  Elland HX5 ....37 B4
Duke Wood Rd HD8..93 B3
Dunbottle Cl WF14..44 A4
Dunbottle La WF14 ..44 A4
Dunbottle Way
  WF14.............44 B4
Dunce Park Cl HX5 ..37 B3
Dundalk Ct [1] WF5 ..48 C3
Dundas St HD1......96 A2
Dunford Rd HD9.....86 B1
Dunnock Rd HD9....80 A4
Dunsmore Dr HD3...50 C2
Dunstan Cl WF5 ....49 A2
Dunstan Gr BD19 ....8 B4
Dyehouse Dr BD19....7 C4
Dyehouse La HD6....26 B3
Dyke Bottom HD8...90 B2
Dyke Cl WF14........30 A1
Dyke End HD7.......64 A1
Dymond Gr WF15....17 A1
Dymond Rd WF15...17 B1
Dymond View WF15 ..17 A1
Dyson's Hill HD9....83 A4
Dyson St
  Brighouse HD6.....13 A1
  Huddersfield HD5...69 A4
Dyson Wood Way
  HD2..............40 C3

E

Ealand Ave WF17 ...11 A1
Ealand Cres WF17...11 A1
Ealand Rd
  Batley, Brown Hill
  WF17.............10 C1
  Batley, Carlinghow
  WF17.............11 A1
Ealing Ct WF17.....19 A4
Earles Ave HD5 .....69 A3
EARLSHEATON 33 C1
Earlsheaton Inf Sch
  WF12.............33 C1
Earlsheaton Tech Coll
  WF12.............33 B2
Earl St WF12........34 B2
Easby Ave WF15.....18 C2

Easedale Gdns HD3..51 A3
Easingwood Dr HD5 .55 B3
East Ave
  Horbury WF4 ......61 B3
  Huddersfield HD3...51 C3
East Bath St WF17...20 A3
EASTBOROUGH.....33 A3
Eastborough Cres
  WF13.............33 A3
Eastborough Jun & Inf
  Sch WF13.........33 A2
East Cl HD2 ....53 B4
East Croft [6] BD12....6 A4
Eastfield HD8.......90 B2
Eastfield Dr HD8....88 B1
Eastfield Rd WF14 ..44 C4
East Fold HD8......92 B2
Eastgate Elland HX5..23 C1
  Honley HD9.......83 A3
East Gr HD5 ....55 C2
Eastlands HD5......69 C2
East Mount [3] HD6..13 A1
East Mount Pl [4]
  HD6..............13 A1
Easton Pl HD3......51 B1
East St Batley WF17..19 C3
  Brighouse, Bailiff Bridge
  HX3..............5 A1
  Brighouse HD6.....26 A3
  Holmfirth HD9.....87 B1
  Huddersfield, Leymoor
  HD7..............65 A2
  Huddersfield, Lindley
  HD3..............51 B3
EAST-THORPE.....43 C2
East-Thorpe Pl
  WF14.............44 A2
East View
  Brighouse HX3 .....5 A1
  Cleckheaton BD19 ..15 A4
  Gildersome LS27 ....4 C3
  Huddersfield HD1...52 B1
  [6] Mirfield WF14 ....43 B4
  Ossett WF5........49 A1
Eastway WF14......29 C1
Eastway Pk WF14 ...30 A1
Eastwood St
  [8] Brighouse HD6...13 B1
  [6] Huddersfield HD5..68 C3
Ebor Gdns WF14....43 B3
Ebury Cl WF17......20 A4
Ebury St WF17......20 A4
Echo St WF15.......29 C4
Edale Ave HD4......76 B3
Edale Cl HD5 ....55 B3
Eddercliffe Cres
  WF15.............17 A4
Eden Ave WF5......48 C4
Edge Ave WF12.....57 C3
Edge Cl
  Dewsbury WF12.....58 A3
  Huddersfield HD7...65 A2
Edge Hill HD7......74 A3
Edge Hill Cl HD5....54 A1
Edge Junc WF12.....57 C3
Edge La WF12.......58 A3
Edgemoor Rd HD9...82 C1
Edge Rd WF12.......58 B3
Edge View
  Dewsbury WF12.....58 A3
  Huddersfield HD7...65 A2
Edgeware Rd HD5 ...69 C4
Edward Cl WF12.....46 A1

Edward Rd WF14 ....43 B3
Edward St
  Brighouse HD6......26 C4
  Brighouse, Waring Green
  HD6..............13 A1
  Liversedge, Knowler Hill
  WF15.............17 A2
  Liversedge, Littletown
  WF15.............17 A3
Eighth Ave WF15....15 B3
EIGHTLANDS.......32 C2
Eightlands Rd WF13 .32 C2
Eland Ho [8] HX5....23 C1
Elder Cl WF17 .....10 C4
Elder Dr WF12......46 C1
Elder Gr HD4.......82 B4
Elder Grove Mews
  HD4..............82 B4
Elder La HD2.......41 C3
Elder Mews HD8....89 B1
Eldon Pl BD19 ......8 B1
Eldon Rd HD1......52 A1
Eldon St
  Batley WF16 ......18 A2
  Ossett WF5........35 C1
Eleanor St
  Brighouse HD6......26 A3
  [2] Huddersfield HD1..53 A2
Eleventh Ave WF15 ..15 C3
Elgin Cl HD4........75 B4
Elim Wlk [5] WF13...32 C2
Elizabeth St
  Elland HX5 ....37 B4
  [1] Elland, West Vale
  HX4..............23 A1
  Huddersfield HD4...67 C1
  Liversedge FW15 ...16 B2
ELLAND...........37 A4
Elland Bridge HX5...23 C1
Elland CE Jun & Inf Sch
  HX5..............23 C1
Elland Hall Farm Cvn
  Pk HX5...........23 B1
Elland Hospl HX5....24 A1
Elland La HX5......24 A1
ELLAND LOWER
  EDGE............25 A1
Elland Rd HD6, HX5...25 B4
Elland Riorges Link
  HX5..............24 A1
ELLAND UPPER
  EDGE............38 B4
Elland Wood Bottom
  HX3, HX5.........23 A3
Ellerslie Ct HD2 ....52 B2
Ellison St HD4......66 C1
Ellistones Gdns HX4 .22 A1
Elm Cl WF5.........49 A1
Elm Ct
  Birkenshaw BD11......2 B2
  Kirkburton HD8.....88 C1
Elmfield Ave HD3 ...65 B3
Elmfield Cl BD11 ....2 A2
Elmfield Dr HD8....91 C2
Elmfield Rd HD2....52 B3
Elmfield Terr [3]
  HD5..............68 C3
Elm Gr
  Cleckheaton BD19 ....9 A2
  Horbury WF4 ......61 A3
  Liversedge WF16 ...17 C3
Elm Mews WF4 .....61 A3
Elm Rd WF13.......31 C2
Elms Hill HD7......72 B2
Elm St
  Huddersfield HD4...68 A2
  Skelmanthorpe HD8..91 C3
Elms View HD7.....72 B2
Elm Terr HD6.......13 B3
Elm Tree Cl WF15 ...30 C4
Elm Way WF17......11 A4

Elmwood Ave HD1...96 A3
Elmwood Cl
[5] Huddersfield
  HD1..............96 A3
  Mirfield WF14.....56 C3
Elmwood Dr HD6 ...12 C1
Elmwood Gr
  Batley WF17 ......20 A1
  Horbury WF4 ......61 B3
Elm Wood Rd HD6..13 B2
Elmwood Terr WF13..32 C3
Elsinore Ave HX5....37 B3
Elsinore Ct HX5.....37 A4
Ely St HX4..........36 C4
Embankment The
  WF14.............43 C3
Emerald St
  Batley WF17.......19 B4
  Huddersfield HD1...53 C2
Emmanuel Terr HD4 .76 B4
Emmet Cl BD11......2 B3
Empsall Row [4]
  HD6..............13 B1
Enfield Cl WF17.....18 C4
Enfield Dr WF17 ....18 C4
Engine La WF4 .....60 B3
Ennerdale Ave
  WF12.............33 B4
Ennerdale Cres
  WF12.............33 B4
Ennerdale Dr HX5 ...24 B1
Ennerdale Rd WF12..33 B4
Enoch La HD4......67 B1
Epsom Way HD5....55 C3
Equilibrium HD3.....51 B2
Ernest St [8] WF13...33 A2
Escroft Cl BD12......6 A3
Eskdale Cl WF12....20 B1
Eton Ave HD5......69 B4
Eunice La HD8......94 A3
Everard St HD4.....66 C2
Exchange HD9.......83 A3
Exchange Ct BD19 ....8 A3
Exchange St
  Cleckheaton BD19 ....8 A3
  [5] Elland HX4.......36 C4
EXLEY............23 A4
Exley Bank HX3.....23 A4
Exley Bank Top HX3 .23 A3
Exley Gdns HX3.....23 A4
Exley La Elland HX5 .23 B2
  Halifax HX5.......23 B3
Eyre St Batley WF17 .20 A2
  Dewsbury WF12....46 A2

F

Factory La HD3 .....66 A2
Fairfax Ave WF11 ....4 A3
Fairfield Ave
  Batley WF16.......18 B3
  [3] Dewsbury WF12 ..33 C2
  Ossett WF5........49 B2
Fairfield Cl WF5 ....49 B2
Fairfield Cres [8]
  WF13.............32 A3
Fairfield Ct WF15 ...16 C2
Fairfield Dr
  Batley WF16.......18 B3
  Ossett WF5........49 B2
Fairfield Rd WF5 ....49 B3
Fairfield Mews [7]
  WF13.............32 A3
Fairfield Mount
  WF5..............49 B2
Fairfield Par WF16...18 B3
Fairfield Rd
  Batley WF16.......18 B3
  Ossett WF5........49 B2
Fairfield Rise HD8 ...89 C3
Fairfield Sch WF16 ..18 B3

Fairfield Terr
[9] Cleckheaton
  BD19..............8 B1
  Dewsbury WF12....33 C2
  Ossett WF5........49 A2
Fairfield Wlk WF5 ...49 B2
Fairlea Ave HD4 ....76 A3
Fairlea Cotts HD4...76 A3
Fair Lea Rd HD4 ....76 A3
Fairless Ave HX3......5 A1
Fairmoor Way WF16 .18 B3
Fairmount Terr
  WF12.............47 A4
Fair St HD1.........67 B2
Fair View WF15.....16 C3
Fairview Ave WF17 ..18 C4
Fairview Cres WF17..19 A4
Fairview Rd WF17 ...19 A4
Fairway Ind Pk
  WF17.............10 C4
Fair Ways WF14.....56 C4
Fairway The HD2 ....39 C2
Falconers Ride HD4 .76 A1
Falcon Rd HD12....46 C4
Falcon St HD4......76 B4
Fall La
  Dewsbury WF13.....46 A4
  Liversedge WF15 ...29 A3
  Marsden HD7......78 C3
Fallow Croft HD2....41 B3
Fall Rd WF14.......29 B2
Fanny Moor Cres
  HD4..............77 B4
Fanny Moor La HD4..77 B4
Faraday Sq [2] HD3 ..65 C2
Far Common Rd
  WF14.............29 C2
Far Dene HD8.......88 A2
Farehill Flats HD4 ...76 B2
Farehill Rd HD4.....76 B2
Far End La HD9......83 B2
Farfield Ave WF17 ...18 C4
Farfield Rd HD5.....69 B1
Farfield Rise BD19 ...18 A3
Farfield St BD19 .....8 A3
Farmhouse Ct HD4 .75 C4
Farm Mount WF4 ...63 C4
Farnlee HD3........51 B3
Farnley Hey HD4....77 B1
Farnley View BD11 ...4 A4
Farrar Ave WF14....43 B4
Farrar Cl HX5.......24 B1
Farrar Dr WF14.....43 B4
Far Richard Cl WF5 .35 A1
Farriers Ct BD11.....3 B4
FARTOWN.........53 B4
FARTOWN GREEN .53 B4
Fartown Green Rd
  HD2..............53 B4
Fartown High Sch
  HD2..............53 C4
Far View Bank HD5 .69 A2
Far View Cres HD5 ..69 A2
Fearnley Ave WF5...35 A1
Fearnley Croft BD19 ..9 B2
Fearnley Ct HD9 ....87 A3
Fearnley Dr WF5....34 C1
Fearnley La HD9....86 C4
Fearnley St WF13...32 B1
Fearnside's Cl [10]
  WF4..............60 C3
Featherbed Cl [4]
  HX4..............36 C4
Feather Bed La [5]
  HX4..............36 C4
Felcote Ave HD5....69 A3
Felks Stile Rd HD4...74 C3
Fell Gr HD2.........40 B2

Fell Greave Cres
HD2 . . . . **40** B2
Fell Greave Rd HD2 . . **40** B2
Fellowsides La WF5 . . **49** A3
Fellowsides Mews
WF5 . . . . **49** A3
Fellows The HD4 . . . . . . **75** B1
Fenay Bankside
HD8 . . . . **70** C1
FENAY BRIDGE **70** B1
Fenay Bridge Rd
HD8 . . . . **70** B2
Fenay Cres HD5 . . . . . **69** C1
Fenay Dr HD8 . . . . **70** B1
Fenay Lea HD5, HD8 . . **70** A1
Fenay Lea Dr HD5 . . . . **70** B2
Fentham Ind Est ⓬
HD6 . . . . **26** A3
Fenton Rd HD1 . . . . **67** B1
Fenton Sq HD1 . . . . **67** B3
Fenton St WF14 . . . . . . **43** C2
Fern Ave HD9 . . . . **80** A3
Fern Cl WF17 . . . . **20** C3
Ferncroft WF15 . . . . . . **15** C2
Ferndale Ct HD2 . . . . . . **40** A2
Ferndale Gr HD2 . . . . . **40** A2
Ferndene Ave WF17 . . . **3** C1
Ferndene Wlk WF17 . . . **3** C1
Fernhurst Cl �4
WF14 . . . . **43** C4
Fernhurst Cres
WF14 . . . . **44** A4
Fernhurst Lea WF14 . . **44** A4
Fernhurst Rd WF14 . . . **44** A4
Fernhurst Way ⑤
WF14 . . . . **43** C4
Fernlea Cl WF16 . . . . . . **18** B1
Fern Lea Flats HD3 . . . **51** A3
Fernlea Gr HD7 . . . . . . **65** A1
Fern Lea Rd HD3 . . . . . **51** A3
Fernleigh Dr HD3 . . . . **65** C3
Fern Rise HX5 . . . . **24** B1
Fern St E HD1 . . . . **68** B4
Fernside Ave HD5 . . . . **69** B2
Fernside Cl HD5 . . . . . . **69** C3
Fernside Cres HD5 . . . **69** C3
Fernside Ct HD5 . . . . . . **69** C3
Fern St HD1 . . . . **53** A3
Fern View BD19 . . . . **9** A3
Ferrand La BD19 . . . . . . **9** A3
Fiddler Hill WF12 . . . . **46** A2
Field Cl WF16 . . . . **18** A4
Fieldcroft Ct ⑧
WF14 . . . . **43** B3
Field End La HD9 . . . . **83** B2
Fieldens Pl WF17 . . . . . **19** A4
Field Head
Batley WF17 . . . . **3** B1
Huddersfield HD7 . . . . . . **64** C3
Shepley HD8 . . . . **90** A3
Fieldhead Cres WF17 . **3** B1
Field Head Farm Ct
HD8 . . . . **90** A3
Fieldhead Gdns
WF12 . . . . **21** B1
Fieldhead Jun & Inf
Sch WF17 . . . . **3** C1
Field Head La WF17 . . . **3** B1
Field Head Par WF17 . . **3** C1
Fieldhead Way
WF16 . . . . **17** C3
Fieldhouse HD9 . . . . . . **86** B2
Fieldhouse Dr HD7 . . . **72** C3
Fieldhouse Rd ②
HD1 . . . . **53** C2
Field Hurst BD19 . . . . . . **6** C1
Field La Batley WF17 . . **20** A2
Brighouse HD6 . . . . **25** C2

Field La *continued*
Dewsbury WF13 . . . . . . **44** C4
Ossett WF5 . . . . **48** C4
Field Lane Jun & Inf
Sch WF17 . . . . **20** A2
Field Lane Prim Sch
HD6 . . . . **25** B1
Field Rd HD9 . . . . **86** B2
Fieldshead Bglws
HD7 . . . . **73** C1
Fields Rd HD8 . . . . **88** A4
Fields Rise HD5 . . . . . **55** C3
Field St WF13 . . . . **45** A4
Fields Way HD5 . . . . . . **55** C3
Field Top Rd HD6 . . . . **25** C3
Field Way HD8 . . . . **90** A2
Fifth Avenue E
WF15 . . . . **15** B3
Fifth Avenue W
WF15 . . . . **15** B3
Filbert St HD1 . . . . **53** A3
Filley Royd BD19 . . . . . **16** B4
Finching Gr WF14 . . . . **30** A2
Finkil St HD6 . . . . **12** C3
Finkle Ct LS27 . . . . **4** C4
Finthorpe La HD5 . . . . **69** C1
Fir Ave WF13 . . . . **44** C3
Fir Bank ⑨ WF13 . . . . **32** A3
Fir Gr WF13 . . . . **44** C3
Fir Par WF13 . . . . **44** C3
Fir Rd HD1 . . . . **66** C4
First Ave
Cleckheaton WF15 . . . . **15** C3
Horbury WF4 . . . . **60** B3
Huddersfield, Dalton
HD5 . . . . **54** C1
Huddersfield, Town End
HD7 . . . . **64** C2
Firth Ave ⑤ HD6 . . . . . **15** A3
Firthcliffe Dr WF15 . . **17** B3
Firthcliffe Gr WF15 . . **17** B3
Firthcliffe La WF15 . . **17** B3
Firthcliffe Mount
WF15 . . . . **17** B3
Firthcliffe Par WF15 . **17** B3
Firthcliffe Pl WF15 . . **17** C3
Firthcliffe Rd WF15 . . **17** B3
Firthcliffe Terr
WF15 . . . . **17** B3
Firthcliffe View
WF15 . . . . **17** B3
Firthcliffe Wlk
WF15 . . . . **17** B3
Firth House La HD6 . . **26** C1
Firth St
Brighouse HD6 . . . . **26** A3
Huddersfield HD1 . . . . . **96** B1
Shepley HD8 . . . . **90** A2
Fir Wlk WF13 . . . . **44** C3
Fisher Gn HD9 . . . . **83** A2
Fisher Gr WF5 . . . . **49** B2
Fisher Way WF15 . . . . **18** B1
Fitzwilliam St HD1 . . . **96** A1
FIXBY **39** C3
Fixby Jun & Inf Sch
HD2 . . . . **39** C2
Fixby Park Dr HD2 . . . **52** C4
Fixby Rd HD2 . . . . **39** C3
Fixby View Yd HD6 . . . **39** A4
Flagship Sq WF12 . . . . **34** A4
Flash La WF14 . . . . **44** A4
Flat Ho HD7 . . . . **73** B2
Flax Meadow HD3 . . . **51** A4
Fleet St HD8 . . . . **92** C2
Fleming Ct HD5 . . . . . . **69** C3
Fleminghouse La
HD5 . . . . **69** C3
Fleming St WF17 . . . . . **19** C3
Fletcher Cres HD6 . . . **39** A4
Fletcher Homes
WF13 . . . . **32** A2

Flint St HD1 . . . . **53** B3
Floreat Cl WF17 . . . . . . **11** A2
Flower Acre HX5 . . . . . **37** B4
Flugel Way HD3 . . . . . . **51** C3
Flush HD15 . . . . **17** C2
Flushdyke Jun & Inf
Sch WF5 . . . . **35** C1
Fold Ct HD8 . . . . **89** B3
Foldings Ave BD19 . . . . **6** C2
Foldings Cl BD19 . . . . . . **6** B2
Foldings Ct BD19 . . . . . **6** B2
Foldings Garth BD19 . . **6** B2
Foldings Gr BD19 . . . . . **6** B2
Foldings Par BD19 . . . . **6** B2
Foldings Rd BD19 . . . . . **6** C2
Foldings The HD8 . . . . **91** C3
Follett Ave HD4 . . . . . . **75** B4
Follingworth Rd
WF17 . . . . **20** C3
FOLLY HALL **96** A1
Folly Hall HD1 . . . . **67** C2
Folly Rd HD2 . . . . **39** C1
Ford Dr WF14 . . . . **43** A4
Forester's Bldgs
HD9 . . . . **83** C2
Forest Rd HD5 . . . . **69** A3
Forest Way HD9 . . . . . **82** C2
Forge La
Batley WF15 . . . . **30** C4
Dewsbury WF12 . . . . . . **46** A2
Horbury WF4 . . . . **61** B2
Liversedge WF15 . . . . . **17** B1
Formby Ave HD2 . . . . . **39** B1
Forrest Ave HD1 . . . . . **52** A1
Forrest Terr WF12 . . . . **47** A4
Forster Dr HD6 . . . . . . **18** B1
Fort Ann Rd WF17 . . . . **20** C2
Fortis Way HD3 . . . . . . **50** B2
Foster Ave HD4 . . . . . . **75** B4
Foundry St
Brighouse HD6 . . . . **26** C3
Dewsbury, Ravensthorpe
WF13 . . . . **45** A3
Dewsbury WF13 . . . . . . **33** A2
Foundry Terr BD19 . . . **8** B1
Fountain Cl WF15 . . . . **29** C3
Fountain Dr WF15 . . . . **29** C3
Fountain Gr HD4 . . . . . **66** B2
Fountains Ave WF17 . **18** C2
Fountain St
Batley WF15 . . . . **18** A3
Liversedge WF15 . . . . . **29** C3
Four Acres WF14 . . . . . **43** C1
Four Lane Ends
WF12 . . . . **58** B4
Fourth Ave WF15 . . . . **15** B3
Foxcroft Dr HD6 . . . . . **25** C3
Fox Ct HX4 . . . . **23** A1
Foxglove Rd
Batley WF17 . . . . **10** B4
Huddersfield HD5 . . . . . **69** A2
Foxlow Ave HD5 . . . . . **54** B2
FOX ROYD **57** A3
Fox Royd HD8 . . . . **90** A3
Fox Royd Ave WF14 . . **43** B4
Fox Royd Dr WF14 . . . **43** B4
Foxroyd La WF12 . . . . **57** A3
Fox Royd La ⑧
WF14 . . . . **43** B4
Fox Royd View ④
WF14 . . . . **43** B4
Fox St Batley WF17 . . . **20** A2
Cleckheaton BD19 . . . . **8** B1
Dewsbury WF13 . . . . . . **45** A3
Huddersfield HD1 . . . . . **96** A2
Fox View WF13 . . . . . . **19** A1
France Fold HD9 . . . . . **83** A3
France Hill HD9 . . . . . . **83** A3
Frances Ave HD4 . . . . . **66** B1
Frances Rd WF12 . . . . **33** C1
Frances St
⑨ Brighouse HD6 . . . . **13** A1

Frances St *continued*
⓬ Elland HX5 . . . . **37** B4
Frances St WF17 . . . . . **20** B2
Francis Ave ◀ HD3 . . **65** C2
Francis St
Batley WF16 . . . . **18** B1
Huddersfield HD3 . . . . . **65** C2
Mirfield WF14 . . . . **43** B3
Francis View WF14 . . . **43** B3
Frank Cl WF12 . . . . **58** A4
Frank La WF12 . . . . **58** A4
Frank Peel Cl ⑥
WF16 . . . . **18** A2
Freakfield La WF15 . . **28** B4
Frederick St
Huddersfield HD4 . . . . . **66** B2
⑤ Liversedge WF15 . . **17** B1
Frederick Walker Gdns
WF17 . . . . **20** A2
Friar Pl HD2 . . . . **41** B3
Friary Ct WF17 . . . . **10** A3
Friendly St ⑧ HD1 . . . **96** B2
Frith House HD6 . . . . . **26** C1
Frost Hill WF15 . . . . . . **17** B2
Fulford Ave HD2 . . . . . **53** A4
Fullwood Dr HD7 . . . . **64** C2
Fulneck Cl HD2 . . . . . . **39** B1
Fulstone Hall Rd
HD9 . . . . **87** C4
Furnace La BD11 . . . . . . **2** A4
Furnbrook Gdns
HD5 . . . . **55** C2
Fusden La BD19 . . . . **9** A3

G

Gagewell Dr WF4 . . . . **61** A4
Gagewell La WF4 . . . . **61** A4
Gagewell View WF4 . . **61** A4
Galloway St ◀ HD1 . . **53** C2
Galpharm Stadium
HD1 . . . . **53** C2
Ganny Rd HD6 . . . . **26** B4
Ganton Way HD2 . . . . **39** B1
Garden Ave WF15 . . . . **17** A4
Garden Cl
Liversedge WF15 . . . . . **17** A4
Ossett WF5 . . . . **49** A1
Garden Cres WF13 . . . **45** A4
Garden Croft WF17 . . . **19** A1
Garden Dr WF13 . . . . . **45** A4
Garden Par ⑧
WF15 . . . . **17** A3
Garden Pl WF13 . . . . . . **31** C3
Garden Rd HD6 . . . . . . **13** A2
Gardens Rd WF13 . . . . **45** B3
Garden St
⑥ Batley WF16 . . . . . . **18** A1
Dewsbury WF13 . . . . . . **45** A3
Huddersfield HD1 . . . . . **67** B2
Garden Terr
Denby Dale HD8 . . . . . . **95** A2
Dewsbury WF13 . . . . . . **45** A4
Garden View WF15 . . . **17** A4
Garden Wlk ②
WF15 . . . . **17** A3
Garfield Pl HD7 . . . . . . **78** C3
Garfit Hill BD19 . . . . . . **10** A2
Garforth Ct WF14 . . . . **30** A1
Garforth St
Huddersfield, Aspley
HD1 . . . . **68** B3
Huddersfield, Netherton
HD4 . . . . **75** B1
Gargrave Cl HD6 . . . . . **25** A1
Garlick St HD6 . . . . **39** A4
Garner La
Honley HD9 . . . . **82** B2
Kirkburton HD8 . . . . **73** C2
Garnett St WF13 . . . . . **18** C1
Garrett Cl HD8 . . . . **91** B3

Garsdale Rd HD4 . . . . **77** A4
Garwick Terr ⑨
HX4 . . . . **23** A1
Gaskell Dr WF4 . . . . . . **60** C4
Gas Works La HX5 . . . **23** C1
Gasworks St
Huddersfield HD1 . . . . . **96** B3
Liversedge WF15 . . . . . **17** B2
Gate Head HD7 . . . . . . **79** B3
Gatehead Bank HD7 . **79** B4
Gatehouse Ent Ctr
HD1 . . . . **67** B1
Gatesgarth Cres
HD3 . . . . **51** A3
GAWTHORPE **34** C3
Gawthorpe Green La
HD5, HD8 . . . . **71** A4
Gawthorpe La
Kirkheaton HD8 . . . . . . **70** C4
Ossett WF5 . . . . **35** B4
Gayle Cl BD12 . . . . **5** C4
Gelderd Rd WL27,
LS27 . . . . **4** C3
Gelder Terr HD5 . . . . . **68** B3
George Ave HD2 . . . . . **52** B2
George St
Batley, Heckmondwike
WF16 . . . . **18** A2
Batley WF17 . . . . **19** C2
Brighouse HD6 . . . . **26** A3
Brighouse HD6 . . . . **26** C4
Cleckheaton BD19 . . . . **8** A2
Dewsbury, Dewsbury
Moor WF13 . . . . **31** C3
Dewsbury, Ravensthorpe
WF13 . . . . **45** A3
Dewsbury WF13 . . . . . . **32** C2
Elland HX5 . . . . **37** B4
⑫ Elland, West Vale
HX4 . . . . **23** A1
Horbury WF4 . . . . **61** A3
⓬ Huddersfield HD1 . . **96** B1
Huddersfield, Lindley
HD3 . . . . **51** B3
Huddersfield, Milnsbridge
HD3 . . . . **66** A3
Huddersfield, Paddock
Brow HD1 . . . . **67** A2
Kirkburton HD8 . . . . **89** B4
⓲ Liversedge WF15 . . **17** A2
Ossett WF5 . . . . **35** A1
Slaithwaite HD7 . . . . . . **72** B3
Georgia Mews WF5 . . **49** B2
Gernhill Ave HD2 . . . . **39** B3
Gervase Rd WF4 . . . . . **60** C4
Ghyllroyd Ave BD11 . . **2** B3
Ghyllroyd Dr BD11 . . . **2** B2
Ghyll The HD2 . . . . **39** C2
Gib Cotts HD9 . . . . **84** B4
Gib La HD8 . . . . **91** C3
Gibson St HD3 . . . . **51** C1
Gilbert Gr HD4 . . . . **66** C1
Gilead Rd HD3 . . . . **50** B1
Giles St HD9 . . . . **84** A2
Gillroyd La HD7 . . . . . . **73** C2
Gilthwaites Cres
HD8 . . . . **95** B4
Gilthwaites Fst Sch
HD8 . . . . **95** B4
Gilthwaites Gr HD8 . . **95** B3
Gilthwaites La HD8 . . **95** B4
Gilthwaites Top
HD8 . . . . **95** B4
Gisbourne Rd HD2 . . . **41** A3
Gladstone Ct ②
WF13 . . . . **32** A3
Gladstone St ⑧ BD19 . **8** A1
Gladwin St WF17 . . . . . **19** B2
Glastonbury Dr HD3 . **65** B3

Glebe Gate WF12 . . . . **58** B3
Glebe Side HD5 . . . . . . **55** C4
Glebe St HD1 . . . . **52** B1
Gledhill Terr WF13 . . **31** C2
Gledholt Bank HD1 . . **67** A3
Gledholt Bsns Pk
  HD1 . . . . **67** A3
Gledholt Rd HD1 . . . . **67** A4
Glen Ave WF17 . . . . . . **19** C4
Glencoe Terr WF15 . . **17** B1
Glendale WF4 . . . . **60** B3
Glendorne Dr HD5 . . **55** C3
Gleneagles Way
  HD2 . . . . **39** B1
Glen Field Ave HD2 . . **41** B1
Glenfields WF4 . . . . . . **63** B3
Glenfields Cl WF4 . . **63** B3
Glenholme Terr
  WF5 . . . . **34** C3
Glenlow Rd WF12 . . . . **20** C1
Glenroyd HD7 . . . . **78** B3
Glenside Cl HD3 . . . . . **52** A2
Glen Side Rd HD7 . . **72** C2
Glen View WF17 . . . . . **11** B4
Glen View Rd HD8 . . **90** C4
Globe Ct WF15 . . . . . . **17** B2
Glyndon Ct HD6 . . . . . **26** B2
Godwin Pl HD2 . . . . . . **41** B3
Gog Hill HX5 . . . . **23** C1
GOLCAR **64** C3
GOLCAR BROW **80** B2
Golcar Brow Rd
  HD9 . . . . **80** A2
Golcar Jun & Inf Sch
  HD7 . . . . **64** C2
Goldcrest Ct HD4 . . . . **82** C4
Golden Sq WF4 . . . . . . **61** A3
Goldfields Ave HX4 . . **22** B2
Goldfields Cl **1**
  HX4 . . . . **22** B2
Goldfields View **2**
  HX4 . . . . **22** B2
Goldfields Way HX4 . . **22** B2
Goldington Ave HD3 . **51** A2
Goldington Dr HD3 . . **51** A2
GOMERSAL **9** B2
Gomersal CE Mid Sch
  BD19 . . . . **9** B3
Gomersal Fst Sch
  BD19 . . . . **9** B3
GOMERSAL HILL
  TOP **9** B2
Gomersal La BD19 . . . . **9** A1
Gomersal Rd WF16 . . **17** C4
Gomersal St Marys CE
  Fst Sch BD19 . . . . **9** B2
Gooder La HD6 . . . . . . **26** B3
Gooder St HD6 . . . . . . **26** A4
Goods La WF12 . . . . . . **33** A1
Goose Gn HD9 . . . . **86** A3
Goose Hill WF16 . . . . **18** A2
Gordale Cl WF17 . . . . **19** B3
Gordon Ave WF5 . . . . **48** C4
Gordon Ct WF14 . . . . **44** B4
Gordon St
  Elland HX5 . . . . **37** B4
  Slaithwaite HD7 . . . . **72** C2
Gordon Terr HD7 . . . . **73** C4
Goring Park Ave
  WF5 . . . . **49** C2
Gorse Rd HD3 . . . . **66** B4
Grace Leather La
  WF17 . . . . **20** B3
Grafton St WF17 . . . . **20** A1
Graham La HD4 . . . . . . **66** A1
Graham St HD1 . . . . . . **67** B3
Gramfield Rd HD4 . . **66** B1
Grampian Cl HD8 . . . . **89** B1
Granby Flats **1**
  HD1 . . . . **67** A3

Grand Cross Rd
  HD5 . . . . **69** A4
Grand Stand HD7 . . . . **64** A3
Grange Ave
  Batley WF17 . . . . **19** B1
  Huddersfield HD2 . . **52** C3
  Marsden HD7 . . . . **79** A3
Grange Bank Cl
  HD5 . . . . **54** A1
Grange Cotts
  Cleckheaton BD19 . . . . **7** C2
  Marsden HD7 . . . . **79** A3
Grange Dr WF5 . . . . . . **49** B1
Grangefield Ave
  WF17 . . . . **19** B1
Grange La HD6 . . . . . . **27** B4
Grange Rd
  Batley, Chidswell
    WF17 . . . . **21** A2
  Batley WF17 . . . . **19** A1
  Cleckheaton BD19 . . . . **7** C2
  Huddersfield HD7 . . . . **65** A4
Grange Road Ind Est
  WF17 . . . . **20** B2
Grange St HD7 . . . . . . **79** A3
Grange Terr HD7 . . . . **79** A3
Grange The HD5 . . . . **54** C1
Grange Valley Rd
  WF17 . . . . **20** C2
Grange View WF12 . . **57** C3
Granny Hall Gr HD6 . . **12** C3
Granny Hall La HD6 . . **12** C3
Granny Hall Pk HD6 . . **12** C3
Granny La WF14 . . . . . **44** A1
Grantley Pl HD2 . . . . . **40** C3
Granville St
  Dewsbury WF13 . . . . **32** B2
  6 Elland HX5 . . . . . . **37** B4
  Liversedge WF15 . . . . **17** B1
Granville Terr **5**
  HD1 . . . . **67** A3
Grasmere Dr HX5 . . . . **24** B1
Grasmere Rd
  Batley WF12 . . . . **33** B4
  Brighouse BD12 . . . . . **6** B3
  Meltham HD9 . . . . **80** C1
Grasscroft Ave HD9 . . **83** A2
Grasscroft Rd
  Honley HD9 . . . . **82** C2
  Huddersfield HD1 . . **52** B1
Grassmere Rd HD1 . . **52** B1
Grassmoor Fold
  HD9 . . . . **83** B1
Grayshon St BD11 . . . . **3** B3
Gray St FW15 . . . . **16** B2
Greatfield Cl WF5 . . **49** A4
Greatfield Dr WF5 . . **49** A3
Greatfield Gdns
  WF5 . . . . **49** A4
Greatfield Rd WF5 . . **49** A3
Great Northern Ret Pk
  HD1 . . . . **96** B3
Great Northern St
  HD1 . . . . **96** B3
Great Pond St WF13 . **45** B3
Great Wood Gdns
  HD8 . . . . **88** B4
Great Wood St
  WF17 . . . . **19** C2
Greave Cl HD2 . . . . . . **40** A2
Greave House La
  HD8 . . . . **70** C1
Greave House Terr
  HD8 . . . . **70** C1
Greaves Croft HD8 . . **70** C1
Greaves Fold HX4 . . **36** B2
Greaves Pl HX4 . . . . . **36** B2
Greaves Rd WF13 . . **33** A3
Greenacre Ave BD12 . . **6** A4
Greenacre Cl **1**
  BD12 . . . . **6** A4

Greenacre Dr BD12 . . . **6** A4
Greenacre Gate
  HD8 . . . . **71** C1
Greenacres WF5 . . . . **35** A3
Greenacres Cl WF5 . **35** A3
Greenacres Dr
  WF17 . . . . **11** A4
Greenacre Way BD12 . . **6** A4
Green Ave WF16 . . . . **18** B2
Green Balk La HD8 . . **88** C4
Green Bank BD19 . . . . **16** C4
Green Cl
  Batley WF17 . . . . **20** B3
  Dewsbury WF13 . . . . **32** A4
Green Cliff HD9 . . . . . **83** A3
Green Cres HD7 . . . . . **65** A3
Green Ct BD19 . . . . **7** C2
Greendale Ct HD9 . . **83** A3
Green Edge HD7 . . . . **64** B4
Green End HD6 . . . . . **26** A3
Greenfield Ave
  Brighouse HX3 . . . . **5** A1
  Huddersfield HD3 . . **51** A1
  Ossett WF5 . . . . **49** C2
Greenfield Cl WF5 . . **49** C2
Greenfield Dr **6**
  BD19 . . . . **6** C2
Greenfield Pl HX3 . . . . **5** A1
Greenfield Rd WF5 . . **49** C2
Greenfields WF16 . . . . **17** C3
Greenfinch Gr HD4 . . **76** A1
Greengates Ave **3**
  BD12 . . . . **5** C3
Greengates Mill
  WF12 . . . . **34** B2
Green Gdns HD7 . . . . **65** A3
Green Head HD7 . . . . **73** A1
Greenhead Ave HD5 . **69** B3
Greenhead Coll HD1 **67** B4
Greenhead Ct HD1 . . **52** B1
Greenhead La
  Brighouse HX3 . . . . . . **39** A4
  Huddersfield HD5 . . **69** B3
Greenhead Rd HD1 . . **67** B4
Green Hill HD2 . . . . . . **40** A2
Greenhill Bank Rd
  HD9 . . . . **87** B3
Greenhill Rd HD3 . . **50** B1
Greenhouse Rd HD2 . **53** A3
Green La
  Bradford, Wyke
    BD12 . . . . **5** C4
  Brighouse, Clifton
    HD6 . . . . **27** C4
  Brighouse, Hove Edge
    HD6 . . . . **12** B3
  Cleckheaton BD19 . . . . **8** A4
  Dewsbury WF13 . . . . **32** A3
  Elland, West Vale
    HX4 . . . . **36** B4
  Horbury WF4 . . . . **61** B2
  Liversedge WF15 . . . . **16** A1
  Meltham HD9 . . . . **80** C1
  Netherton, Overton
    WF4 . . . . **62** A4
  Netherton WF4 . . . . . **63** C3
Green Lane Cl WF4 . . **62** B4
Green Lane Terr
  HD7 . . . . **64** B4
Greenlea Ct
  Honley HD9 . . . . **83** A3
  Huddersfield HD5 . . **69** C3
Green Lea Mills (Ind
  Units) HD5 . . . . **69** B3
Green Lea Rd HD5 . . **69** B4
Green Mount HD5 . . **68** C4
Green Park Ave
  Halifax HX3 . . . . **22** C4
  Horbury WF4 . . . . **60** B4
  Ossett WF5 . . . . **49** A1
Green Park Dr HX3 . . **22** C4

Green Park Gate
  HX3 . . . . **22** C4
Green Park Rd HX3 . . **22** C4
Green Royd WF15 . . . . **17** A3
Green Royd HX4 . . . . . **36** B4
Greenroyd Ave BD19 . . **8** A4
Greenroyd Cl HX3 . . . . **22** B4
Greenroyd Croft
  HD2 . . . . **52** B3
Greens End Rd HD9 . . **80** B2
GREENSIDE **69** C3
Greenside
  Cleckheaton BD19 . . . . **8** B1
  Denby Dale HD8 . . . . **95** B4
  2 Liversedge WF16 . . **17** C2
  Skelmanthorpe HD8 . . **91** A1
Greenside Ave HD5 . . **69** C3
Greenside Cres HD5 . **69** C3
Greenside Dr HD5 . . **69** C3
Greenside Est WF14 . **30** C1
Greenside Inf Sch
  HD5 . . . . **69** C2
Greenside Mount
  WF14 . . . . **30** B1
Greenside Rd WF14 . . **30** B1
Green St
  4 Elland HX4 . . . . . . **36** A2
  Huddersfield HD1 . . **96** A1
  Meltham HD9 . . . . **80** B2
Green Terr
  Dewsbury WF13 . . . . **32** A4
  Mirfield WF14 . . . . . . **43** B4
Green The
  Batley WF17 . . . . **10** C4
  Huddersfield HD2 . . **40** C3
  Marsden HD7 . . . . **78** C3
  Mirfield WF14 . . . . . . **43** A4
  Ossett WF5 . . . . **49** A2
Greenton Ave BD19 . . **6** B3
Greenway
  Honley HD9 . . . . **83** A3
  Huddersfield HD3 . . **65** B3
Greenwood Ave
  WF12 . . . . **33** C1
Greenwood Bldgs
  HD5 . . . . **55** C2
Greenwood St
  Dewsbury, Savile Town
    WF12 . . . . **46** B4
  12 Dewsbury WF12,
    WF13 . . . . **32** B2
  Huddersfield HD4 . . **67** C2
GREETLAND **22** A2
Greetland Prim Sch
  HX4 . . . . **22** B1
Gregory Dr HD8 . . . . **88** C1
Gregory Springs La
  WF14 . . . . **44** A1
Gregory Springs Rd
  WF14 . . . . **44** A1
Gregory St WF17 . . . . **20** B3
Greyfriars Ave HD2 . . **41** A2
Grey Gables WF4 . . . . **63** C4
Greystone HD4 . . . . . . **75** A4
Greystone Ave HX5 . . **37** A3
Greystone Ct HD6 . . **26** A1
Greystones Dr WF5 . . **49** A1
Griffe Dr BD12 . . . . . . **5** C3
Griffe Head Cres **2**
  BD12 . . . . **5** C4
Griffe Head Rd BD12 . **5** C4
Griffe Rd BD12 . . . . . . **5** C3
Griffe Terr BD12 . . . . . **5** C3
Grimescar Mdws
  HD2 . . . . **52** A4
Grimscar Rd HD2 . . **38** C1
Grimscar Ave HD2 . . **52** C3
Grisedale Ave HD2 . . **52** C3
Grosvenor Ave HD8 . **71** A1
Grosvenor Rd
  Batley WF17 . . . . **20** A4

Grosvenor Rd continued
  Huddersfield HD5 . . **69** B4
Grosvenor St
  2 Batley WF16 . . . . **18** A3
  Dewsbury WF12 . . . . **32** C1
  Elland HX5 . . . . **37** B4
Grosvenor Terr **1**
  WF16 . . . . **18** A2
Grosvenor Way HD8 . **71** A1
Grove Cl BD19 . . . . . . **9** B3
Grove Cotts HD6 . . . . **25** B4
Grove Farm WF17 . . **20** C1
Grove Gdns WF12 . . **47** C4
Grove House Dr
  HD8 . . . . **93** A3
Grove La BD19 . . . . . . **9** B3
Grove Nook HD3 . . . . **65** B4
GROVE PLACE **69** A4
Grove Rd
  Batley WF16 . . . . **18** B1
  Elland HX5 . . . . **24** B1
  Horbury WF4 . . . . **60** C3
  Huddersfield HD1 . . **96** B3
Groves Hall Rd
  WF13 . . . . **31** C2
Grove Sq BD19 . . . . . . **9** B3
Grove St
  Batley, Heckmondwike
    WF16 . . . . **18** B2
  Batley, Norristhorpe
    WF15 . . . . **30** C4
  Brighouse HD6 . . . . . **26** B4
  Dewsbury WF13 . . . . **32** C2
  Huddersfield HD3 . . **65** B4
  Mirfield WF14 . . . . . . **44** A4
  Ossett WF5 . . . . **48** C2
  Slaithwaite HD7 . . . . **72** B3
Grove Terr
  Birkenshaw BD11 . . . . **2** A2
  Brighouse HD6 . . . . . **25** B4
Grove The
  Batley, Brookroyd
    WF17 . . . . **11** A1
  Batley, Nunroyd
    WF16 . . . . **17** C4
  Huddersfield HD2 . . **53** B4
  Meltham HD9 . . . . **81** A1
Guernsey Rd WF14 . . **44** A1
Guildford St WF5 . . **48** C2
GULLY **86** B2
Gully Terr HD9 . . . . . **86** B2
Gunson Cres WF5 . . **48** C4
Gynn La HD9 . . . . **83** C3

H

Haddon Cl BD19 . . . . . **9** B2
Hadfield Rd WF16 . . **18** A3
Hadrian's Cl HD3 . . **50** B2
Haggroyd La HD9 . . **84** C4
HAGGS HILL **49** C3
Haggs Hall Rd WF5 . . **49** C3
Hagg Wood Rd HD4 . **84** C4
Haigh House Hill
  HD3 . . . . **37** A1
Haigh La HD9 . . . . **84** A2
Haigh Row HD8 . . . . . **91** C4
Haigh's Sq HD5 . . . . **54** A1
Haigh St
  16 Brighouse HD6 . . **13** A1
  Elland HX4 . . . . **22** B1
  Huddersfield HD1 . . **67** B1
Half House La HD6 . . **12** A3
Half Moon St **13**
  HD1 . . . . **96** A2
Halifax Ho WF17 . . . . **19** A1

Halifax Rd
Batley WF13,
WF17. . . . .**32** B4
Brighouse, Hartshead
Moor Top HD6 . . . .**6** B1
Brighouse, Hove Edge
HD6 . . . .**12** B3
Brighouse, Waring Green
HD6 . . . .**13** A1
Cleckheaton WF15 . . . .**15** C3
Elland HX5 . . . .**23** B1
Halifax HX3, HX5 . . . .**23** B2
Slaithwaite HD7 . . . . . .**64** A3
Hallas Gr HD5 . . . .**69** B3
Hallas Rd HD8 . . . .**89** B4
Hall Ave HD1 . . . .**67** B3
Hall Bower HD4 . . . . . .**77** A3
Hall Bower La HD4. . . .**77** A3
Hall Cl
Liversedge WF15 . . . . .**17** A1
Meltham HD9 . . . .**81** A2
Ossett WF5 . . . .**34** B3
HALL CLIFFE. **61** A4
Hall Cliffe Cres WF4 .**60** C4
Hall Cliffe Ct WF4. . . .**60** C4
Heron Cl WF4 . . . .**60** C4
Hall Cliffe Rd WF4 . . .**60** C4
Hall Cliffe Rise WF4. .**61** A4
Hall Croft WF4. . . . . . .**63** C4
Hallcroft Cl 6 WF4 . . .**61** A3
Hallcroft Dr WF4. . . . .**61** A3
Hall Cross Gr HD5 . . .**68** C1
Hall Cross Rd HD5 . . .**68** C1
Hall Dr WF15 . . . .**30** B4
Halliley Gdns 2
WF13 . . . .**32** C2
Halliley St WF13 . . . . .**32** B2
Hall La
Dewsbury WF12 . . . . . .**58** B4
Kirkburton HD8 . . . .**88** B1
Slaithwaite HD3,
HD7 . . . .**64** A4
Hall Lee Rd HD3 . . . . .**51** C3
Hallows Ct 4 HD5 . . . .**69** B1
Hall Park Ave WF15 . .**30** A4
Hall St
5 Brighouse HD6 . . . .**26** B4
Huddersfield HD3. . . . . .**50** C1
Halton Cl HD5 . . . .**69** B2
Hambledon Ave
HD9 . . . .**81** A1
Hammerstone Leach La
HX5 . . . .**36** C3
Hammerstones Rd
HX5 . . . .**36** C4
Hammerton Rd HD2 . .**53** A4
Hammond St HD2 . . . .**53** B3
Hampshire St 5
HD5 . . . .**68** C4
Hampson St WF17 . . . .**11** A1
Hamza St WF17 . . . . . .**19** B2
Hanby Cl HD8 . . . .**70** B2
Handel St HD7 . . . .**64** C2
Handel Terr 2 HD5 . . .**68** C3
HANGING HEATON . . .**73** A4
Hanging Heaton CE
Jun & Inf Sch
WF17 . . . .**20** C1
Hanging Royd HD7 . . .**64** C1
Hanging Stone Rd
HD4. . . . .**76** B1
Hanging Wood Way
BD19 . . . .**7** C4
Hangram St 2 HD6. . .**26** B4
Hanover Ct 6 WF13 . .**32** A3
Hanover Gdns WF13 . .**32** B2
Hanover Pl WF17 . . . . .**20** A3

Hanover St
Batley WF17 . . . .**19** C3
Dewsbury WF13 . . . . . .**32** B2
Hanson Ct BD12 . . . . . .**5** B4
Hanson La HD4 . . . . . .**76** A4
Hanson Mount BD12 . .**5** C4
Hanson Rd
Brighouse HD6 . . . .**25** B2
Meltham HD9 . . . .**80** A1
Hardy Pl HD6 . . . .**12** B3
Hardy St HD6 . . . .**13** B1
Harefield Dr WF7 . . . .**11** A3
Harefield Pk HD2 . . . .**52** A4
Hare Park Ave
WF15 . . . .**15** C2
Hare Park Cl WF15 . . .**15** C2
Hare Park Dr WF15 . . .**15** C2
Hare Park La WF15 . . .**15** C2
Harewood Ave
WF16 . . . .**18** B1
Harewood Gr WF16 . . .**18** B1
Harewood Mount
HD9. . . . .**81** A2
Harley Pl HD6 . . . .**26** A3
Harley St 7 HD6. . . . .**26** A3
Harpe Inge HD5 . . . . . .**54** B1
Harp Rd HD3 . . . .**66** A3
Harriet St HD6. . . . . . .**13** A2
Harrington Ct HD9. . . .**81** A1
Hartington St WF17 . .**19** C1
Hartley St WF15 . . . . .**17** A1
Hartley Gr WF13 . . . . .**32** C3
Hartley St WF13 . . . . .**32** C3
HARTSHEAD **28** C3
Hartshead Hall La
WF15 . . . .**29** A3
Hartshead Jun & Inf
Sch WF15 . . . .**28** C4
Hartshead La WF15 . .**28** C4
HARTSHEAD MOOR
SIDE **15** A4
HARTSHEAD MOOR
TOP **6** B1
Hart St HD4 . . . .**76** C4
Harvest Mews WF5 . . .**49** A1
Harvey Royd HD5 . . . . .**69** C2
Harwood Cl HD5. . . . . .**69** B3
Hassocks La HD9 . . . .**82** B2
Hassocks Rd HD9 . . . .**80** A3
Haughs La HD3 . . . . . .**51** A1
Haughs Rd HD3 . . . . . .**51** A1
Havelock St WF13 . . . .**45** A3
Havercroft WF5. . . . . .**49** A3
Havercroft Way
WF17 . . . .**18** C3
Hawes Ave HD3 . . . . . .**66** A4
Hawke Ave WF16 . . . .**18** B2
Hawkincroft Rd
WF4 . . . .**60** B3
Hawkroyd Bank Rd
HD4. . . . .**82** C4
Haworth Cl WF14 . . . .**43** B4
Haworth Rd WF17 . . . .**10** C4
Hawthorn Ave WF14 .**19** A1
Hawthorn Cl HD6 . . . .**13** C1
Hawthorne Cl HD8. . . .**70** C1
Hawthorn Terr
HD4. . . . .**66** B2
Hawthorne Way
HD8. . . . .**89** B1
Hawthorn Rd HD7 . . . .**72** B3
Hawthorns The
WF5 . . . .**49** A1
Hawthorn Terr
Huddersfield HX1. . . . . .**53** B2
Ossett WF5 . . . .**49** A1
Hayburn Gdns WF17 .**19** B3
Hayburn Rd WF17. . . . .**19** A3
Hayfield Ave HD3 . . . .**51** A1
Hayfield Cl HD9. . . . . .**87** A2
Hayson Cl WF12 . . . . .**33** C3

Haywood Ave HD3 . . .**51** C1
Hazel Ave WF12. . . . . .**34** B1
Hazel Cl
Birkenshaw BD11. . . . . .**2** A4
Dewsbury WF12 . . . . . .**34** B1
Hazel Cres WF12. . . . .**34** B1
Hazel Dr WF12. . . . . . .**34** B1
Hazel Gr
Batley WF17 . . . .**19** A2
Brighouse HX3 . . . .**5** A1
Huddersfield, Brackenhall
HD2. . . . .**40** A3
Huddersfield, Cowlersley
HD7 . . . .**74** B4
Headfield CE Jun Sch
WF12 . . . .**46** B3
Headfield La WF12. . . .**46** B3
Headfield Rd
Dewsbury WF12 . . . . . .**46** C3
Huddersfield HD4. . . . . .**67** C1
Headfield View
WF12 . . . .**46** C2
Headland La WF12. . . .**47** B4
Headlands Ave WF5. . .**48** B3
Headlands CE Jun & Inf
Sch WF15 . . . .**17** A2
Headlands Cl WF15 . . .**17** B1
Headlands Gr WF5. . . .**48** B3
Headlands Pk WF5. . . .**48** B3
Headlands Rd
Huddersfield HD1. . . . . .**96** A3
Liversedge WF15 . . . . .**17** A2
Ossett WF5 . . . .**48** B3
Headlands St WF15 . . .**17** A1
Headlands The
WF15 . . . .**17** A1
Headlands Wlk WF5 .**48** B3
Headwall Gn HD7. . . . .**64** A1
Healds Ave WF15 . . . .**17** B2
Healds Rd WF13 . . . . .**32** A4
HEALEY. **48** B1
Healey Cl WF17 . . . . . .**18** C3
Healey Cres WF5 . . . .**48** C1
Healey Dr WF5 . . . . . .**48** C2
Healey Farm HD8 . . . .**89** A2
Healey Green La
HD5 . . . .**56** C1
Healey Jun & Inf Sch
WF17 . . . .**18** C3
Healey La WF17. . . . . .**19** B3
Healey Lane Bsns Ctr
WF17 . . . .**18** C2
Healey Lane Mills Bsns
Ctr WF17 . . . .**19** A3
Healey Rd WF5 . . . . . .**48** C1
Healey St WF17 . . . . . .**18** C3
Healey View WF5 . . . .**48** C2
Healey Wood Cres
HD6. . . . .**26** A3
Healey Wood Gdns
HD6. . . . .**26** B2
Healey Wood Gr
HD6. . . . .**26** B2
Healey Wood Rd
HD6. . . . .**26** B3
Heath Cl
Dewsbury WF12 . . . . . .**34** B2
Slaithwaite HD7 . . . . . .**74** A1
Heathcliffe Cl WF17. . .**3** C1
Heathdale Ave HD2 . . .**52** C3
Heather Ave HD9 . . . . .**80** C1
Heather Cl WF5. . . . . .**49** B1
Heather Ct
Batley WF17 . . . .**10** B1
Huddersfield HD3. . . . . .**50** C2
Heatherfield Cres
HD1. . . . .**66** C4
Heatherfield Rd
HD1. . . . .**66** C4
Heather Fold HD8 . . . .**91** B1

Heathergrove Fold
HD5. . . . .**54** A1
Heather Rd HD9 . . . . .**80** B1
Heather View
Elland HX5 . . . .**24** B1
Ossett WF5 . . . .**48** C3
HEATHFIELD. **24** B2
Heathfield WF14 . . . . .**43** B4
Heathfield Ave HX5 . .**24** B1
Heathfield Grange 4
HX5. . . . .**24** A1
Heathfield Ind Est
HX5. . . . .**37** C4
Heathfield Mews
HD7. . . . .**65** A2
Heathfield Rd HD7. . . .**65** A2
Heathfield St HX5 . . . .**37** C4
Heath Gr
Batley WF17 . . . .**20** C2
Huddersfield HD4. . . . . .**76** A4
Heath House La
HD7. . . . .**64** A2
Heath House Mill
HD7. . . . .**64** B2
Heath Mount Rd
HD6. . . . .**26** A2
Heath Rd
Dewsbury WF12 . . . . . .**34** B2
Huddersfield HD7 . . . . .**74** A2
Slaithwaite HD7 . . . . . .**74** A2
Heath St WF15 . . . . . .**30** B4
Heath Wlk WF12 . . . . .**34** B2
Heathwood Dr HD7 . . .**64** B3
Heaton Ave
Cleckheaton BD19 . . . . .**7** C1
Dewsbury WF12 . . . . . .**33** B2
Kirkheaton HD5 . . . .**55** C3
Heaton Avenue Fst Sch
BD19. . . . .**7** C1
Heaton Dr HD5 . . . . . .**55** C4
HEATON FIELDS **55** B3
Heaton Fold La HD1 .**66** C4
Heaton Gdns HD1. . . . .**66** C4
Heaton Gr BD19 . . . . . .**7** C1
Heaton Grange
WF17 . . . .**20** B1
Heaton Moor Rd
HD5. . . . .**55** C3
Heaton Rd
Batley WF17 . . . .**11** C1
Huddersfield HD1. . . . . .**66** C4
Heaton St
4 Brighouse HD6 . . . .**26** A4
Cleckheaton BD19 . . . . .**8** B2
Heatons Yd HD6 . . . . . .**26** B3
Heator La HD8. . . . . . .**90** C1
Hebble Mount HD9 . . .**80** C1
Hebble St
Dewsbury WF13 . . . . . .**45** B3
4 Huddersfield HD1 . .**53** B2
Hebden Ct HD3 . . . . . .**51** B1
HECKMONDWIKE **31** A4
Heckmondwike Gram
Sch WF16 . . . .**18** A2
Heckmondwike Rd
Batley WF13 . . . .**31** C3
Dewsbury WF13 . . . . . .**31** C2
HEIGHT **74** A2
Heights Ct WF15 . . . . .**15** B3
Heights Dr HD7. . . . . .**73** C2
Heights La WF16 . . . . .**18** B1
Heights The HD9 . . . . .**86** C1
Helene Ct HD3 . . . .**50** B2
Helen St HD1 . . . .**67** A1
Helen Terr HD6 . . . . . .**12** C1
Hellewell's Row
WF4 . . . .**59** C3
Helme CE Jun & Inf
Sch HD9. . . . .**80** C1
Helme La HD9 . . . .**80** B3
Helme Pk HD9 . . . .**80** B3

Helmet La HD9 . . . . . .**80** B2
Helm La WF14 . . . .**42** C3
Helston Dr HD9 . . . . . .**82** C2
Helted Way HD5. . . . . .**69** A1
Henley Ave WF12 . . . . .**58** A4
Henley Croft HD5 . . . .**69** A4
Henley Rd WF12 . . . . .**58** A4
Henrietta St 2
WF17 . . . .**19** C3
Henry Frederik Ave
HD4. . . . .**82** A4
Henry Ralph Ave
HD4. . . . .**75** B3
Henry St
Batley WF17 . . . .**32** C4
Brighouse HD6 . . . .**13** A2
Huddersfield HD1. . . . . .**96** A2
Heppenstall St HD4. . .**68** A2
Hepworth Cl WF14 . . . .**44** B4
Hepworth Cres HD9. . .**87** B1
Hepworth Dr WF14 . . .**44** B4
Hepworth La WF14. . . .**44** A4
Hepworth Rd HD9 . . . .**87** B1
Hepworths Bldgs
HD2. . . . .**40** C1
Heritage Ct HD9 . . . . .**80** B3
Heritage Rd WF17 . . . .**19** C2
Hermitage Pk HD8. . . .**88** B4
Heron Cl WF13 . . . .**45** A4
Hesketh Pl HX3 . . . .**5** A1
Hever Gr HD5 . . . .**55** A1
Hexham Gn HD3 . . . . .**65** B3
Heybeck La WF3,
WF12 . . . .**21** C3
Hey Cliff Rd HD9. . . . .**86** B3
Hey Cres HD9. . . . .**80** B2
Hey La
Huddersfield,
Lowerhouses HD5 . . .**68** C1
Kirkburton HD9. . . . .**77** A1
Hey St HD6 . . . .**13** B2
Heys The HD9. . . . .**80** C4
Heywood Bottom
HD8. . . . .**95** B3
Hick La WF17. . . . .**20** A3
High Ash Ave HD8 . . . .**93** C3
High Bank Cl HX5. . . . .**24** C1
High Bank Fst Sch
WF15 . . . .**15** B3
Highbridge La HD8 . . .**92** B2
High Brooms HD2 . . . .**52** B3
HIGHBURTON. **88** B1
Highburton CE Fst Sch
HD8. . . . .**88** B2
Highbury Sch HD6. . . .**25** B1
Highbury Terr 12
WF12 . . . .**33** A2
High Cl
Huddersfield HD5. . . . . .**69** A1
Ossett WF5 . . . .**35** A3
Slaithwaite HD7 . . . . . .**74** A2
Highcliffe Ave HD2 . . .**52** C4
Highcliffe Rd WF17 . . .**19** C1
High Crest HD7 . . . . . .**74** A4
Highcroft WF17. . . . . .**19** C1
Highcroft Cres HD5. . .**69** B1
Highdale WF12 . . . . . .**33** B4
Highfield Ave
Brighouse HD6 . . . .**5** B2
Elland HX4 . . . .**22** B1
Meltham HD9 . . . .**80** B3
Highfield Cres
Meltham HD9 . . . .**80** B3
Netherton WF4 . . . .**62** A4
Highfield Ct WF15 . . . .**29** C4
Highfield Dr
Batley WF17 . . . .**10** B4
Liversedge FW15 . . . . .**16** B1
Highfield Gdns
WF12 . . . .**46** C1
Highfield Gr HX5 . . . . .**23** B2

Highfield Grange
WF4 . . . .**60** C3
Highfield La
Batley WF13 . . . .**18** C2
Lepton HD8. . . . .**70** C3
Meltham HD9 . . . .**80** A3
Highfield Mount
WF12 . . . .**58** A3
Highfield Rd
Brighouse HD6 . . . .**25** B2
Cleckheaton BD19 . . . . .**7** C1
Elland HX5 . . . .**37** B4
Horbury WF4 . . . .**60** C3
Kirkburton HD8. . . . . . .**88** B1
Meltham HD9 . . . .**80** B3
Netherton WF4. . . . . . .**63** B3
Highfields
Huddersfield HD1. . . . .**52** C1
Netherton WF4 . . . .**63** B3
Highfield Sch WF5. . .**35** A3
Highfields Rd HD1 . .**52** C1
Highfield Terr
Cleckheaton BD19 . . . . .**7** C1
Dewsbury WF12 . . . . . .**46** C1
Highgate Ave HD8 . .**71** B1
Highgate Cres HD8 .**71** A1
Highgate Dr HD8 . . .**71** B1
Highgate La
Kirkheaton HD5 . . . . . .**56** A3
Lepton HD8. . . . .**71** A1
Highgate Rd 🔟
WF12 . . . .**33** A2
Highgate St WF17 . . .**20** C1
Highgate Terr 🔢
WF12 . . . .**33** A2
Highgate Wlk HD8 . .**71** B1
High Gn HD8 . . . .**88** C4
High House Edge
HD7. . . . .**73** B1
High House La HD7 .**73** B2
High La
Holmfirth HD9. . . . . . .**86** B1
Huddersfield HD4. . . . .**77** B3
Highlands WF5 . . . . .**48** B3
Highlands Ave HD5 .**69** B1
Highlands The
WF15 . . . .**16** A3
High Lea HD7. . . . . . .**78** C3
Highley Hall Croft
HD6. . . . .**14** A1
Highley Pk HD6. . . . .**27** B4
High Mdws
Dewsbury WF12 . . . . . .**57** B3
Elland HX4 . . . .**22** C1
Highmoor Cres HD6 .**14** A1
Highmoor La
Brighouse, Clifton
HD6 . . . .**14** B2
Brighouse HD6 . . . .**14** C3
Cleckheaton HD6 . . . . .**15** A4
High Rd WF12 . . . .**33** B1
High Ridge WF4 . . . .**63** C4
Highroyd HD8 . . . .**71** B1
Highroyd Cres 🔢
HD5. . . . .**68** C3
Highroyd La HD5 . . . .**68** C4
High St
Batley, Birstall
WF17. . . . .**10** B3
Batley, Hanging Heaton
WF17. . . . .**18** C2
Batley WF16 . . . .**18** B2
Brighouse HD6 . . . .**13** B1
Clayton West HD8. . . . .**93** B3
Cleckheaton BD19 . . . . .**8** A2
Dewsbury, Daw Green
WF12, WF13 . . . .**32** B1
Dewsbury, Earlesheaton
WF12. . . . .**33** C1
Dewsbury, Overthorpe
WF12. . . . .**57** B3

High St *continued*
Dewsbury, Overthorpe
WF12. . . . .**57** C3
🔟 Elland, West Vale
HX4 . . . .**23** A1
Honley HD9. . . . .**83** A2
Horbury WF4 . . . .**60** C3
Huddersfield HD1. . . . .**96** A1
Huddersfield, Paddock
HD1. . . . .**67** A3
Ossett WF5. . . . .**34** C3
Slaithwaite HD7 . . . . . .**64** A3
HIGHTOWN. **16** A3
Hightown Fst Sch
WF15 . . . .**15** C3
HIGHTOWN
HEIGHTS **15** B4
Hightown La HD9 . . .**86** A3
Hightown Rd WF15 . .**16** A4
Hightown View
WF15 . . . .**16** A3
High Wood Rd WF17 . .**4** A2
Higson Ct HD5. . . . . .**55** A1
Higson Row HD8 . . . .**93** B4
Hilberoyd Rd WF17 . .**20** A3
Hilda St WF5 . . . .**49** A2
Hillary St 🔢 WF13 . . .**18** C1
Hill Cres WF17. . . . . .**11** A3
Hillcrest Ave
Batley WF17 . . . .**19** A3
Ossett WF5. . . . .**34** C2
Hillcrest Flats HD1. .**67** B2
Hillcrest Mount BD19 . **6** C1
Hill Crest Rd WF12. . .**46** B3
Hill End WF12 . . . .**33** B2
Hill End Cl HX3 . . . . . . **5** A4
Hillesley Rd WF12. . . .**21** A1
Hillgarth WF12 . . . . . .**46** C1
Hill Gr HD3. . . . .**50** C3
Hill Grove Lea HD8. . .**50** C3
Hillhead Dr WF17 . . . .**11** A3
HILLHOUSE. **53** B3
Hillhouse La HD1 . . .**53** B2
Hill Pk WF14. . . . .**56** C4
Hill Rise WF17 . . . . . .**20** C2
HILL SIDE **55** B1
Hillside HD8. . . . .**95** B3
Hillside Ave HD2. . . .**53** B4
Hillside Cres HD4. . . .**77** A4
Hillside Rise WF15 . . .**17** A1
Hillside View HD7. . . .**74** A3
Hillside Works Ind Est
HD9. . . . . **8** A4
Hill St
Cleckheaton BD19 . . . . . **7** C1
Holmfirth HD9. . . . . . .**87** B1
Hill Top HD8 . . . .**93** B3
Hill Top Ave HD2 . . . .**38** A2
Hill Top Bank HD4. . .**82** A4
Hill Top Cres WF14 . .**56** C3
Hill Top Croft HD4 . .**82** A4
Hill Top Dr HD3 . . . . .**51** A2
Hill Top Est WF16 . . .**18** B2
Hill Top Farm HD8 . .**89** A1
Hill Top Fold HD7 . . .**72** B3
Hill Top Rd
Huddersfield, Grove
Place HD5 . . . .**68** C4
Huddersfield HD3. . . . .**50** C1
Huddersfield, Paddock
HD1. . . . .**67** A3
Slaithwaite HD7 . . . . . .**72** C3
Hill Top Terr HD8. . . .**93** B3
Hill Tree Pk HD4 . . . .**74** C3
Hinchcliffe Ave WF5 .**49** B3
Hind Ct HD9 . . . .**80** A3
Hindley Rd WF15 . . . .**17** A1
Hind St BD12 . . . . **5** C4
Hions Cl HD6 . . . .**26** A2

Hipperholm &
Lightcliffe High Sch
& Sports Coll HX3 . . . **5** A1
Hirst Ave WF16 . . . . . .**18** A4
Hirstlands Ave WF5 . .**34** C1
Hirstlands Dr WF5 . . .**34** C2
Hirst Rd WF13 . . . .**32** C3
Hirst St WF14. . . . .**43** C1
Hobart Rd WF12 . . . . .**33** C3
Hob La HD4 . . . .**75** A4
Hobson Fold 🔢 BD12 . . **6** A4
Hodgson La BD11. . . . .**2** C4
Hodgson Terr WF12 . .**46** C4
Hoffman St HD3 . . . . .**65** C2
Holays HD5. . . . .**54** B1
Holden Ing Way
WF17 . . . . **4** A2
Holdsworth Ct 🔢
BD19 . . . . **8** A2
Holdsworth St BD19 . . **8** A2
Holland St WF17. . . . .**20** A3
Hollin Ave HD3 . . . . . .**51** C2
Hollinbank La WF16. .**18** B3
Hollin Edge HD8 . . . . .**95** B3
Hollin Hall HD7 . . . . .**64** B3
Hollin Hall La
Huddersfield HD7. . . . .**64** C3
Huddersfield, Scapegoat
HD7. . . . .**64** B3
Kirkheaton WF14 . . . . .**56** A4
Hollin House La
Clayton West HD8. . . . .**93** C1
Holmfirth HD9. . . . . . .**87** C3
Hollinroyd Rd WF12. .**33** B2
Hollins Ave WF13 . . . .**18** C1
Hollins Glen HD7 . . . .**72** C2
Hollins Hey Rd HX4 . .**36** C2
Hollins Rd 🔢 WF13 . .**31** C4
Hollins Row HD7 . . . .**72** C2
Hollin Terr HD3 . . . . .**51** C1
Hollowgate HD9 . . . . .**86** A3
Hollow The HD9 . . . . .**80** B2
Holly App WF5. . . . . . .**35** C2
Holly Bank
Elland HX5 . . . .**37** A3
Kirkheaton HD5 . . . . . .**55** B2
Hollybank Ave
Batley WF17 . . . .**11** C1
Denby Dale HD8 . . . . . .**94** A3
Holly Bank Ct HD3 . . .**51** A1
Holly Bank Ho 🔢
HD6. . . . .**25** C2
Holly Bank Pk HD6. . .**25** C2
Holly Bank Rd
Brighouse HD6 . . . .**25** C2
Huddersfield HD3. . . . .**51** C3
Holly Bank Sch
WF14 . . . .**29** B2
Holly Dene WF5 . . . . .**34** C1
Hollyfield Ave HD3. . .**51** A1
Holly Gr Batley WF17. .**19** B1
Huddersfield HD3. . . . .**51** C3
Holly Mede WF5 . . . . .**35** A2
Hollynsmill HX4 . . . . .**23** A1
Hollyns Terr 🔢 HX4 . .**22** C1
Holly Rd HD1 . . . .**67** A2
Holly Terr HD1. . . . . . .**53** B2
Holmcliffe Ave HD4. .**76** B3
Holmdale Cres HD9. .**84** A2
Holmdene Dr WF14 . .**43** C4
Holme Ave HD5. . . . . .**69** A3
Holmebank Mews
HD9. . . . .**85** A4
Holme Field WF5 . . . .**34** C1
Holmefield Rd HD3 . .**65** A4
Holme La HD7. . . . .**89** C3
Holme Leas Dr WF5. .**34** C1
Holme Mills Ind Est
HD3. . . . .**65** B2
Holme Pl 🔢 HD1 . . . . .**52** A1
Holmeside Cl HD4 . . .**76** B2

Holme St
Brighouse HX3 . . . . **5** A1
Liversedge WF15 . . . . .**17** B2
Holme Valley Bsns Ctr
HD4. . . . .**76** A2
Holme Way WF5 . . . . .**34** C1
Holmfield HD8 . . . . . .**93** B3
Holmfield Ave HD8 . .**93** B3
Holmfield Cl HD8 . . . .**93** B3
Holmfield Dr HD7. . . .**65** B3
Holmfield Rd HD8 . . .**93** B3
Holmfield Terr HD8 . .**93** B3
HOLMFIRTH **86** B3
Holmfirth Jun & Inf
Sch HD9. . . . .**86** A2
Holmfirth Rd HD9. . . .**80** C1
Holt Ave HD2 . . . .**36** B2
Holtby Gr HX3 . . . .**4** B2
Holyoake Ave
Batley WF17 . . . .**19** A3
Linthwaite HD7. . . . . . .**73** B2
Holyoake Terr
Horbury WF4 . . . .**60** A3
Slaithwaite HD7 . . . . . .**73** C3
Holy Spirit RC Prim
Sch WF16 . . . .**18** A2
Holy Trinity CE Prim
Sch WF5 . . . .**48** C4
Holywell HD7. . . . .**73** C3
HOLYWELL GREEN . .**36** A2
Holywell Green Prim
Sch HX4. . . . .**36** A2
Homestead The
WF16 . . . .**18** B2
Homes The HD2 . . . . .**41** B1
Honey Head La HD9. .**83** A1
Honeysuckle Dr
WF12 . . . .**46** C1
Honley Bsns Ctr
HD9. . . . .**83** B2
Honley CE Inf Sch
HD9. . . . .**83** A3
Honley CE Jun Sch
HD9. . . . .**83** A2
Honley High Sch & Coll
HD9. . . . .**83** B3
Honley Sq WF4 . . . . . .**60** C3
Honley Sta HD9 . . . . .**83** C3
Honoria St HD1. . . . . .**53** A3
Hood St HD4 . . . .**76** B2
Hoods The HD6 . . . . . .**25** C1
Hope St
Dewsbury WF13 . . . . . .**32** C3
Huddersfield HD3. . . . .**66** A3
Ossett WF5. . . . .**49** B1
Hope Terr HD7. . . . . . .**64** C1
Hopewell St WF17 . . .**19** B4
Hopkinson Rd HD2 . .**40** A2
Hopton Ave WF14 . . . .**56** B4
Hopton Dr WF14 . . . . .**56** B4
Hopton Hall La
WF14 . . . .**56** C3
Hopton La WF14. . . . .**56** C4
Hopton New Rd
WF14 . . . .**43** C1
Hopton Prim Sch
WF14 . . . .**43** B2
Horace Waller VC Par
WF12 . . . .**34** A4
HORBURY **61** A4
HORBURY BRIDGE . .**59** C3
Horbury Bridge CE Jun
& Inf Sch WF4 . . . . . .**60** A3
HORBURY
JUNCTION. **61** B1
Horbury Mews WF4. .**60** B4
Horbury Prim Sch
WF4 . . . .**61** B3
Horbury Rd WF5. . . . .**49** A1
Horbury Sch WF4. . . .**61** B3

Horncastle St 🔢
BD19. . . . . **8** B1
Horner Ave WF17 . . . .**18** C4
Horner Cres WF17 . . .**18** C4
Horse Bank Dr HD4 . .**67** A1
Horsley Fold HD6. . . .**27** B4
Horton St
Batley WF16 . . . .**18** A1
Ossett WF5. . . . .**48** B4
Hostingley La WF12. .**59** A4
Houghton's
Almshouses 🔢
HD5. . . . .**69** B1
Houghton St HD6 . . . .**13** B1
Houldsworth Ave
WF16 . . . .**10** B1
Hoults La HX4 . . . .**22** C2
Hove Ct 🔢 WF16. . . . .**18** A2
HOVE EDGE **12** C3
Howard Ave HD3 . . . .**51** C1
Howard Pk BD19. . . . . . **8** B1
Howard Pl WF17 . . . . .**19** C1
Howard Rd HD3 . . . . .**51** C1
Howard St
Batley WF17 . . . .**19** C1
Ossett WF5. . . . .**35** A1
Howard Villas BD19 . . **8** B1
Howard Way HD9 . . . .**80** C1
Howarth La HD1. . . . . .**67** A1
Howden Cl HD4. . . . . .**74** B4
HOWDEN CLOUGH . .**11** B4
Howden Clough Ind Est
WF17 . . . . **4** B1
Howgate Rd HD7 . . . .**72** B2
Howley St WF17 . . . . .**20** A4
Howley Wlk WF17. . . .**20** B4
Howroyd's Yd WF5. . .**34** C3
Hoylake Ave HD2 . . . .**39** B1
Hoyle Beck Cl HD7. . .**73** C3
Hoyle Head Mills Ind
Est WF12 . . . .**33** C3
Hoyle House Fold
HD7. . . . .**73** C3
Hoyle Ing HD7 . . . .**73** C3
Hubert St HD3. . . . . . .**50** B3
HUDDERSFIELD **96** B2
Huddersfield Gram Sch
HD3. . . . .**86** B4
Huddersfield New Coll
HD3. . . . .**50** C1
Huddersfield
Observatory ★
HD4. . . . .**74** B2
Huddersfield Rd
Batley WF17 . . . .**10** B2
Brighouse HD6 . . . .**26** B1
Dewsbury, Ravensthorpe
WF13. . . . .**44** C2
Dewsbury, West Town
WF13. . . . .**32** B1
Holmfirth HD9. . . . .**86** A4
Honley HD9. . . . .**83** B3
Huddersfield HD3,
HX5 . . . .**37** C3
Kirkburton HD8. . . . . . .**89** C2
Huddersfield Royal
Infmy HD3. . . . .**51** C2
Huddersfield Sta
HD1. . . . .**96** A2
Huddersfield Tech
Coll
Huddersfield HD1. . . . .**96** A1
Huddersfield, Salford
HD4. . . . .**76** B4
Huddersfield Tech Coll
(Annexe) HD1 . . . . . .**52** C1
Huddersfield Tech Coll
(Brunel Ho) HD2. . . .**54** B4

Huddleston Ct
Dewsbury WF12 . . . . . .**33** C2
Mirfield WF14. . . . .**43** C2
Hudroyd HD5 . . . .**69** B1
Hulbert Croft HD5 . . .**69** B2
Hullenedge Gdns
HX5 . . . .**36** C4
Hullenedge La HX5 . .**36** C4
Hullenedge Rd HX5 . .**37** A4
Hullen Rd HX5. . . . . . .**36** C4
Humber Cl HD7. . . . . . .**73** C3
Humber Pl WF4. . . . . . .**60** C4
Hume Crest 8
WF17 . . . .**19** C3
Hungerford Rd HD3. .**52** A2
Hunston Ave HD3 . . . .**51** B1
Huntingdon Ave
HD2. . . . .**41** B2
Huntingdon Rd HD6 .**26** C3
Huntock Pl HD6 . . . . .**12** C3
Huntsman's Cl HD4 . .**75** C2
Hurst Knowle HD5 . . .**69** C2
Hurst La WF14 . . . .**44** A2
Hurstwood HD2 . . . . .**41** A2
Hustings The WF15 . .**16** C2
Hutchinson La 11
HD6. . . . .**26** B4
Hutton Dr WF16 . . . . .**18** B2
Hyrst Garth WF17. . . .**32** B4
Hyrstlands Rd WF17 .**19** C1
Hyrstmount Jun Sch
WF17 . . . .**19** C1
Hyrst Wlk WF17. . . . . .**19** C1

I

Ibbotson Flats 6
HD1. . . . .**96** B2
Illingworth St WF5. . .**48** C3
Imperial Arc 23 HD1 .**96** A2
Imperial Rd HD1,
HD3. . . . .**52** A1
Independent Ho
WF16 . . . .**18** B2
Indus Cl WF16 . . . .**18** B2
Industrial Ave WF17 .**10** A3
Industrial St
Brighouse HD6. . . . .**13** B1
13 Brighouse, Scholes
BD19. . . . .**6** C2
Horbury WF4 . . . .**61** B2
Huddersfield HD4. . . .**67** C2
Liversedge FW15. . . . .**16** B2
Industrial Terr HD5 .**69** C3
Infirmary Rd WF13. . .**32** B3
Ingdale Dr HD9 . . . . . .**86** B4
Ingfield Ave
Huddersfield HD5. . . .**68** C4
Ossett WF5. . . . .**49** A4
Ingfield Terr HD7 . . . .**72** C3
Ingham Cl WF14 . . . . .**44** B2
Ingham Croft WF14 . .**44** B2
Ingham Garth WF14 .**44** B3
Ingham Rd WF12 . . . . .**46** C1
Ing Head HD7 . . . .**72** A3
Ing La HD4 . . . .**67** C1
Ingle Ct HD8 . . . .**70** C2
Ingleton Rd HD4 . . . . .**77** A4
Inglewood Ave HD2. .**51** C3
Ings Cres
Dewsbury WF12 . . . . . .**57** B4
Liversedge WF15 . . . . .**17** B2
Ings La WF12 . . . .**57** B4
Ings Mill WF5 . . . .**49** A4
Ings Mill Ave HD8 . . .**93** B4
Ings Mill Dr HD8 . . . . .**93** B3
Ings Mill Yd WF16. . . .**18** A2

Ings Rd
Batley, Heckmondwike
WF16. . . . .**18** A2
Batley WF17 . . . .**19** A4
Dewsbury WF13 . . . . . .**33** B3
Huddersfield HD5. . . . .**69** C2
Liversedge WF15 . . . . .**17** B3
Ings Rise WF17 . . . .**19** B4
Ings The
Brighouse HX3 . . . . . .**13** A4
Clayton West HD8. . . .**93** B3
Ings Villa WF15 . . . . . .**30** C4
Ings Way HD8 . . . .**71** B1
Ings Way W HD8 . . . . .**71** A1
Ingwell Terr BD19. . . . .**8** B1
Ingwood Par HX4. . . . .**36** B4
Inkerman Ct HD8 . . . . .**95** B2
Inkerman Way HD8 . .**95** A4
Inner Hey HD7 . . . .**79** A3
Intake HD7 . . . .**65** A3
Intake La
Batley WF17 . . . .**10** C1
Meltham HD4 . . . .**74** B1
Ossett WF5. . . . .**49** A3
Iron St BD19. . . . .**7** C1
Islamia Girls High Sch
HD1. . . . .**67** A2
Island Dr HD9 . . . .**85** A4
Island View WF12 . . . .**46** A4
Ivy Mount HD2. . . . . . .**72** B3
Ivy St Brighouse HD6 .**12** C1
Huddersfield, Moldgreen
HD4, HD5 . . . .**68** B3
Huddersfield, Paddock
HD4 . . . .**66** B2
Ivy Terr HD6 . . . .**12** C1

J

Jacinth Ct HD2 . . . . . .**53** C4
Jack Hill HD2 . . . .**53** A3
Jack La WF17 . . . .**33** A4
Jackroyd La
Huddersfield HD4 . . . .**77** A4
Mirfield WF14 . . . .**56** B4
JACKSON BRIDGE . . .**87** C2
Jacobs Ct WF4 . . . .**61** B2
Jacob's Row HD4 . . . . .**67** B1
Jacquard Cl BD19 . . . . .**5** B1
Jade Pl HD2 . . . .**53** C4
Jaggar La HD9 . . . .**83** A2
JAGGER DEAN **36** B1
Jagger Green Dean
HX4 . . . .**36** A1
Jagger Green La
HX4 . . . .**36** B1
Jaggar La HD5 . . . .**55** A2
Jail Rd WF17 . . . .**18** C3
James Mason Ct 11
HD1. . . . .**52** A1
James St
Batley WF17 . . . .**19** B2
Birkenshaw BD11. . . . . .**2** A4
Brighouse HD6 . . . . . .**13** A2
Dewsbury WF13 . . . . . .**32** B3
Elland, Holywell Green
HX4 . . . .**36** A2
Elland HX5 . . . .**37** C4
Huddersfield HD7. . . . .**64** C2
Liversedge WF15 . . . . .**17** B1
Mirfield WF14 . . . .**30** A1
Slaithwaite HD7 . . . . . .**72** C3
Jason Terr WF17 . . . . . .**11** A4
Jay House La HD6 . . . .**14** A3
Jenkin Dr WF4 . . . .**60** B3
Jenkin La WF4 . . . .**60** B3
Jenkin Rd WF4 . . . .**60** C3
Jenkinson St WF17 . . .**32** C4
Jenny La WF14 . . . .**30** B1
Jensen Ave WF13 . . . .**18** C1

Jepson La HX5 . . . . . .**37** B4
Jeremy La WF16 . . . . . .**18** A2
Jersey Cl WF12 . . . . . .**33** C4
Jerusalem Rd HD7. . .**73** A1
Jesmond Gr WF13 . . .**32** B3
Jessamine St WF13 . .**44** C3
Jessop Ave HD5 . . . . .**69** C1
Jessop Fold HD9 . . . . .**83** A3
Jilley Royd La HD2. . .**39** C2
Jill La WF14 . . . .**31** A2
Jim La HD1. . . . .**66** C4
Joan Royd WF16 . . . . .**18** A4
John Booth Cl
WF15 . . . .**29** C4
John Carr Ave WF4 . .**60** C4
John Haigh Rd HD7 . .**72** C2
John Nelson Cl 9
WF17 . . . .**10** C3
John Ormsby V C Way
WF12 . . . .**34** A4
Johns La HX5. . . . .**37** B2
Johnson St WF14 . . . .**43** C1
John St
5 Batley, Birstall
WF17. . . . .**10** B3
9 Batley, Heckmondwike
WF16. . . . .**18** A1
Brighouse HD6 . . . . . .**13** A1
2 Dewsbury,
Eastborough WF12 . .**33** B3
Dewsbury, Ravensthorpe
WF13. . . . .**45** A3
Dewsbury WF13 . . . . . .**32** C4
Elland HX5 . . . .**37** B4
Elland, Lindhead HX4. .**22** C1
Huddersfield HD3. . . . .**66** A2
John William St
3 Cleckheaton
BD19. . . . .**8** A2
14 Elland HX5. . . . .**37** B4
Huddersfield HD1. . . . .**96** A2
Liversedge, Mill Bridge
WF15. . . . .**17** C2
1 Liversedge WF15 . . .**17** B2
Josephine Rd HD4 . . .**65** C1
Jos La HD8 . . . .**90** A2
Jos Way HD8 . . . .**90** A2
Jubilee Ave HD8 . . . . .**90** C4
Jubilee La HD4 . . . . . .**65** C1
Jubilee Mount HD6 . .**25** C4
Judy Haigh La
WF12 . . . .**57** C2
Judy La HD2. . . . .**40** A1
Julian St HD5. . . . .**69** A3
Jumble Dyke 5
HD6. . . . .**25** C4
Jumble Wood HD8. . .**70** C1
Junction 25 Bsns Pk
WF14 . . . .**43** B3
Junction La WF5. . . . .**49** C2
Junction Rd 3
WF13 . . . .**32** B1
Juniper Gr HD4. . . . . .**82** B4
Juniper Grove Mews
HD4. . . . .**82** B4
Justin Way HD4 . . . . .**74** C3

K

Kaffir Rd HD2. . . . . . .**52** A1
Karon Dr WF4 . . . .**61** A3
Kaye La HD7. . . . .**65** A1
Kaye's Fst Sch HD8. .**93** B3
Kaye St Batley WF16 . .**18** A1
Dewsbury WF12 . . . . . .**46** C1
Keats Dr HD6 . . . .**31** B4
Keat St HD4 . . . .**67** A2
Kebble St HD2 . . . .**52** A1
Keir Hardie Cl WF16 .**17** C2
Keldregate HD2 . . . . .**41** A2
Kelloe St BD19. . . . .**8** A3

Kelso Gr HD5 . . . .**69** C4
Kelvin Ave HD5 . . . . .**69** A4
Kelvin Rd HX5 . . . .**37** A4
Kemps Way HD9 . . . . .**87** B1
Ken Churchill Dr
WF4 . . . .**49** C1
Kenilworth Cl WF14 .**43** B4
Kenilworth Dr HX3. .**13** A4
Kenmore Ave BD19 . . .**7** C2
Kenmore Cl BD19 . . . .**7** C2
Kenmore Cres BD19 . .**7** C2
Kenmore Dr BD19 . . . .**7** C2
Kenmore Gr BD19. . . . .**7** C2
Kenmore Rd BD19 . . . .**7** C2
Kenmore View BD19 . .**7** C2
Kenmore Way BD19. . .**7** C2
Kennedy Ave HD2. . . .**39** C3
Kennedy Cl WF12 . . . .**20** C1
Kensington Cl WF17 .**19** B2
Kensington Gdns
HX5 . . . .**37** A4
Kentmere Ave BD12. .**6** B3
Kent Wlk 3 WF13 . . . .**32** B2
Kenyon Bank HD8 . . .**95** A2
Kertland St WF12 . . . .**32** C1
Kester Rd WF17. . . . . .**18** C3
Kestrel Bank HD4 . . .**76** A1
Kestrel View
Cleckheaton BD19 . . . .**8** A3
Shelley HD8 . . . .**89** B1
Keswick Ave HD3 . . . .**51** A3
Kew Hill HD3 . . . .**37** B1
Kew Hill Bottom
HD3. . . . .**37** B1
Kidroyd HD5. . . . .**68** C2
Kidroyd La HD5. . . . . .**69** A2
Kilburn Cl HD5 . . . . . .**68** C3
Kilburn La WF13 . . . . .**32** C3
Kiln Ave WF14 . . . .**29** C1
Kiln Brow HD7. . . . . . .**65** A2
Kiln Ct HD3. . . . .**50** B3
Kilner Bank HD5. . . . .**53** C1
Kiln Fold HD6 . . . .**14** A1
Kiln Hill HD7 . . . .**72** C2
Kiln Hill Ind Est
HD7. . . . .**72** C2
Kiln La 10 WF13. . . . . .**33** A2
Kilnsey Hill WF17 . . . .**33** A4
Kilpin Hill La WF13. . .**18** C1
Kilroyd Ave BD19 . . . . .**8** A4
Kilroyd Dr BD19 . . . . . .**8** B4
Kimberley St
Brighouse HD6 . . . . . .**13** B1
Dewsbury WF12 . . . . . .**46** A2
Kinder Ave HD4. . . . . .**74** B4
King Cliffe Flats 4
HD1. . . . .**53** A2
King Cliffe Rd HD1,
HD2. . . . .**53** A3
King Edward St
WF12 . . . .**46** A1
Kingfisher Cres
WF13 . . . .**45** A4
Kingfisher Gr HD4 . . .**76** A1
King's Bridge Rd
HD4. . . . .**68** A2
Kings Cl WF5 . . . .**34** C1
Kings Croft WF5 . . . . .**34** C2
Kings Ct Batley WF15 .**30** C4
Skelmanthorpe HD8 . .**91** C3
Kings Dr WF17 . . . .**10** B4
Kingsgate Ctr HD1. . .**96** B2
Kings Head Dr 2
WF14 . . . .**43** B4
Kings Head Rd
WF14 . . . .**43** B4
Kings Lea
Batley WF15 . . . .**30** C4
Halifax HX3. . . . .**22** B4

Kings Lea *continued*
Ossett WF5. . . . .**34** C2
Kingsley Ave
Birkenshaw BD11. . . . . .**2** B2
Huddersfield HD1. . . . .**67** A2
Kingsley Cl BD11 . . . . .**2** B2
Kingsley Cres BD11 . . .**2** B2
Kingsley Dr BD11 . . . . .**2** B2
Kingsmead WF5 . . . . .**34** C2
Kings Meadow WF5. .**34** C1
King's Mill La HD1. . .**96** B1
Kings Paddock WF5 .**34** C1
King St Batley WF16 . .**18** A2
Birkenshaw BD11. . . . . .**3** C4
Brighouse HD6 . . . . . .**26** B4
Cleckheaton BD19 . . . .**8** B2
Elland HX5 . . . .**37** C4
Horbury WF4 . . . .**60** A3
Huddersfield HD1. . . . .**96** B2
Huddersfield, Oakes
HD3. . . . .**51** C2
Mirfield WF14. . . . .**43** C2
Ossett WF5. . . . .**49** A2
Skelmanthorpe HD8 . .**91** C3
Kingston Ave HD5 . . .**69** A4
Kingsway
Batley WF17 . . . .**10** B4
Birkenshaw BD11. . . . . .**3** C4
1 Dewsbury WF12 . . .**33** A2
Ossett WF5. . . . .**48** B4
Kingsway Cl WF5 . . . .**34** C1
Kingsway WF5 . . . . . .**34** C1
Kingsway Ho 3
WF5 . . . .**48** C4
Kinnaird Cl
Batley WF17 . . . .**20** C3
Halifax HX5. . . . .**23** C2
Kipling Cl HD4. . . . . . .**66** C1
Kirby Row HD5 . . . . . .**55** C3
KIRKBURTON **89** A4
Kirkburton CE Fst Sch
HD8. . . . .**89** B4
Kirk Cl WF12 . . . .**34** B2
Kirkgate
Batley, Birstall
WF17. . . . .**10** A3
Batley, Hanging Heaton
WF17. . . . .**20** C1
Huddersfield HD1. . . . .**96** B2
KIRKHEATON **55** C3
Kirkheaton Prim Sch
HD5. . . . .**55** B4
Kirklands WF15. . . . . .**17** A2
Kirk Lea Cres HD3 . . .**51** C3
Kirkley Ave BD12 . . . . .**5** C3
Kirkstone Ave HD5 . .**68** B4
Kirkstone Dr BD19 . . . .**9** B2
Kirkwood Dr HD3 . . . .**51** B2
Kirkwood Gn HD3 . . . .**51** B2
Kistvaen Gdns HD9 . .**80** A3
Kitchen Fold HD7. . . .**72** C2
KITSON HILL. **29** C1
Kitson Hill Cres
WF14 . . . .**43** B4
Kitson Hill Rd WF14. .**29** C1
Knaresborough Dr
HD2. . . . .**53** A4
Knave Cl WF4. . . . .**61** C4
Knightsbridge Ct 18
HD6. . . . .**13** A1
Knight St HD1 . . . .**96** B3
Knoll Cl WF5 . . . .**35** B1
Knoll La HD9 . . . .**85** B2
Knotty La HD8 . . . .**71** C1
KNOWL **43** B3
Knowl Bank HD7. . . . .**65** A2
Knowle Ave HD5. . . . .**69** A3
Knowle La
Bradford BD12 . . . .**6** A4
Meltham HD9 . . . .**81** B2

Knowle Park Ave
HD8 . . . . .90 B2
Knowler Cl WF15 . . . .17 A3
Knowle Rd
Kirkheaton HD5 . . . . .55 C2
Slaithwaite HD7 . . . . .72 C3
KNOWLER HILL 17 A3
Knowler Hill WF15 . . .17 A3
Knowler Way WF15 . .17 A3
Knowle Sch WF14 . . .43 C4
Knowles Croft 8
WF13 . . . . .31 C4
Knowles Hill 6
WF13 . . . . .31 C4
Knowles Hill Inf Sch
WF13 . . . . .31 C4
Knowles Hill Rd
WF13 . . . . .31 C4
Knowles La
Batley WF17 . . . . .19 B2
Cleckheaton BD19 . . . . .9 B4
Knowles Rd
Batley WF17 . . . . .19 B2
Brighouse HD6 . . . . . .26 B2
Knowle The HD8 . . . . .90 B2
Knowl Gr WF14 . . . . .43 C3
Knowl Rd
Huddersfield HD7 . . . .65 A2
Mirfield WF14 . . . . . . .43 C3
Knowl The 11 WF14 . .43 B3

L

Laburnum Ct WF4 . . . .60 B3
Laburnum Gr
Brighouse HX3 . . . . . .13 A4
Cleckheaton BD19 . . . . .9 A4
Horbury WF4 . . . . .60 B3
Huddersfield HD7 . . . .65 B3
Skelmanthorpe HD8 . .91 C2
Laburnum Rd WF13 . .31 B4
Laburnum Terr
Brighouse HX3 . . . . .5 A4
Huddersfield HD1 . . . .53 B2
Lacey St
Dewsbury WF13 . . . . . .32 B2
Horbury WF4 . . . . .61 B4
Lacy Way HX5 . . . . . .24 A2
Lady Anne Bsns Pk
WF17 . . . . .20 B4
Lady Ann Rd WF17 . . .20 B3
Ladybower Ave HD4 .74 B4
Lady Cl WF5 . . . . .34 C2
Lady Heton Ave
WF14 . . . . .43 B4
Lady Heton Cl WF14 .43 A4
Lady Heton Dr
WF14 . . . . .43 A4
Lady Heton Gr
WF14 . . . . .43 A4
Lady House La HD4 . .76 C2
Lady La HD5 . . . . .55 A1
Ladywell La WF15 . . .15 B1
Ladywood Way
WF13 . . . . .45 A2
Laithe Croft WF17 . . .20 B3
Laithe Croft Rd
WF17 . . . . .20 B3
Laithes Croft WF12 . .33 B1
Lakeside HD7 . . . . . . .79 A3
Lakeside Ct HD3 . . . . .51 B2
Lake View HD4 . . . . . .76 A2
Lamb Cote Rd HD2 . .40 C4
Lambert Cl HX4 . . . . . .23 A1
Lambert St 2 HX4 . . .23 A1
Lamb Hall Rd HD3 . . .50 B2
Lamplands WF17 . . . .20 A4
Lancaster Cres HD5 . .69 B2
Lancaster La HD9 . . . .85 A3
Lands Beck Way
WF15 . . . . .16 C2

Land's Bldgs WF5 . . . .35 A1
Lane Court No 1 6
HD6 . . . . .13 B1
Lane Court No 2 7
HD6 . . . . .13 B1
Lane & Dowry Rd
HD7 . . . . .72 B1
Lane Hackings HD8 . .94 C4
Lane Hackings Gn
HD8 . . . . .94 C4
Lane Head HD9 . . . . . .83 A2
Lane Head La HD8 . . .89 B4
Lane Head Rd HD8 . . .90 A1
Lane Ings HD7 . . . . . . .79 A3
Laneside HD8 . . . . . . .89 C4
Lane Side HD5 . . . . . .55 C1
Lane Side La HD5 . . . .56 A1
Lane Top HD7 . . . . . . .74 A3
Langdale Ave BD12 . . .6 B3
Langdale Dr HD5 . . . .54 A1
Langdale Rd HD12 . . .33 C4
Langdale St HX5 . . . . .37 B4
Langley La HD8 . . . . . .93 A3
Langley Terr HD3 . . . .51 A2
Langsett Croft HD2 . .41 A3
Langton Cl BD19 . . . . . .9 A4
Lansdowne Cl WF17 .19 C4
Larch Cl Batley WF17 .11 A4
Kirkheaton HD5 . . . . .55 B3
Liversedge WF15 . . . .17 C1
Larch Dale HD2 . . . . . .39 C2
Larch Rd HD1 . . . . . . .66 C3
Larkfield Ct 11 HD6 . .13 A1
Lark Hill WF17 . . . . . . .11 A2
Lark Hill Ave BD19 . .15 B4
Lark Hill Cl BD19 . . . .15 B4
Lark Hill Dr BD19 . . . .15 B4
LASCELLES 70 B4
Lascelles Hall Rd
HD5 . . . . .70 B4
Lascelles Rd WF13 . . .18 B1
Last of the Summer
Wine Exhibition Mus
The★ HD9 . . . . .86 A3
Latham Ct BD19 . . . . . .9 B4
Latham La BD19 . . . . . .9 A4
Latham Lea BD19 . . . . .9 A4
Laund Rd HD3 . . . . . . .50 B3
Laura St 8 HD6 . . . . .26 A3
Laurel Bank
Brighouse BD12 . . . . . .5 C2
Skelmanthorpe HD8 . .91 C3
Laurel Cl HX5 . . . . .37 A4
Laurel Ct WF5 . . . . . . .48 B4
Laurel Dr WF17 . . . . . .11 A1
Laurel Gr WF17 . . . . . .10 C1
Laurel Mount WF16 . .18 A2
Laurels The WF12 . . . .33 C1
Lavender Croft
WF16 . . . . .18 B2
Lavender Ct HD4 . . . . .82 B4
Laverhills WF15 . . . . .16 A3
Laverock Cres HD6 . .12 C3
Laverock La HD6 . . . .12 C3
Laverock Pl HD6 . . . . .12 C3
Laycy Cl WF5 . . . . .48 C4
Lawnhurst Mews
WF13 . . . . .18 C1
Lawns The
Batley WF16 . . . . .18 B2
Middlestown WF4 . . . .62 B4
Lawrence Batley
Theatre HD1 . . . . .96 B1
Lawrence Cres
WF16 . . . . .18 A4
Lawrence Mews
HD1 . . . . .67 A4
Lawrence Rd HD1 . . . .67 A4
Lawson Rd HD6 . . . . . .26 B4
Law St Batley WF17 . .10 C2
Cleckheaton BD19 . . . . .8 A2

Lawton St HD4 . . . . . .67 C1
Laygarth Dr HD5 . . . .70 B4
Lea Cl HD6 . . . . .13 A2
Lea Croft WF14 . . . . . .43 C4
Lea Dr HD8 . . . . .90 B2
Leafield Ave HD3 . . . .65 A4
Leafield Bank HD3 . . .65 A4
Leafield Cl HD2 . . . . . .40 C2
Lea Head HD8 . . . . . . .90 A2
Leak Hall Cres HD8 . .95 A3
Leak Hall La HD8 . . . .95 B3
Lea La HD4 . . . . .82 A4
Leamington Terr
WF12 . . . . .46 C4
Lea Rd WF17 . . . . .10 C2
Lea Rise HD9 . . . . .83 A1
Learoyd St HD1 . . . . . .96 B3
Leas Ave HD9 . . . . . . .84 A1
Leas Gdns HD9 . . . . . .87 B2
Lea Side Gdns HD3 . .50 B1
Lea St
Huddersfield, Fartown
HD1 . . . . .53 A3
Huddersfield HD1 . . . .53 A2
Huddersfield, Prince Royd
HD3 . . . . .51 C3
Lea Terr HD8 . . . . .91 C3
Lea View WF17 . . . . . .10 C2
Ledgard Bridge Mills
Ind Units WF14 . . . . .43 C1
Ledgard Wharf 1
WF14 . . . . .43 C1
Lee Ct
10 Liversedge
WF15 . . . . .17 A3
Ossett WF5 . . . . .49 B2
Leeds Old Rd WF16 . .18 A4
Leeds Rd
Batley WF17 . . . . .11 B4
Dewsbury WF12 . . . . . .33 B3
East Ardsley WF12 . . .21 B3
Huddersfield HD2 . . . .54 C4
Liversedge WF16 . . . .17 C3
Ossett, Chickenley
WF5 . . . . .34 C2
Ossett, Gawthorpe
WF5 . . . . .34 C3
Leeds Road Ret Pk
HD1 . . . . .53 C2
Leefield Rd WF17 . . . .18 B4
Leef St 8 HD5 . . . . . . .68 C4
Lee Gn WF14 . . . . .43 C4
Lee Head HD2 . . . . . . .52 C2
Leeke Ave WF4 . . . . . .60 C4
Lee La HD8 . . . . .89 A4
Lee Mills Ind Est
HD9 . . . . .87 A2
Lee Rd WF13 . . . . .44 C3
Lees Ave WF12 . . . . . .46 B2
Lees Cl HD5 . . . . .54 C1
Lees Dr WF12 . . . . . . .46 B2
Lees Hall Rd WF12 . . .46 B1
Lees Holm WF12 . . . . .46 B2
Lees House Rd
WF12 . . . . .46 B3
Leeside Ave HD2 . . . . .40 B2
Leeside Com Prim Sch
WF16 . . . . .18 B4
Leeside Rd WF16 . . . .18 B4
Lees Mill La HD7 . . . .73 A3
Lee St Brighouse HD6 .13 A2
Dewsbury WF13 . . . . . .45 A4
Liversedge WF15 . . . .17 A3
Lee Way HD8 . . . . .88 B1
Leith Ct WF12 . . . . . . .58 A3
Lemans Dr WF13 . . . .18 C1
Le Marchant Ave
HD3 . . . . .51 C2
Leonard St HD2 . . . . . .53 B3
Leopold St WF5 . . . . . .49 C2
LEPTON 71 A1

Lepton CE Jun & Inf
Sch HD8 . . . . .70 C1
Lesley Way HD4 . . . . .74 C3
Leslie St HD2 . . . . .53 A3
Leveret Way WF17 . . .11 B3
Lewes Fold 2
WF16 . . . . .18 A2
Lewisham Rd HD7 . . . .72 C3
Leyburn Ave HD5 . . . .54 B1
Leygards La HD9 . . . . .80 A1
Leyland Croft HD2 . . .41 A4
Leyland Rd WF17 . . . .10 B3
LEYMOOR 65 A3
Leymoor Rd HD7 . . . .65 A3
Library Cl HD8 . . . . . . .71 A1
Lichfield Rd HD12 . . . .33 C2
Lidgate Cl WF13 . . . . .32 A4
Lidgate Gdns WF13 . .32 C4
Lidgate La WF13 . . . . .32 C4
Lidget St HD3 . . . . .51 B3
Lidgett La HD8 . . . . . . .91 B2
Lidgett Rise HD8 . . . . .91 B2
Lightcliffe Rd
Brighouse HD6 . . . . . .13 A2
Huddersfield HD4 . . . .66 C2
Lightenfield La HD4 . .75 C1
Lighthouse The 5
HD3 . . . . .52 A1
Lightridge Cl HD2 . . . .39 B3
Lightridge Rd HD2 . . .39 B3
Lilac Cl HD6 . . . . .13 C1
Lilac Ct HD2 . . . . .41 B1
Lilac Gr BD19 . . . . .9 A3
Lilac Wlk HD7 . . . . . . .65 A3
Liley La WF14 . . . . .56 C2
Lillands Ave HD6 . . . .25 C4
Lillands La HD6 . . . . . .25 C4
Lillands Terr HD6 . . . .25 C4
Lime Gr HD7 . . . . .65 A3
Lime St
Cleckheaton BD19 . . . . .7 C1
Huddersfield HD1 . . . .67 A2
Ossett WF5 . . . . .49 A2
Lime Tree Ave
Batley WF17 . . . . .19 A2
Elland HX5 . . . . .37 C4
Lincoln Ave
Batley WF16 . . . . .18 A3
Liversedge WF15 . . . .29 C4
Lincoln Ct HD5 . . . . . .55 A1
Lincoln Dr WF15 . . . . .30 A4
Lincoln Gr
Huddersfield HD5 . . . .69 C2
Liversedge WF15 . . . .29 C4
Lincoln Rd WF12 . . . . .33 C3
Lincoln St HD1 . . . . . . .68 B4
Lincroft Ave HD5 . . . .69 A3
Lincs Wold WF15 . . . .15 B2
Linden Cl
Brighouse HD6 . . . . . .13 C1
Dewsbury WF12 . . . . . .34 B1
Linden Rd
Elland HX5 . . . . .37 A4
Huddersfield HD2 . . . .52 C3
LINDLEY 51 B3
Lindley Ave HD3 . . . . .51 A4
Lindley CE Inf Sch
HD3 . . . . .51 B3
Lindley Jun Sch
HD3 . . . . .51 B3
Lindley Lodge HD3 . . .51 B3
Lindley Moor Rd
HD3 . . . . .50 B4
Lindley Rd HX5 . . . . . .37 B2
Lindley St HD3 . . . . . . .65 C3
LINDWELL 22 C2
Lindwell Ave 5
HX4 . . . . .22 C1
Lindwell Gr 2 HX4 . . .22 C1
Lindwell Pl 1 HX4 . . .22 C1
Linefield Rd WF17 . . .20 A3

Lineham Ct WF15 . . . .30 A4
Linfit Fold HD7 . . . . . .72 C2
Linfit La HD7 . . . . .73 A2
Lingards Rd HD7 . . . . .72 A1
Link Rd
Dewsbury WF12 . . . . . .33 A1
Huddersfield HD1 . . . .66 C4
Links Ave BD19 . . . . . . .8 A4
Linnet Ct WF14 . . . . . .30 A2
LINTHWAITE 73 C4
Linthwaite Ardron CE
Jun & Inf Sch HD7 . .74 A3
Linthwaite Bsns Ctr
HD7 . . . . .73 C3
Linthwaite Clough Jun
& Inf Sch HD7 . . . . . .73 C3
Linton Ave WF17 . . . .19 A3
Linton Cl WF15 . . . . . .16 C3
Linton Gr
Batley WF16 . . . . .18 B1
Brighouse HD6 . . . . . .25 B2
Lionel St WF5 . . . . .49 A2
Lipscomb St HD3 . . . .66 A3
Listerdale WF15 . . . . .17 B3
Lister's Rd HD2 . . . . . .40 A1
Lister St
Brighouse HD6 . . . . . .13 A1
Huddersfield HD5 . . . .69 A3
Listing Ave WF15 . . . .17 B3
Listing Ct WF15 . . . . . .17 B3
Listing Dr WF15 . . . . . .17 B3
Listing La BD19,
WF15 . . . . .17 B4
Little Bradley HX4 . . .36 B4
Little Brunswick St 6
HD1 . . . . .96 A3
Littlefield Gr WF5 . . . .49 A4
Littlefield Rd WF5 . . . .49 A3
Little Green La
WF16 . . . . .17 C3
Little Hallas HD8 . . . . .89 B4
Little La HD9 . . . . .86 C4
Little London HD7 . . . .73 B1
Littlemoor Gr WF14 . .43 B3
Littlemoor Rd 2
WF14 . . . . .43 B3
LITTLE THORPE 29 A4
Littlethorpe Hill
WF15 . . . . .29 A3
Littlethorpe Rd
WF15 . . . . .29 A4
LITTLETOWN 17 B3
Littletown Jun & Inf
Sch WF15 . . . . .17 A4
Littlewood Croft
HD4 . . . . .76 C4
Little Wood Dr BD19 . .8 A4
Little Woodhouse
HD6 . . . . .26 A4
LIVERSEDGE 17 A4
Liversedge Hall La
WF15 . . . . .17 A1
Lobley St WF16 . . . . . .18 B2
Lockbridge Way
HD3 . . . . .66 A2
Locksley Rd HD6 . . . . .27 A3
Lock St WF12 . . . . .46 C2
Lock View HX5 . . . . . . .24 A2
Lock Way WF13 . . . . . .45 A2
LOCKWOOD 75 C4
Lockwood Ave
WF14 . . . . .30 B1
Lockwood Cl HD3 . . . .51 C1
Lockwood Rd HD1 . . . .67 B1
Lockwood Scar HD4 . .74 C4
Lockwood Sta HD1 . .67 A1
Lockwood's Yd 21
HD1 . . . . .96 A4

Lodge Ave HX5 . . . . . .24 C1
Lodge Cl HD4. . . . . . . .76 A3
Lodge Dr Elland HX5 . .24 C1
Mirfield WF14 . . . . . . .44 B2
Lodge Farm Cl
WF12 . . . . .46 C2
Lodge Hill Rd WF5 . . .35 A2
Lodge La WF15 . . . . . .30 C4
Lodge Pl HX5. . . . . . . .24 C1
Lodge The HD8. . . . . . .91 C3
Lodge The HD7 . . . . . .74 A4
Logwood St HD1. . . . . .67 C2
Lombardi Ct WF5 . . . . .49 B2
Lombardy Cl HD9 . . . .83 A1
London Rd HD7. . . . . .72 C3
Longbow Cl HD2. . . . .40 C3
Longcauseway
WF12 . . . . .33 A2
Long Croft St HD7 . . . .65 A2
Long Cswy WF12. . . . .46 C1
Longden Ave HD4. . . . .75 C4
Longdon Ave HD8 . . . .71 A1
Longdon Wlk HD8 . . . .71 A1
Long Fallas Cres
HD6. . . . . .26 B2
Longfield HX4 . . . . . . .36 A2
Longfield Ave
Huddersfield, Grove
Place HD5 . . . . .54 A1
Huddersfield, Leymoor
HD7. . . . . .65 A3
Longfield Cl HD5 . . . . .54 A1
Longfield Ct WF16 . . . .18 B2
Longfield Rd WF16. . . .18 A2
Long Grove Ave
HD5. . . . . .69 A4
Long Heys HX4 . . . . . .36 B4
Long Hill Rd HD2 . . . .40 B2
Long La
Clayton West HD8 . . .93 B4
Dewsbury WF12 . . . . .47 B3
Honley HD9 . . . . .83 B1
Huddersfield HD5. . . .54 B1
Shepley HD8 . . . . . . .90 A2
Shepley, Thunder Bridge
HD8 . . . . .89 B1
Longlands Ave HD7 . .72 A3
Longlands Cl WF5 . . .49 A4
Longlands Rd
Batley WF13 . . . . .32 A4
Ossett WF5. . . . . .49 A4
Slaithwaite HD7 . . . . .72 A3
Longlands Trad Est
WF5. . . . . .49 A4
LONGLEY 77 C4
Longley Ct HD4. . . . . .68 B1
Longley La HD4. . . . . .77 C4
Longley Rd HD5 . . . . . .68 C2
Longley Sch HD5 . . . . .68 B2
Long Ridge HD6 . . . . .26 A1
Longroyd Cres HD7 . .72 A3
Longroyd Cl HD6 . . . .25 C3
Longroyde Gr HD6 . . .25 C2
Longroyde Jun Sch
HD6. . . . . .25 C3
Longroyde Rd **3**
HD6. . . . . .26 A3
Longroyd Farm
WF4 . . . . .59 A1
Longroyd La HD1 . . . .67 B3
Longroyd Pl HD1 . . . .67 C3
Long Tongue Scrog
La
Kirkheaton HD5 . . . . .56 B1
Lepton HD5 . . . . .71 B4
Long Wall HX5. . . . . . .37 A4
LONGWOOD 65 B4

LONGWOOD EDGE . .50 B1
Longwood Edge Rd
HD3. . . . . .50 B2
Longwood Gate
HD3. . . . . .65 B4
Longwood House Rd
HD2. . . . . .39 C1
Longwood Rd HD3. . . .66 B3
Lonsbrough Ave
WF16 . . . . .18 A3
Lonsbrough Flats **7**
HD1. . . . . .96 B1
Lonsdale Ave **3**
WF17 . . . . .10 C1
Lonsdale Terr **8**
WF15 . . . . .17 A2
Lord's La HD6 . . . . . . .26 B3
Lord St Batley WF13 . .18 C2
Dewsbury WF12 . . . . .34 B1
Huddersfield HD1. . . .96 B2
Slaithwaite HD7 . . . . .72 B3
Love La WF5. . . . . .48 B4
Low Cliff Wlk WF16 . .31 B4
LOW COMMON 49 C3
Lowdale WF12. . . . . . . .33 B4
Lower Bower La **1**
WF13 . . . . .31 C4
LOWER CLOUGH 73 C2
Lower Common La
HD8. . . . . .93 A2
Lower Cross St **1**
WF13 . . . . .32 C3
Lower Crow Nest Dr
HX3 . . . . .5 B1
LOWER
CUMBERWORTH . .91 A1
LOWER DENBY 95 C1
Lower Denby La
HD8. . . . . .95 C1
Lower Edge Rd HD6,
HX5. . . . . .25 A1
Lower Exley HX3. . . . .23 A3
Lower Finkil St HD6. .12 C3
Lower Fitzwilliam St
HD1. . . . . .96 B3
Lower Fold
Brighouse HD6 . . . . . .39 B4
Honley HD6. . . . . .83 A3
Lower Gate HD3 . . . . .66 B3
Lower Grange HD2 . .41 A4
Lower Greave Rd
HD9. . . . . .84 C2
Lower Green Ave **11**
BD19. . . . . .6 C2
Lower Hagg HD9 . . . .84 C3
Lower Hall Cl WF15 . .16 C2
Lower Hall Cres
HD5. . . . . .70 B4
Lower Hall Dr WF15. .16 C2
Lower Hall La WF15. .16 C2
Lower Hall Mount
WF15 . . . . .16 C2
Lower Hall Rd HD5. . .70 B4
Lower Haughs HD7 . .64 A3
Lower Hey HD9 . . . . . .80 B3
LOWER HOPTON. . . .43 C1
LOWERHOUSES 68 C2
Lowerhouses **1** 68 C1
Lowerhouses CE Jun &
Inf Sch HD5 . . . . . . .68 C1
Lowerhouses La
HD5. . . . . .68 C1
Lowerhouses Rd
HD3. . . . . .66 A4
Lower La
Cleckheaton BD19 . . . .9 B1
Honley HD9. . . . . .82 C2
Lower Lark Hill BD19 . .7 B1
Lower Mill Mews
HD9. . . . . .80 A2

Lower Newlands
HD6. . . . . .26 B3
Lower North St
WF17 . . . . .19 B2
Lower Peel St WF13. .32 C3
Lower Pk HD4 . . . . . . .76 C1
LOWER POPELEY . . .17 C3
Lower Putting Mill
HD9. . . . . .95 C4
Lower Quarry Rd HD2,
HD5. . . . . .41 C4
Lower Reins HD9 . . . .83 B4
Lower Skircoat La
HX3. . . . . .22 C4
Lower Slaids HD7. . . .74 B3
LOWER SOOTHILL . .20 B3
Lower Sunny Bank Ct
HD9. . . . . .80 A2
Lower Viaduct St
HD1. . . . . .96 B3
Lower Wellgate **3**
HX4 . . . . .22 C1
Lower Wellhouse Rd
HD7. . . . . .64 C1
Lower Whitegate Rd
HD4. . . . . .68 A1
Lower Wyke Gn BD12 . .5 B2
Lower Wyke La BD12. .5 C2
Lowfield Rd WF13 . . . .31 C2
Lowfields Bsns Pk
HX5. . . . . .24 A2
Lowfields Cl HX5 . . . .24 A2
Lowfields Way HX5 . .24 A2
Low Fold
Brighouse BD19 . . . . . .6 C2
Denby Dale HD8 . . . . .94 C4
Kirkheaton HD5 . . . . .55 B2
Low Gate
Holmfirth HD9. . . . . . .86 B2
Kirkburton HD8. . . . . .89 B4
Low Hills La HD3 . . . .51 A3
Low House Fold
WF15 . . . . .16 C2
Low La Batley WF17. . .10 B3
Brighouse HD6 . . . . . .13 C4
Middlestown WF4. . . .59 A2
LOWLANDS. 44 A1
Lowlands Rd WF14. . .44 A2
Low Mill La WF13 . . . .45 A2
Low Mill Rd WF5. . . . .48 B1
Low Mills Ind Est
WF13 . . . . .44 C2
Lowood La WF17 . . . . .3 C1
Low Rd
Dewsbury, Dewsbury
Moor WF13 . . . . .31 C2
Dewsbury, Earlsheaton
WF12. . . . . .33 B3
Dewsbury, Overthorpe
WF13. . . . . .57 B3
Huddersfield HD4. . . .76 B2
Low St WF13 . . . . .32 C3
Low Town HD8. . . . . . .89 B4
Low Westwood La
HD7. . . . . .73 C4
Loxley St WF17 . . . . . .11 A1
Luck La HD1, HD3 . . . .66 C4
Lucy La HD4 . . . . .71 A3
Luddite House **8**
WF15 . . . . .17 A3
Ludwell Cl WF12. . . . .54 A2
Ludwood Cl HD9. . . . .83 C3
Luke La HD9. . . . . .85 A3
Lumb La
Huddersfield HD4. . . .77 C2
Liversedge WF15 . . . .29 C4
Lumley Rd WF12. . . . .33 B4
Lund Dr WF14 . . . . . . .18 B1
Luther Pl HD2 . . . . . . .52 B2
Luton St HD4 . . . . .65 B1

Lydbrook Pk HX3 . . . .22 A3
Lydgate HD8 . . . . .71 C1
Lydgate Cl HD9 . . . . . .87 B4
Lydgate Dr HD8 . . . . .71 C1
Lydgate Jun & Inf Sch
WF17 . . . . .20 C3
Lydgate Rd
Batley WF17 . . . . .20 C3
Shepley HD8 . . . . .90 A2
Lydia Gr WF5 . . . . .49 C2
Lyndale Cres WF16 . .18 B2
Lyndale Mews WF13 .18 C1
Lyndhurst Ave HD6 . .26 A1
Lyndhurst Grove Rd
HD6. . . . . .26 A1
Lyndhurst Rd
Brighouse HD6 . . . . . .26 A2
Huddersfield HD3. . . .51 B2
Lynfield Dr WF15 . . . .15 B3
Lynndale Ave HD2 . . .52 C3
Lynton Ave HD1 . . . . .67 B4
Lynton Terr **6** BD19. . .6 B4
Lynwood Cl BD11. . . . .2 B2
Lytham Way HD3 . . . .51 B2

M

MacAulay Rd HD2 . . .52 C3
MacAulay St **25** HD1 .96 A2
Macham St HD1 . . . . .67 B2
Madni Muslim Girls
High Sch WF12 . . . . .46 C4
Mag Dale HD9 . . . . . . .83 A4
Magnolias WF17. . . . .10 C1
Main Ave HD4 . . . . . . .65 B1
Maizebrook HD6 . . . .31 C3
Malham Ave HD6 . . . .25 B2
Malham Dr
Batley WF17 . . . . .19 A3
Liversedge WF15 . . . .29 C3
Malham Rd HD6 . . . . .25 B1
Malin Rd WF12 . . . . . .20 C1
Mallards Cl WF16 . . . .18 A1
Mallard Way HD7 . . . .72 B2
Mallinson St WF13 . . .32 A3
Maltings The
Cleckheaton BD19 . . . .7 C2
Mirfield WF14 . . . . . . .43 B3
Shepley HD8 . . . . .90 B3
Malvern Rd
Dewsbury WF12 . . . . .33 C3
Huddersfield HD4. . . .68 A2
Malvern Rise HD4 . . .68 A1
Manchester Rd HD4 .66 B2
Manchester Rd
Marsden HD7. . . . . . . .78 B3
Manchester Rd
(Slaithwaite) HD7. . .72 C2
Manchester Road
(Linthwaite) HD7 . . .73 C3
Manley St HD6. . . . . . .13 A1
Mannerley Gr BD19 . .17 B4
Mann's Bldgs WF17 . .11 B4
Manor Ave WF5. . . . . .49 B1
Manor Cl WF5 . . . . . . .49 B1
Manor Croft HD8 . . . .91 C3
Manor Croft Gdns
WF12 . . . . .33 B2
Manor Ct WF5 . . . . . . .49 B1
Manor Dr
Mirfield WF14 . . . . . . .29 A1
Ossett WF5. . . . . .49 B1
Skelmanthorpe HD8 . .91 C2
Manor Farm Dr
WF17 . . . . .20 C3
Manorfield Dr WF4 . .60 C4
Manorfield Inf Sch
WF17 . . . . .19 A2
Manor Garth Rd
WF12 . . . . .33 C1
Manor Gdns WF12 . . .34 A4

Manor Gr WF5 . . . . . . .49 B1
Manor Hos HD9 . . . . .81 A2
Manor La WF5 . . . . . . .49 B1
Manor Park Gdns
BD19. . . . . .2 B1
Manor Park Way
Cleckheaton BD19 . . .16 B4
Lepton HD8. . . . . .88 A2
Manor Pk
Batley WF12 . . . . .21 B1
Mirfield WF14 . . . . . . .28 C1
Manor Pl **1** WF4 . . . .60 C3
Manor Rd
Batley WF17 . . . . .20 C3
Dewsbury WF13 . . . . .32 B1
Horbury WF4 . . . . .60 C3
Huddersfield HD7. . . .64 C2
Ossett WF5. . . . . .49 B2
Manor Rise
Huddersfield HD4. . . .68 A2
Skelmanthorpe HD8 . .91 C2
Manor St
Brighouse BD19 . . . . .14 C4
Dewsbury WF13 . . . . .33 A2
Huddersfield HD4. . . .68 A2
Manorstead HD8 . . . .91 C2
Manor Way WF17 . . . .19 A2
Manse Dr HD4. . . . . . .65 C1
Mansion Gdns HD4 . .76 B3
Maple Ave HD3, HD7. .65 B3
Maple Cl HD5. . . . . . . .55 C3
Maple Croft HD4. . . . .82 B4
Maple Ct WF5 . . . . . . .49 A1
Maple Fold HX5 . . . . .37 A3
Maple Gr
Cleckheaton BD19 . . . .9 A3
Huddersfield HD2. . . .39 C3
Maple Rd WF12. . . . . .34 B1
Maple St HD5 . . . . . . .68 B3
Maple Wlk WF12. . . . .34 B1
Maplin Ave HD3 . . . . .50 C3
Maplin Dr **1** HD3. . . .50 C3
Mapplewell Cres
WF5 . . . . .49 A3
Mapplewell Dr WF5. .49 A3
Marcus Way HD3 . . . .50 A3
Mardale Rd WF12. . . .33 B4
Margetson Rd BD11. . .4 A3
Marie Cl HD5 . . . . .70 B4
Marina Terr HD7 . . . . .65 A3
Marion St HD6 . . . . . .13 A1
Market Ave **9** HD1 . .96 B1
Market Pl
Batley, Birstall
WF17 . . . . .10 C3
Batley, Heckmondwike
WF16 . . . . .18 A1
6 Batley WF17 . . . . .19 C3
1 Cleckheaton BD19. . .8 B1
Dewsbury WF13 . . . . .33 A2
Honley HD9. . . . . .83 A2
Huddersfield HD1. . . .96 A2
Marsden HD7 . . . . . . .78 C3
Meltham HD9 . . . . . . .80 B2
Ossett WF5. . . . . .48 C3
Slaithwaite HD7 . . . . .72 B2
Market Sq **5** WF17 . .19 C3
Market St
Batley, Birstall
WF17 . . . . .10 B3
Batley, Heckmondwike
WF16 . . . . .18 A1
Brighouse HD6 . . . . . .26 B4
Cleckheaton BD19 . . . .8 B1
3 Dewsbury WF13 . .33 A2
Holmfirth HD9. . . . . . .86 A3
Huddersfield HD1. . . .96 A2
Huddersfield, Milnsbridge
HD3. . . . . .66 A3
Huddersfield, Paddock
HD1. . . . . .67 A3

Market Wlk
🏢 Holmfirth HD9 . . . . .86 A3
Marsden HD7 . . . . .78 C3
Markham St WF17 . . . .19 B2
Mark St
Huddersfield HD1 . . . . . .67 A3
Liversedge WF15 . . . . . .17 B2
Marlbeck Cl HD9 . . . .83 A1
Marlborough Gdns
WF13 . . . . .32 B4
Marlborough Ho 🏢
HX5 . . . . .23 C1
Marlborough Rd
HD2 . . . . .40 A3
Marlborough St
WF5 . . . . .48 B3
Marlbro'Terr 🏢
WF13 . . . . .32 B4
Marled Cl WF16 . . . . . .18 A3
Marling Rd HD2 . . . . . .38 A1
Marlo Rd WF12 . . . . . .34 A4
Marlow Cl HD5 . . . . . . .69 B4
Marmaville Ct WF14 . .44 B2
MARSDEN 78 B2
Marsden Inf Sch
HD7 . . . . .79 A3
Marsden Jun Sch
HD7 . . . . .79 A3
Marsden La HD7 . . . . . .79 A4
Marsden St HD8 . . . . . .91 C3
Marsden Sta HD7 . . . . .78 C3
MARSH Cleckheaton . . .8 B1
Huddersfield 52 A1
Marsh HD9 . . . . .83 A2
Marshall Mill Ct
HD8 . . . . .93 A2
Marshall St WF14 . . . .43 C1
Marsham Gr HD3 . . . . .51 C1
Marsh Gdns HD9 . . . . .83 A2
Marsh Grove Rd
HD3 . . . . .52 A2
Marsh La BD11 . . . . . . .2 A3
Marsh Mills Bsns Ctr 🏢
HD3 . . . . .52 A1
Marsh Platt La HD9 . .83 B3
Marsh Rd HD9 . . . . . . .87 A1
Marsh St BD19 . . . . . . .16 B4
Marsland Ct BD19 . . . . .8 A4
Marten Dr HD4 . . . . . .75 C1
Marten Gr HD4 . . . . . . .76 A1
Martin Bank Wood
HD5 . . . . .68 C3
Martin Green La
HX4 . . . . .22 A1
Martin St
Batley WF17 . . . . .10 B3
Brighouse HD6 . . . . . . .13 B1
Mayfield Gdns WF5 . .49 B3
Mary St HD6 . . . . .13 A2
Maryville Ave HD6 . . . .12 B3
Mason Ct HD4 . . . . .75 A4
Matherville HD8 . . . . .91 C2
Matlock St HD4 . . . . . .66 B2
Matterdale Cl WF12 . .33 B4
Matterdale Rd WF12 .33 B4
Matthew Gr HD9 . . . . .80 A2
Matthew La HD9 . . . . .80 B2
Matty Marsden La
WF4 . . . . .60 A4
Maude St HX4 . . . . .23 A1
Maurice Ave HD6 . . . . .12 C2
Mavis Ave WF13 . . . . . .45 C4
Mavis Rd WF13 . . . . . . .18 C1
Mavis St WF13 . . . . . . .45 C4
Maxwell Ave WF17 . . .32 C4
Mayfield Ave
Brighouse HD6 . . . . .5 B2
Huddersfield HD5 . . . . . .69 B4
Mayfield Ct WF5 . . . . . .49 A1
Mayfield Gdns WF5 . .34 C2

Mayfield Gr
Brighouse HD6 . . . . .5 B2
Huddersfield HD5 . . . . . .69 B4
Mayfield Terr 🏢
BD19 . . . . .8 B1
Mayman Cl WF17 . . . .19 C3
Mayman La WF17 . . . .19 B3
Maynes Cl WF12 . . . . .57 C4
Maypole Rd HD2 . . . . . .40 B2
May St
Cleckheaton BD19 . . . . . .8 A3
Huddersfield HD4 . . . . . .67 A2
Mayster Gr HD6 . . . . . .25 C2
Mayster Rd HD6 . . . . . .25 C1
Maythorne Ave
WF17 . . . . .19 A2
Mazebrook BD19 . . . . .8 B4
Mazebrook Ave BD19 .8 B4
Mazebrook Cres
BD19 . . . . .8 B4
Meadow Bank
Dewsbury WF13 . . . . . .31 C2
Holmfirth HD9 . . . . .86 C4
Meadow Bank Cres
WF14 . . . . .43 A3
Meadow Cl
Batley WF17 . . . . .11 A3
Liversedge WF15 . . . . . .29 C3
Meadowcroft HD9 . . . .82 C2
Meadow Croft
Birkenshaw,
Drighlington BD11 . . . .3 A4
Huddersfield HD2 . . . . . .41 B3
Meadow Ct
Brighouse HD6 . . . . . . .27 B4
Ossett WF5 . . . . .34 C1
Meadow Dr WF15 . . . .29 C3
Meadowgate WF5 . . . .34 C1
Meadow Gn HD7 . . . . .73 C2
Meadow La
Dewsbury WF13 . . . . . .32 C3
Liversedge WF15 . . . . . .29 C3
Slaithwaite HD7 . . . . . . .72 B3
Meadowlands BD19 . . .6 B3
Meadow Pk HD5 . . . . . .55 B4
Meadow St HD1 . . . . . .52 A1
Meadows The HD8 . . . .95 A2
Meadow View WF4 . . .63 B3
Meadow View
Bradford BD12 . . . . .5 C3
Ossett WF5 . . . . .34 C1
Skelmanthorpe HD8 . . . .92 A2
Mead St HD1 . . . . .53 A3
Mead Way HD8 . . . . . . .88 B1
Meal Hill HD7 . . . . .72 B4
Meal Hill La
Holmfirth HD9 . . . . .87 C1
Slaithwaite HD7 . . . . . . .72 B4
Mean La HD9 . . . . .80 C2
Mearhouse Bank
HD9 . . . . .87 B2
Mearhouse Terr
HD9 . . . . .87 B2
Medlock Rd WF4 . . . . .60 C3
Medway HD5 . . . . .55 B4
Meg La HD3 . . . . .66 A3
Melbourne St 🏢
WF15 . . . . .17 B1
Mellor Mill La HX4 . . . .36 A2
Melrose Cl HD5 . . . . . .69 C4
Melrose St HX5 . . . . . . .37 A4
Melrose Terr HX5 . . . . .37 B4
MELTHAM 80 C3
Meltham CE Prim Sch
HD9 . . . . .80 C1
Meltham Hall HD9 . . .81 A2
Meltham House La
HD9 . . . . .87 C2
Meltham Mills Ind Est
HD9 . . . . .81 A2

Meltham Mills Rd
HD9 . . . . .81 A2
Meltham Moor Prim
Sch HD9 . . . . .80 A3
Meltham Rd
Honley HD9 . . . . .82 B1
Huddersfield HD1,
HD4 . . . . .67 B1
Marsden HD7 . . . . .79 C4
Melton St WF17 . . . . . .19 B4
Melton Way WF15 . . . .29 C3
Mendip Ave HD3 . . . . . .51 A3
Mendip Rd WF12 . . . . .33 C3
Mercer Cl HD4 . . . . . . .75 B1
Merlin Ct
Batley WF17 . . . . .11 A2
Huddersfield HD4 . . . . . .76 A1
Merton St HD1 . . . . . . .96 A1
Methuen Oval 🏢
BD12 . . . . .5 C3
Mexborough Ho 🏢
HX5 . . . . .23 C1
Middle Dean St 🏢
HX4 . . . . .36 C4
Middlegate WF17 . . . .10 B3
Middle Hall Cl WF15 . .16 C2
Middlemost Cl HD2 . . .52 C3
Middle Rd
Dewsbury, Earlsheaton
WF12 . . . . .33 B1
Dewsbury WF12,
WF13 . . . . .32 B1
MIDDLESTOWN 58 C1
Middlestown Jun & Inf
Sch WF4 . . . . .59 A1
Middleton Ct
Cleckheaton BD19 . . . . .16 C4
Liversedge WF15 . . . . . .16 B2
Midland St HD1 . . . . . . .53 B2
Mile End HD9 . . . . .80 B2
Milford Gr BD19 . . . . . . .2 A1
Milford St HD1 . . . . . . .96 A1
Mill Ave HD5 . . . . .55 A1
Mill Bank Rd HD9 . . . . .81 A1
MILL BRIDGE 17 B2
Millbridge Jun & Inf
Sch WF15 . . . . .17 B2
Millbrook Gdns
WF13 . . . . .19 A1
Mill Cl HD9 . . . . .80 B2
Miller Hill HD8 . . . . . . .95 B2
Miller Hill Bank
HD8 . . . . .95 B2
Millers Croft WF17 . . .11 B3
Millers Ct WF15 . . . . . .30 B4
Millfield Cl HD3 . . . . . . .51 C1
Millfield Rd WF4 . . . . . .61 B2
Millfields WF5 . . . . .48 B3
Mill Forest Way
WF17 . . . . .20 C2
Millgate Elland HX5 . . .23 C1
Huddersfield, Yews Hill
HD1 . . . . .67 A3
Mill Gr HD6 . . . . .12 C2
Mill Hill La
Brighouse HD6 . . . . . . .12 C2
Liversedge HD6 . . . . . . .27 C3
Mill La
Batley, Hanging Heaton
WF17 . . . . .20 B1
Batley, Howden Clough
WF17 . . . . .11 B4
Birkenshaw BD11 . . . . . .2 A4
Brighouse HD6 . . . . . . .26 B4
Dewsbury WF12 . . . . . .34 A1
Elland HX4 . . . . .36 B2
Huddersfield HD5 . . . . . .42 A3
Mill Lane Jun & Inf Sch
WF17 . . . . .20 A1
Mill Moor Rd HD9 . . . .80 A4
Mill Rd WF13 . . . . .32 C4

Mill Royd St HD6 . . . .26 B2
Mill St E WF12 . . . . . . .46 C4
Mill St W WF12 . . . . . .32 C1
Mill St Batley WF17 . . .10 B2
Elland HX3 . . . . .22 A3
Huddersfield HD4 . . . . . .67 A2
Mill Stables HD9 . . . . . .81 A2
Millstone Rise WF15 . .30 B4
Millwater Ave WF12 . .46 A3
Millwright Cl HD7 . . . .78 B3
Milner Cl HX4 . . . . .22 C1
Milner La HX4 . . . . .22 C1
Milner St
Huddersfield HD1 . . . . . .67 A1
Ossett WF5 . . . . .34 C3
Milner Way WF5 . . . . . .49 A4
Miln Rd HD1 . . . . .53 A2
MILNSBRIDGE 65 C2
Milroyd Cres WF17 . . .11 A4
Milton Ave WF15 . . . . .17 C1
Milton Cl WF15 . . . . . . .17 C1
Milton Dr WF15 . . . . . .30 C4
Milton Gdns WF15 . . . .30 C4
Milton Gr WF13 . . . . . .32 C4
Milton Pl WF5 . . . . .35 A1
Milton Rd WF15 . . . . . .17 C1
Milton Sq WF16 . . . . . .18 A2
Milton St 🏢 WF16 . . . .18 A3
Milton Terr BD19 . . . . . .7 C2
Milton Wlk 🏢 WF13 . .32 C2
Minerva St HD4 . . . . . . .66 B1
Mini Market 🏢 HD1 . .53 C2
Minstead Ave HD6 . . . .25 A1
Minster Cl HX4 . . . . . . .22 B1
Mint St HD1 . . . . .52 A1
Miramar HD2 . . . . .40 C3
MIRFIELD 30 B2
Mirfield Free Gram &
Sixth Form The
WF14 . . . . .29 C1
MIRFIELD MOOR 29 B1
Mirfield Sta WF14 . . . .43 C1
Miry La
Cleckheaton WF15 . . . .15 C3
Holmfirth, Netherthong
HD9 . . . . .84 A2
Mission St HD6 . . . . . . .26 C3
Mistral Cl BD12 . . . . .5 C4
Mistral Gr WF15 . . . . . .15 B3
Mitchell Ave
🏢 Dewsbury
WF13 . . . . .32 B4
Huddersfield HD5 . . . . . .70 A3
Mitchell St HD6 . . . . . . .13 A1
Mitre St
Dewsbury WF13 . . . . . .32 A2
Huddersfield HD1 . . . . . .52 B1
Moat Hill WF17 . . . . . . .11 A4
Moat Hill Farm Dr
WF17 . . . . .11 A4
MOLDGREEN 68 B3
Moldgreen Com Prim
Sch HD5 . . . . .68 C3
Moles Head HD7 . . . . . .64 B4
Mona St HD7 . . . . .72 B3
Monkfield WF14 . . . . . .43 A4
Monk Ings WF17 . . . . .10 B3
Monk Ings Ave WF17 . .9 B4
Moon Cl 🏢 WF17 . . . .10 C3
Moor Bottom
Cleckheaton BD19 . . . . . .7 B1
Honley HD9 . . . . .83 A2
Moor Bottom La
Elland HX4 . . . . .22 A2
Halifax HX3 . . . . .22 A3
Moorbottom Rd
HD1 . . . . .67 B2
Moor Cl HD4 . . . . .75 B3
Moor Cottage Cl
HD4 . . . . .75 C1
Moor Crest Rd HD4 . .66 B1

Moorcroft
Dewsbury WF13 . . . . . .32 A3
Huddersfield HD7 . . . . . .64 C3
Ossett WF5 . . . . .48 C4
Moorcroft Avenues
HD7 . . . . .64 C3
Moorcroft Ct 🏢
WF5 . . . . .48 C4
Moorcroft Dr WF13 . .31 C3
Moorcroft Rd WF13 . .31 C3
MOOREND 8 A3
Moorend CE Fst Sch
BD19 . . . . .7 C3
Moor End La WF13 . . .31 C4
Moor End Rd HD4 . . . .67 A1
Moor End Tech Coll
HD4 . . . . .75 C4
Moorfield BD11 . . . . . . .2 C2
Moorfield Ave BD19 . . .6 B1
Moorfield Rd HD1 . . . . .53 B3
MOOR FIELDS 3 B2
Moorfield View
WF15 . . . . .17 B1
Moorfield Way BD19,
LS29 . . . . .6 B1
Moorgate Flats HD9 . .80 B2
Moorhead Cl HD9 . . . . .80 B2
Moor Hey La HD2,
HX5 . . . . .38 B3
Moor Hill Ct HD3 . . . . .50 C2
Moor Hill Rd HD3 . . . . .50 C3
Moor La
Birkenshaw BD11 . . . . . .2 C1
Cleckheaton BD19 . . . . . .9 B4
Holmfirth HD9 . . . . .85 C2
Huddersfield HD4 . . . . . .75 C1
Kirkburton HD8 . . . . . . .88 C1
Moorland Cl HD7 . . . . .74 A1
Moorland Dr BD11 . . . . .2 B4
Moorland Mount
BD19 . . . . .15 B4
Moorland Rd BD11 . . . .3 B4
Moorland Rise HD9 . .80 A2
Moorlands HD9 . . . . . . .86 C1
Moorlands Ave
🏢 Dewsbury
WF13 . . . . .32 C3
🏢 Mirfield WF14 . . . . .43 B4
Ossett WF5 . . . . .34 C2
Moorlands Ave N
WF13 . . . . .32 B3
Moorlands Ave W
WF13 . . . . .32 B3
Moorlands Cres
Holmfirth HD9 . . . . .86 C1
Huddersfield HD3 . . . . . .50 A3
Moorlands Ct 🏢
HX4 . . . . .22 B2
Moorlands Ind Ctr
BD19 . . . . .8 A2
Moorlands Prim Sch
HD3 . . . . .50 A3
Moorlands Rd
Dewsbury WF13 . . . . . .32 B2
Elland HX4 . . . . .22 B2
Huddersfield HD3 . . . . . .50 A3
Moorlands Terr
WF13 . . . . .32 B3
Moorlands View
HD8 . . . . .93 C3
Moor Park Ave HD4 . .75 B3
Moor Park Ct 🏢
WF12 . . . . .33 B3
Moor Park Gdns
WF12 . . . . .33 B3
Moor Park La WF12 . .33 B3
Moor Royd HD9 . . . . . .82 C1
MOORSIDE 3 C3

Moorside
Cleckheaton, Hartshead
  Moor Side BD19 . . . . . .**15** A4
Cleckheaton, West End
  BD19 . . . .**7** C1
Moorside App BD11. . .**3** C3
Moorside Ave
  Batley WF13 . . . .**31** C4
  Birkenshaw, Drighlington
  BD11 . . . .**3** C3
  Huddersfield HD4 . . . . .**66** C2
Moorside Cl BD11 . . . .**3** C3
Moorside Cres
  Batley WF13 . . . .**31** C4
  Birkenshaw BD11 . . . . .**3** C3
Moorside Dr BD11 . . . .**3** C3
Moorside End WF13 .**31** C4
Moorside Gdns BD11 .**3** C3
Moorside Gn BD11 . . . .**3** C3
Moorside Mount
  BD11 . . . .**3** B3
Moorside Paddock
  BD19 . . . .**15** B4
Moorside Par BD11 . . .**3** C3
Moorside Pl WF13 . .**31** C4
Moorside Rd
  Batley WF13 . . . .**31** C4
  Birkenshaw BD11 . . . . . .**3** B3
  Honley HD9 . . . .**82** C1
  Kirkheaton HD5 . . . .**55** C3
Moorside Rise BD19 . .**7** B1
Moorside Terr BD11. . .**3** C3
Moorside Vale BD11. . .**3** C3
Moorside View BD11 . .**3** C3
Moorside Wlk BD11. . .**3** C3
MOOR TOP **29** B2
Moortop BD11. . . . .**3** B4
Moor Top
  Birkenshaw BD11 . . . . . .**3** A4
  Mirfield WF14 . . . .**43** A4
Moor Top Rd HD5 . . . .**55** C4
Moor View
  Batley WF16 . . . .**31** B4
  Meltham HD9 . . . .**80** A3
  Mirfield WF14 . . . .**30** A3
Morlands Cl WF13 . . .**18** C1
Morley Fold HD8 . . . .**95** A2
Morley La HD3. . . . . . .**65** C2
Mortimer Ave WF17. .**18** C3
Mortimer Rise WF5 . .**49** B4
Mortimer Row WF4 . .**60** B3
Mortimer St
  Batley WF17 . . . .**18** C3
  Cleckheaton BD19 . . . . .**8** A1
Mortimer Terr
  WF17 . . . .**18** C3
Morton Cl HD5 . . . . . .**69** C1
Morton Gr WF12 . . . . .**46** A1
Morton Way HD3 . . . .**50** B3
Morton Wood Gr
  HD9 . . . .**87** A1
Moss St HD4 . . . .**68** A2
MOUNT **50** A3
Mountain Cres
  WF12 . . . .**57** C4
Mountain Rd WF12 . .**57** C4
MOUNTAIN TOP **46** C1
Mountain Way HD5 . .**55** C1
Mount Ave
  Batley, Nunroyd
  WF16. . . . .**18** B4
  3 Batley WF17 . . . . . .**20** A1
  Huddersfield HD3 . . . . .**50** A3
Mountbatten Gdns
  HD3. . . . .**51** B1
Mount Cres BD19 . . . .**8** A2
Mountfield Ave HD5 .**70** A2

Mountfield Rd HD5 . .**70** A3
Mount Gdns BD19 . . . . .**8** A2
Mountjoy Rd HD1. . . .**52** C1
Mountjoy Sch HD1 . .**52** C1
Mount La HD6 . . . .**39** A4
MOUNT PLEASANT .**19** B2
Mount Pleasant
  Brighouse HD6 . . . .**39** A4
  Dewsbury WF13 . . . . . .**33** B1
  Huddersfield HD1. . . . .**67** B1
Mount Pleasant Jun &
  Inf Sch HD1 . . . .**67** B1
Mount Pleasant La
  HD8. . . . .**70** B2
Mount Pleasant St **1**
  HD5. . . . .**68** C4
Mount Rd HD1. . . . . . .**52** A1
Mount Scar View
  HD9. . . . .**87** A2
Mount St
  Batley WF17 . . . .**20** A1
  Cleckheaton BD19 . . . . .**8** A2
  6 Huddersfield,
    Milnsbridge HD3. . . . .**65** C2
  Huddersfield, Rashcliffe
    HD1, HD4 . . . .**67** B1
Mount Terr WF17 . . .**19** C1
Mount The WF17 . . . .**10** B4
Mount View Ct BD19 . .**7** C2
Mount Zion HD5 . . . . .**68** B4
Mowat Cl WF15 . . . . .**15** B3
Mucky La HX5 . . . .**36** C2
Muffit La BD19 . . . . . .**10** A2
Mug Mill La WF12 . . .**58** A2
Muirlands The HD2 . .**41** A3
Mulberry Cl HD7 . . . . .**65** A3
Mulberry St HD5 . . . . .**68** B3
Mulberry Terr HD1 . .**53** B2
Mullion Ave HD9 . . . .**82** C2
Murray Rd HD2 . . . . .**52** C2
Musgrave St **2**
  WF17 . . . .**10** B3
Myers Croft HD5 . . . .**69** B4
Myrtle Ave WF13 . . . .**45** A3
Myrtle Gr HD3 . . . . . .**66** A4
Myrtle Rd
  Dewsbury WF13 . . . . . .**45** A3
  Elland HX5 . . . .**37** B4
  Huddersfield HD7. . . . .**64** C2
Myrtle St HD1 . . . .**96** B3

N

NAB **43** A4
Nabbs La HD7 . . . .**72** B3
Nab Cres HD9 . . . .**80** A2
Nabcroft La HD4 . . . . .**66** C1
Nabcroft Rise HD4. . .**66** C2
Nab End BD12 . . . .**6** A4
Nab End La HX4 . . . . .**23** A1
Nab La Batley WF17. . .**11** B4
  Mirfield WF14 . . . .**43** B4
Nab The WF14 . . . . . .**43** A4
Nairn Cl HD4 . . . .**75** B4
Naomi Rd HD4 . . . .**76** C4
Napier Rd HX5. . . . . . .**37** A4
Navigation Cl HX5 . . .**24** A2
Navigation Gdns
  WF12 . . . .**46** A2
Navigation Rd WF12 .**46** A2
Navigation Rise
  HD3. . . . .**66** B2
Naylor Cl WF13 . . . . . .**33** A3
Naylor's Bldgs **5**
  BD19. . . . .**8** A1
Naylors Ct FW15. . . . .**29** C4
Naylor St
  Dewsbury WF13 . . . . . .**32** B4
  Ossett WF5. . . . .**34** C2
Neale Rd **3** HD1. . . . . .**67** B1
Near La HD9. . . . .**80** C2

Ned La HD7 . . . .**72** B2
NEILEY **83** C2
Nell Gap Ave WF4. . . .**58** C1
Nell Gap Cres WF4. . .**62** B4
Nell Gap La
  Middlestown WF4. . . . .**58** C1
  Middlestown WF4. . . . .**62** B4
Nelson St
  Batley, Birstall
    WF17. . . . .**10** C3
  Batley WF17 . . . .**19** A3
  Dewsbury WF13 . . . . . .**32** C2
  Huddersfield HD1. . . . .**67** B2
  Liversedge WF15 . . . . . .**17** B1
Neptune Way HD2 . . .**41** B1
Neston Way WF5 . . . .**35** A3
Nether Cl HD5 . . . .**54** B2
Nether Cres HD5 . . . . .**54** B2
Nethercroft WF17. . . .**20** B3
Netherend Rd HD7. . .**72** B3
Netherfield Ave
  WF4 . . . .**63** B3
Netherfield Cl HD8 . .**89** B4
Netherfield Cres
  WF4 . . . .**63** B3
Netherfield Ind Pk
  WF13 . . . .**45** A3
Netherfield Pl
  Cleckheaton BD19 . . . . .**8** B1
  Netherton WF4. . . . . . .**63** B4
Netherfield Rd
  WF13 . . . .**45** A3
Nether Hall Ave
  HD5. . . . .**54** B2
Netherlea Dr HD9. . . .**84** A1
Netherley Dr HD7. . . .**78** B1
Netherly Brow WF5 . .**49** A1
Nether Moor Rd
  HD4. . . . .**75** B2
NETHEROYD HILL. . .**39** C1
Netheroyd Hill Rd
  HD2. . . . .**39** C1
NETHERTHONG. **84** A2
Netherthong Prim Sch
  HD9. . . . .**84** A2
NETHERTON. **75** C1
  Huddersfield. **75** C1
  Wakefield **63** C4
Netherton Fold HD4 .**82** A4
Netherton Hall Dr
  WF4 . . . .**63** C4
Netherton Hall Gdns
  WF4 . . . .**63** C4
Netherton Infant Sch
  HD4. . . . .**75** C1
Netherton Jun & Inf
  Sch WF4 . . . .**63** C4
Netherton La WF4 . . .**60** A1
Netherton Moor Rd
  HD4. . . . .**82** C4
Netherwood Cl HD2 .**39** C1
Nettleton Ave WF14. .**43** B3
Nettleton Chase
  WF5 . . . .**34** C3
Nettleton Hill Rd
  HD7. . . . .**64** A4
Nettleton Rd
  Huddersfield HD5. . . . .**55** A2
  Mirfield WF14. . . . .**43** B3
Nettleton's Almshouses
  3 HD5 . . . .**69** B1
Nettleton St WF5 . . . .**48** B4
Nettleton Terr HD5. . .**55** A2
Neville Gr HD5 . . . . . .**69** B2
Neville St BD19 . . . . . .**8** B1
Nevins Rd WF13 . . . . .**44** C4
New Ave HD5 . . . .**55** B3
Newbury Rd HD6 . . . .**25** C1
Newbury Wlk HD5 . . .**55** C3
Newcastle Cl BD11. . . .**3** A3
Newcombe St HX5. . . .**37** C4

New Fold HD9 . . . .**86** A3
NEW GATE. **86** B2
Newgate WF14 . . . . . .**43** C2
Newgate La HD9. . . . .**80** C2
Newgate St WF17. . . .**20** C1
New Grove Dr HD5. . .**54** B1
New Hall App WF4 . . .**62** A2
New Hall La WF4 . . . . .**62** A2
New Hall Way WF4 . . .**62** A1
Newhaven Bsns Ctr
  HD3. . . . .**66** A3
New Hey Moor Hos
  HD8. . . . .**90** B4
New Hey Rd
  Huddersfield HD2,
    HD6. . . . .**38** C3
  Huddersfield, Marsh HD2,
    HD3. . . . .**51** C1
  Huddersfield, Salendine
    Nook HD3 . . . .**50** B2
New House HD7 . . . . .**72** B1
Newhouse Pl **2**
  HD1. . . . .**96** A3
New House Rd HD2 . .**40** C2
New La
  Cleckheaton BD19 . . . .**15** A4
  Halifax, Copley HX3 . . .**22** B4
  Skelmanthorpe HD8 . . .**92** A2
  Slaithwaite, Scapegoat
    Hill HD7. . . . .**64** A4
New Laithe Cl HD4. . .**77** B4
New Laithe Hill HD4 .**77** B4
New Laithe La HD9 . . .**86** B3
New Laithe Rd HD4 . .**77** B4
Newland Ave HD2 . . .**52** C3
Newland Ct HD2 . . . . .**52** C3
Newland Rd HD5 . . . .**55** B1
Newlands Ave HD8 . .**93** B3
Newlands Cl HD6 . . . .**26** B3
Newley Ave WF17. . . .**10** C2
Newlyn WF17 . . . .**19** A1
New North Par HD1 . .**96** C1
New North Rd
  Huddersfield HD1. . . . .**52** C1
  Liversedge WF16 . . . . .**17** C3
  Slaithwaite HD7 . . . . . .**72** C4
New Poppelwell La
  BD19. . . . .**6** C2
New Rd
  7 Bradford BD19 . . . . . .**6** A4
  Elland, Greetland
    HX4 . . . .**22** B1
  Horbury WF4 . . . .**61** A3
  Kirkheaton HD5 . . . . . .**55** B4
  Middlestown WF4. . . . .**59** A1
New Rd E BD19 . . . .**6** C2
New Road Sq HD6 . . .**39** A4
New Row
  Bradford, Wyke
    Common BD12 . . . .**6** A4
  Elland HX4 . . . .**36** B2
  13 Holmfirth HD9. . . . . .**86** A3
NEW SCARBORO' . . .**43** C3
NEWSOME **76** C3
Newsome Ave HD4 . .**76** C4
Newsome High Sch &
  Sports Coll HD4 . . . .**76** B3
Newsome Jun Sch
  HD4. . . . .**76** C3
Newsome Rd HD4 . . . .**68** A1
Newsome Rd S HD4. .**76** C3
Newsome St WF13. . .**32** B3
New St
  Batley, Hanging Heaton
    WF17. . . . .**20** B1
  Batley WF17 . . . .**19** C3
  Brighouse, Bailiff Bridge
    HD6. . . . .**5** B1
  Brighouse, Clifton
    HD6. . . . .**27** A4
  Clayton West HD8. . . . .**92** C2

New St continued
  Dewsbury WF12 . . . . . .**33** C3
  Honley HD9. . . . .**83** B2
  Horbury WF4 . . . .**61** A3
  Huddersfield HD1. . . . .**96** A1
  Huddersfield, Leymoor
    HD7 . . . .**65** A2
  Huddersfield, Milnsbridge
    HD3. . . . .**65** C2
  Huddersfield, Netherton
    HD4 . . . .**75** B1
  Huddersfield, Paddock
    HD1. . . . .**67** A3
  Kirkheaton HD5 . . . . . .**55** C2
  Liversedge BD19 . . . . .**16** C3
  Meltham HD9 . . . .**80** B2
  Ossett WF5. . . . .**49** A3
  Skelmanthorpe HD8 . . .**91** C3
  Slaithwaite HD7 . . . . . .**72** C3
New Tanhouse **8**
  WF14 . . . .**43** B3
Newton Pk HD6 . . . . .**12** C4
NEWTOWN **83** B3
New Way WF17 . . . . . .**19** C3
Nibshaw La BD19 . . . . .**9** A2
Nibshaw Rd BD19. . . . .**9** A2
Nidderdale Ho
  WF17 . . . .**19** C1
Nields Jun & Inf Sch
  HD7. . . . .**72** B2
Nields Rd HD7 . . . .**72** B2
Nile St HD1. . . . .**67** B3
Ninth Ave HX5 . . . . . .**15** B3
Nixon Cl WF12. . . . . . .**58** B3
Noble Ct HD4. . . . .**82** B4
NOOK **11** A3
Nook Gn WF12. . . . . . .**57** C4
Nooks The HD8 . . . . . .**90** A2
Nook The BD19 . . . .**8** B2
Nook Wlk WF13. . . . . .**31** C2
Nopper Rd HD4 . . . . . .**74** B2
Norcross Ave HD3 . . .**51** B1
Norfield HD2 . . . .**39** C2
Norfolk Ave WF17. . . .**19** B1
Norfolk Cl HD1 . . . . . .**52** C1
Norfolk St WF17 . . . . .**19** B2
Norfolk Wlk **5**
  WF13 . . . .**32** B2
Norgarth Cl WF17. . . .**20** C3
Norham Gr BD12 . . . . .**6** A4
Norman Ave **4** HX5. .**37** C4
Norman Dr WF14 . . . .**43** B4
Norman Gr HX5 . . . . .**37** C4
Norman Pl **7** WF4 . . .**61** A3
Norman Rd
  Denby Dale HD8 . . . . . .**95** A2
  Huddersfield HD2. . . . .**53** A3
  Mirfield WF14. . . . .**43** B4
Norman St HX5 . . . . . .**37** C4
Norman Terr HX5 . . . .**37** C4
Normanton St WF4 . .**61** B2
Norquest Ind Pk
  WF17 . . . .**11** A4
Norridge Bottom **10**
  HD9. . . . .**86** A3
Norris Cl HD5 . . . .**69** C2
NORRISTHORPE **30** B4
Norristhorpe Ave
  WF15 . . . .**30** A4
Norristhorpe Jun & Inf
  Sch WF15 . . . .**30** B4
Norristhorpe La
  WF15 . . . .**30** B4
North Ave WF4 . . . . . .**61** B3
North Bank Rd
  Batley WF17 . . . .**19** A4
  6 Huddersfield HD2 . .**52** C3
North Carr HD5. . . . . .**54** B1
North Carr Croft
  HD5. . . . .**54** B1
Northcote WF5 . . . . . .**34** C3

North Cross Rd HD2 .52 C4
North Cut HD6. . . . . . . .25 C3
North Dean Bsns Pk
HX3. . . . . .22 A3
North Dean Rd HX3. .22 A3
North Dean Wood
(Nature Trail)★
HX3. . . . . .22 A3
North Dr HD7. . . . . . . .65 A2
Northfield Ave
Huddersfield HD1. . . . .67 A2
Ossett WF5. . . . . .48 C4
Northfield CI ◼
HX5. . . . . .37 B4
Northfield Gr HD1 . .67 B1
Northfield La
Horbury WF4 . . . . .61 B3
Kirkburton HD8. . . . . . .88 B2
North Field La HD8 . .91 C3
Northfield Pl WF13 . .32 C3
Northfield Rd
Dewsbury WF13. . . . . .32 B3
Ossett WF5. . . . . .35 A1
Northfield St WF13 . .32 C3
Northfield Terr HD7. .72 C4
Northgate
Cleckheaton BD19 . . . .8 A1
Dewsbury WF13. . . . . .33 A2
Elland, Holywell Green
HX4 . . . . .36 A2
Elland HX5 . . . . .23 C1
Honley HD9. . . . . .83 C4
Horbury WF4 . . . . .60 C3
Huddersfield, Almondbury
HD1, HD5. . . . . .69 B1
Huddersfield HD1. . . . .96 B3
Liversedge WF16 . . . . .17 C2
North Gate HD5,
WF14 . . . . .43 A1
North Hill Dr HD5. . . .55 C2
North King St WF17 . .20 A2
North Lodge Fold
WF13 . . . . .18 C1
NORTH MOOR 42 C1
North Moor La HD5,
WF14 . . . . .55 C4
NORTHORPE 44 B4
Northorpe Ct WF14 . .44 B4
Northorpe La WF14 . .30 C1
North Park St WF13. .32 A3
North Pl WF14. . . . . . .30 A1
North Rd
Dewsbury WF13. . . . . .45 A4
Kirkburton HD8. . . . . . .88 B1
North Rise HD2. . . . . .53 C4
North St
Batley, Heckmondwike
WF16. . . . . .18 A1
Batley WF17 . . . . .19 B4
Dewsbury WF13. . . . . .32 C3
Elland, Holywell Green
HX4 . . . . .36 A2
�4 Elland, West Vale
HX4 . . . . .23 A1
Huddersfield, Paddock
HD1. . . . . .66 C3
Huddersfield, Rashcliffe
HD1. . . . . .67 A1
Mirfield WF14. . . . . . . .43 B2
Northstead WF13. . . .31 A1
North Terr WF17 . . . .10 C3
Northumberland St
HD1. . . . . .96 B2
North Vale Ct BD19. . . .5 B1
North View
Dewsbury WF12. . . . . .46 C4
◼ Elland HX4. . . . . . . .36 A2

North View Terr
◼ Dewsbury, Chapel
Fold WF13. . . . . .31 C4
◼ Dewsbury WF13 . .32 B4
Northway WF14. . . . . .29 C1
Northway Cres
WF14 . . . . .29 C1
Northway Gdns
WF14 . . . . .29 C1
Northwood Pk HD8 . .88 B1
Norton Cl HX5. . . . . . .37 B3
Norton St HX5. . . . . . .37 B4
Nortonthorpe Hall Sch
HD8. . . . . .92 C2
Nortonthorpe Ind Est
HD8. . . . . .92 C2
Norwood Ave BD11 . . .2 B2
Norwood Bsns Pk
BD12. . . . . .5 B4
Norwood Cres BD11 . .2 B2
Norwood Dr
Batley WF17 . . . . .10 C2
Birkenshaw BD11. . . . . .2 B2
Norwood Gr BD11 . . . .2 B2
Norwood Pk HD2 . . . .52 A3
Norwood Rd HD2 . . . .52 B4
Norwood Terr HX3 . . . .5 A4
Nova La WF17 . . . . . . .10 A4
Nowell Pl HD5. . . . . . .69 B2
Nowell St WF13 . . . . . .32 B3
Nowell's Yd WF13. . . .32 B2
Nuffield Hospl HD2. .52 B3
Nunlea Royd HX3 . . . .13 A4
Nunnery La HD6 . . . . .25 A1
NUNROYD 18 A3
Nunroyd WF16. . . . . . .18 A3
Nursery Gr WF12 . . . .46 C2
Nursery Lodge Ct
HD5. . . . . .54 C1
Nursery St
Dewsbury WF12. . . . . .46 B2
Huddersfield HD2. . . . .53 A3
Nursery Wood Rd
WF17 . . . . .20 A1
Nussey Ave WF17 . . . .10 B4
Nutter La BD19, WF17. .9 C4
Nutter St BD19 . . . . . . .7 C1

◯

Oak Ave
Huddersfield HD5. . . . .69 A3
Huddersfield, Leymoor
HD7. . . . . .65 A3
Meltham HD7 . . . . .80 A3
Oakdale Cres HD3 . . .51 A2
Oakdean HD2 . . . . . . .39 C2
Oak Dr HD7 . . . . .64 C1
Oaken Bank Cres
HD5. . . . . .68 B2
Oakenshaw Ct BD12 . .5 C4
OAKES 51 B1
Oakes Ave HD9 . . . . . .85 A4
Oakes Fold HD8 . . . . .71 C1
Oakes Gdns HX4. . . . .36 A2
Oakes La
Brockholes HD9 . . . . . .85 B3
Honley HD9. . . . . .85 A4
Oakes Rd HD3 . . . . . . .51 B2
Oakes Rd S HD3 . . . . .51 B1
Oakfield Cl HX5. . . . . .37 A4
Oakfield Dr WF14. . . .43 B1
Oakfield Gr HD8 . . . . .91 C2
Oakfield Rd HD2. . . . .52 B3
Oakhill Rd WF17. . . . .11 A1
Oak Hill Rd HD6 . . . . .13 B1
Oakland Crest WF4 . .58 C1
Oakland Ct
Batley WF17 . . . . .19 C4

Oakland Ct continued
Kirkburton HD8. . . . . . .88 C1
Oakland Dr WF4 . . . . .63 B3
Oakland Rd WF4. . . . .63 B3
Oaklands HD6 . . . . . . .25 C3
Oaklands Dr
Batley WF17 . . . . .20 C3
Huddersfield HD5. . . . .69 B3
Oakleigh Gdns
WF18 . . . . .43 B1
Oak Rd HD2 . . . . .41 C3
Oak Rise BD19. . . . . . . .8 A4
Oakroyd Cl
Birkenshaw BD11. . . . . .2 A3
Brighouse HD6 . . . . . . .13 B3
Oakroyd Ct HD8 . . . . .89 C4
Oakroyd Dr
Birkenshaw BD11. . . . . .2 A2
Brighouse HD6 . . . . . . .13 B3
Oak Scar La HD9. . . . .87 A1
Oaks Green Mount
HD6. . . . . .25 C1
Oaks Rd WF17 . . . . . . .20 B2
Oak St Batley WF16 . .18 A2
Elland HX5 . . . . .37 B4
Oak Terr HD2 . . . . .53 B4
Oak Tree Ave
Holmfirth HD9. . . . . . . .87 A1
Lepton HD8. . . . . .70 C1
Oak Tree Rd HD8. . . . .70 C1
Oak Tree Terr HD8. . . .70 C1
Oak View Terr ◼
WF17 . . . . .10 C2
Oakway BD11. . . . . .2 B2
OAKWELL 3 A1
Oakwell Ave WF17 . . .18 C4
Oakwell Cl BD11. . . . . .4 A3
Oakwell Hall★ WF17. .3 A1
Oakwell Hall Ctry Pk★
WF17 . . . . .3 A1
Oakwell Hall Visitor
Ctr★ WF17 . . . . .9 C4
Oakwell Ind Pk WF17. .4 A2
Oakwell Rd BD11 . . . . .4 A3
Oakwell Way WF17 . . .4 A1
Oakwood Ave BD11. . . .2 A2
Oakwood Cotts ◼
WF5 . . . . .48 C3
Oakwood Gr WF4. . . . .61 B4
Oakwood Rd WF17. . . .20 B3
Oastler Ave HD1 . . . . .67 B4
Oastler Gr WF14 . . . . .43 C4
Oastler St WF13 . . . . . .32 B2
Oates St WF13 . . . . . . .32 C2
Occupation La
Batley WF13 . . . . .18 C1
Dewsbury WF12. . . . . .34 B1
Honley HD9. . . . . .85 B3
Occupation Rd
Huddersfield, Edgerton
HD3. . . . . .51 C2
Huddersfield, Newsome
HD4. . . . . .76 C4
Huddersfield, Sheepridge
HD2. . . . . .40 B1
Ochrewell Ave HD2 . .41 A1
Oddfellows St
◼ Brighouse HD6 . . . .13 B2
Brighouse, Scholes
BD19. . . . . .6 C2
Mirfield WF14. . . . . . . .43 C3
Oddfellows Villas
HD5. . . . . .55 C2
Ogden La ◼ HD6 . . . .25 C2
Old Bank HD7 . . . . . . .72 B2
Old Bank Fold ◼
HD5. . . . . .68 C3
Old Bank Jun & Inf Sch
WF14 . . . . .30 A1

Old Bank Rd
Dewsbury WF12. . . . . .33 B2
Mirfield WF14. . . . . . . .30 A1
Old Church St ◼
WF5 . . . . .48 C3
Old Earth HX5 . . . . . . .24 B1
Old Earth Prim Sch
HX5. . . . . .24 C1
Old Farmyard The
HD5. . . . . .42 B2
Oldfield HD9 . . . . .84 A3
Oldfield Cl WF5. . . . . .35 A2
Old Fieldhouse La
HD2. . . . . .54 A3
Oldfield La
Batley WF16 . . . . .18 A1
Clayton West HD8. . . . .93 B3
Oldfield Rd HD9 . . . . .84 A3
Oldfield St HD4. . . . . .67 A2
Oldgate HD1 . . . . .96 B2
Old Hall Mews
WF17 . . . . .11 C1
Old Hall Rd WF17 . . . .11 C1
Old La
Birkenshaw BD11. . . . . .2 B3
Brighouse HD6 . . . . . . .13 B1
Huddersfield, Brackenhall
HD2. . . . . .40 C3
Huddersfield, Scapegoat
Hill HD7. . . . . .64 B3
Old Lane Ct ◼ HD6 . .13 B1
Old Leeds Rd HD1 . . .96 B2
OLD LINDLEY 36 C1
Old Lindley Rd HD3 . .50 A4
Old Mill View WF12 . .46 A3
Old Mill Yd WF5. . . . . .48 B1
Old Moll Rd HD4. . . . .82 C3
Old Mount Rd HD7. . .78 B1
Old Popplewell La
BD19. . . . . .6 B2
Old Power Way HX5 . .24 A2
Old Railway Goods Yd
The HD3. . . . . .65 C3
Old Rd WF4. . . . . .62 A4
Old Robin ◼ BD19. . . .8 A1
Oldroyd Way WF13. . .32 B2
Old School La HD5. . . .69 B1
Old School The
WF14 . . . . .43 A4
Old South St HD1. . . .96 A2
Old Turnpike HD9. . . .83 B2
Old Wakefield Rd ◼
HD5. . . . . .55 C2
Old Westgate WF13 . .32 C2
Oliver Ct BD11. . . . . . . .3 A3
Oliver Gdns WF14. . . .29 C1
Oliver La HD7 . . . . .78 C3
Oliver Mdws HX5 . . . .24 B1
Oliver Rd WF16 . . . . . .18 B3
Olive St HD1. . . . . .53 B3
Olney St HD7 . . . . .72 C3
Omar St WF16 . . . . . . .17 C2
Opus Point HX3 . . . . . .22 C4
Orange Terr HD1. . . . .53 B2
Orchard Cl
Horbury WF4 . . . . .60 C4
Meltham HD9 . . . . .81 A1
Orchard Croft
Batley WF17 . . . . .19 A1
Dewsbury WF12. . . . . .46 B3
Horbury WF4 . . . . .61 A3
Orchard Ct HD3. . . . . .65 B4
Orchard Lees HD5 . . .55 C2
Orchard Pl HD9. . . . . .86 C4
Orchard Rd HD5. . . . . .55 C2
Orchard St W HD3 . . .65 C3
Orchard St
Dewsbury WF12. . . . . .46 C4
Huddersfield HD4. . . . .67 C2
Orchards The
◼ Brighouse HD6 . . . .25 C2

Orchards The continued
Cleckheaton BD19 . . . . .9 C2
Orchard Terr HD4 . . . .68 A2
Orchard The
Huddersfield HD7. . . . .64 C2
Mirfield WF14. . . . . . . .30 B1
Ossett WF5. . . . . .48 C3
Orchard Way HD6. . . .13 A2
Orchid Gr HD4. . . . . . .82 B4
Orlando Cl WF14. . . . .29 C1
Osborne Ave WF4. . . .61 B4
Osborne St ◼ HD5. . .68 C3
Osborne Terr WF17 . .19 C4
Osprey Dr HD4 . . . . . .76 A1
OSSETT 49 A4
Ossett Gawthorpe Jun
& Inf Sch WF5. . . . . .34 C3
Ossett La WF12 . . . . . .47 C4
Ossett Sch WF5 . . . . . .48 C1
OSSETT SPA. 49 C2
OSSETT STREET
SIDE 35 A2
Ottiwells Terr HD7 . . .78 C2
Our Lady of Lourdes RC
Prim Sch HD2 . . . . . .40 B2
Outcote Bank HD1. . .96 A1
Outdoor Ind Est
HD3. . . . . .51 B2
Outfield Cl WF16. . . . .18 C2
Out La HD9. . . . . .84 C2
Ouzelwell Cres
WF12 . . . . .46 A1
Ouzelwell La WF12. . .45 C1
Ouzelwell Rd WF12 . .46 A2
Ouzelwell Terr
WF12 . . . . .45 C2
Oval The
Cleckheaton WF15 . . .15 C3
Holmfirth HD9. . . . . . . .84 A1
Overcroft The ◼
WF4 . . . . .60 C3
Overhall Cl WF14 . . . .44 A4
Overhall Pk WF14. . . .44 A4
Overhall Rd WF14. . . .44 A4
Overland Ind Est
LS27 . . . . .4 C3
OVERTHORPE 57 C4
Overthorpe Ave
WF12 . . . . .57 C3
Overthorpe CE Jun &
Inf Sch WF12 . . . . . .57 B4
Overthorpe Rd
WF12 . . . . .46 C1
OVERTON 62 A4
Owen's Terr HD9. . . . .82 C1
Owlar Bars Rd HD9 . .80 B3
Owler Ings Rd HD6. . .26 A4
Owler La WF17 . . . . . . .3 C1
Owler Mdws WF16. . .17 C3
Owlers Cl HD2. . . . . . .41 B3
Owlet Hurst La
WF15 . . . . .30 B4
Owl La
Batley, Chidswell
WF12. . . . . .21 A1
Ossett WF5. . . . . .34 B3
Owl Mews HD5. . . . . . .70 B4
Oxfield Ct HD5. . . . . . .55 A1
Oxford Cl BD19 . . . . . . .9 B2
Oxford Dr BD19. . . . . . .9 B2
Oxford Grange BD19 . .9 C2
Oxford Pl HD1. . . . . . .67 A1
Oxford Rd
Batley WF17 . . . . .10 A1
Cleckheaton BD19 . . . . .9 B4
Dewsbury WF13. . . . . .32 B3

Oxford St
Batley, Mount Pleasant
  WF17. . . . .**19** B2
Huddersfield HD1. . . . . .**96** B3
Oxford Terr WF17 . . . .**20** A2
Oxford Wlk BD19 . . . . . **9** B2
Oxley Rd HD2. . . . .**40** B2
Oxleys Sq HD3. . . . . . .**50** A3

P

Pack Fold HD7 . . . . . .**73** B2
Packhores Ct HD7 . . .**78** C3
Pack Horse Ctr HD1 .**96** B2
PADDOCK **66** C2
PADDOCK BROW . . .**66** C2
Paddock Cl
Birkenshaw BD11. . . . . . **3** B3
Bradford BD12 . . . . **5** C3
Paddock Dr BD11. . . . . **3** B3
Paddock Foot HD1. . . .**67** A4
Paddock Jun & Inf Sch
  HD1. . . . .**66** C3
Paddock The
🅓 Brighouse BD19 . . . . . **6** C2
Dewsbury WF12. . . . . . .**47** B4
Kirkheaton HD5 . . . .**55** C1
Page St HD1. . . . .**96** B1
Paget Cres HD2. . . . . .**52** A3
Paleside La WF5. . . . . .**35** A1
Palesides Ave WF5. . . .**35** A2
Palm St HD4. . . . .**68** A2
Parade The WF17 . . . .**19** A2
Paris HD9 . . . .**87** A1
Paris Rd HD9 . . . .**87** A2
Park Ave
Batley WF17 . . . .**20** A4
Birkenshaw BD11. . . . . . **3** B4
Clayton West HD8. . . . .**93** B4
Dewsbury WF13. . . . . . .**32** B1
Elland HX5 . . . .**37** A4
Huddersfield HD1. . . . . .**67** B4
Liversedge WF15 . . . . . .**30** A4
Mirfield WF14. . . . .**44** A2
Shelley HD8 . . . .**89** B1
Park Cl Batley WF17 . .**19** B1
Birkenshaw BD11. . . . . . **3** B4
Shelley HD8 . . . .**89** B1
Park Croft
Batley WF17 . . . .**19** B2
Dewsbury WF13. . . . . . .**32** A2
Park Ct WF5. . . . .**49** B2
Park Dr Batley WF17 . .**11** A1
Huddersfield HD1. . . . . .**52** B1
Mirfield WF14. . . . .**44** A3
Shelley HD8 . . . .**89** B1
Park Dr S HD1. . . . . . .**67** B4
Parker La WF14. . . . . .**44** A3
Parker Rd
Dewsbury WF12. . . . . . .**46** B2
Horbury WF4 . . . .**61** B3
Parker St WF16. . . . . .**18** A2
Parkfield Ave
🅓 Elland HX5. . . . .**37** B4
Mirfield WF14. . . . .**44** B2
Parkfield Cres WF14 .**44** B2
Parkfield Croft
  WF14 . . . .**44** B2
Parkfield Dr WF5 . . . .**49** C3
Parkfield View WF5 . .**49** C3
Parkfield Way WF14 . .**44** A2
Parkgate HD8 . . . .**76** B2
Park Gdns WF5 . . . . . .**49** B2
Park Gr Horbury WF4 .**60** B4
Huddersfield HD1. . . . . .**67** B4
Mirfield WF14. . . . .**44** B2
Park Hill HD2. . . . .**41** B4

Park House Dr
  WF12 . . . .**46** C2
Parkin La HD9 . . . .**80** C2
Parkin's Almshouses 🅓
  HD5. . . . .**69** B1
Parkin Sq HD7. . . . . . .**64** A3
Parkin St WF15 . . . . . .**15** C3
Park La Halifax HX3. . .**23** B4
Huddersfield HD4. . . . . .**76** C1
Huddersfield, Town End
  HD7. . . . .**64** C2
Meltham HD9 . . . .**80** C2
Parkland Ave HD3 . . .**65** A4
Parklands WF5 . . . . . .**49** B2
Parklands Ave WF4 . .**60** A3
Parklands Cres WF4 .**60** A3
Parklands Ct WF4. . . .**60** A3
Parklands Dr WF4 . . .**60** A3
Parklands Wlk HD8 . .**89** B1
Park Lane E HD7. . . . .**64** C2
Park Lane W HD7. . . . .**64** C2
Park Lea HD2. . . . .**41** B4
Park Lodge View
  HD8. . . . .**91** C2
Park Mill Way HD8. . .**93** B4
Park Nook HX3 . . . . . .**23** C4
Park Par WF13. . . . . . .**32** B1
Park Rd
Batley, Bank Foot
  WF17. . . . .**20** A3
🅓 Batley WF16 . . . . . .**18** A2
Clayton West HD8. . . . .**93** B4
Dewsbury, Earlsheaton
  WF12. . . . .**33** C1
Dewsbury, Ravensthorpe
  WF13. . . . .**45** B4
Dewsbury, Westborough
  WF13. . . . .**32** B3
Dewsbury WF12. . . . . . .**46** B4
Huddersfield, Lockwood
  HD4. . . . .**67** A2
Huddersfield, Milnsbridge
  HD4. . . . .**66** A2
Park Rd W HD4. . . . . .**66** C2
Park Road Jun & Inf
  Sch WF17 . . . .**20** A3
Park Row 🅓 HD6 . . . .**26** B4
Parkside
Cleckheaton BD19 . . . . . **8** B1
Middlestown WF4. . . . . .**62** C4
Park Side
Cleckheaton BD19 . . . . . **9** A1
Holmfirth HD9. . . . .**87** B2
Kirkheaton HD5 . . . .**55** C3
Park Sq WF5 . . . .**49** B2
Park St
Batley, Brown Hill
  WF17. . . . .**10** B2
Batley, Nunroyd
  WF17. . . . .**18** A2
Brighouse HD6 . . . .**26** B4
Cleckheaton, Gomersal
  BD19 . . . . **9** C2
Cleckheaton, Hartshead
  Moor Side BD19 . . . . .**15** B4
Dewsbury WF13. . . . . . .**33** A3
Horbury WF4 . . . .**60** C3
Ossett WF5. . . . .**49** B2
Slaithwaite HD7 . . . .**64** B4
Parkstone HD2 . . . . . .**41** B4
Park View
Cleckheaton BD19 . . . . . **7** C1
Dewsbury, Thornhill
  WF12. . . . .**58** A4
Dewsbury WF12. . . . . . .**33** C2
Holmfirth HD9. . . . .**86** A3
Marsden HD7 . . . .**79** A3
Mirfield WF14. . . . .**44** A4
Parkwood Cl HD8. . . .**89** B1
Parkwood Ct HD7. . . .**65** B4

Parkwood Rd HD3,
  HD7. . . . .**65** A4
Parsonage La HD6. . .**26** A4
Partridge Cres
  WF12 . . . .**58** B3
Pastures Way HD7 . . .**64** C3
Pateley Cres HD2. . . .**53** A4
Patterdale Dr HD5 . . .**68** C4
Patterdale Rd WF12. .**38** B4
Paul La HD5. . . . .**42** B2
Pavement St 🅓 BD19 . **8** B1
Pavilion Ct WF12 . . . .**47** C4
Pavilion Way HD9. . . .**80** C2
Peace Hall Dr HD8. . . .**70** B3
Peak View WF13 . . . . .**31** C4
Pearl St WF17 . . . .**19** A4
Pearson St
Cleckheaton, Hartshead
  Moor Side BD19 . . . . .**15** A4
Cleckheaton, Marsh
  BD19 . . . .**16** B4
Pear St HD4. . . . .**67** A2
Pear Tree Mews
  HD4. . . . .**67** A2
Peaseland Ave BD19 . **7** C1
Peaseland Cl BD19. . . . **8** A1
Peaseland Rd BD19. . . . **8** A1
Peat Ponds HD3 . . . . .**50** B3
Peckett Cl HD3 . . . . . .**51** C1
Peebles Cl HD3. . . . . . .**51** B3
Peel Ave WF17 . . . .**19** C3
Peel Cl WF4 . . . .**61** A3
Peel St Horbury WF4 . .**61** A3
Huddersfield HD1. . . . . .**96** A1
Liversedge WF16 . . . . . .**17** C2
Marsden HD7 . . . .**78** C3
Peep Green Rd
  WF15 . . . .**28** C4
Pembroke Ct HD4 . . . .**75** A4
Penfield Rd BD11. . . . . **3** C4
Penistone Rd
Kirkburton HD8. . . . .**89** A3
Lepton HD8. . . . .**70** B1
Penn Dr WF15 . . . .**16** A4
Penn Gr WF15 . . . .**16** A4
Pennine Cres HD3 . . . .**50** B2
Pennine Dr HD8 . . . . . .**92** C3
Pennine Gdns HD7. . . .**73** C3
Pennine Rd HD2. . . . . .**33** B2
Pennine Rise HD8 . . . .**92** C3
Pennine View
Batley WF17 . . . .**11** A4
Kirkheaton HD5 . . . .**55** C4
Slaithwaite HD7 . . . .**73** C3
Pennine Way HD8 . . . .**92** C3
Penny La HD5. . . . .**70** A3
Penny Spring HD5. . . .**69** A1
Penrhyn Gdns HD4 . . .**66** B2
Penryn Ave HD5. . . . . .**55** C2
Pentland Inf Sch
  WF12 . . . .**46** C3
Pentland Rd WF12. . . .**46** C4
Pepper Royd St
  WF13 . . . .**33** A3
Percival Ct HD3. . . . . .**65** B4
Percival St HD3. . . . . .**65** B4
Percy St HD2 . . . .**53** A3
Peregrine Ct HD4. . . . .**76** A1
Peridot Fold HD2. . . . .**53** C4
Permain Ct HD4 . . . . . .**68** A2
Perseverance Mills
  HD4. . . . .**67** B1
Perseverance St
  HD4. . . . .**67** C1
Perseverance Terr
  WF17 . . . .**19** C1
Perseverence St
  HD4. . . . .**65** C1
Peter Hill WF17. . . . . .**33** A4
Pheasant Dr WF17 . . . . **4** A1

Phoenix Ct WF17 . . . .**20** C3
Phoenix St HD6. . . . . .**26** B4
Pickard Way WF13 . . .**32** B3
Pickering Ct HD2 . . . .**53** A3
Pickering Dr WF5. . . . .**34** C3
Pickering La WF5. . . . .**34** C3
Pickersgill St WF5 . . . .**34** C2
Pickford Sq 🅓 HD3 . .**65** C2
Pickford St HD3 . . . . . .**65** C2
Pickhill Rd HD9. . . . . . .**80** B3
Picklesfield WF17. . . . .**32** B4
Pickles La HD8 . . . .**92** A2
Pickles St WF17 . . . . . .**32** B4
Pickle Top HD7 . . . .**72** A4
Picton Way HD5 . . . . . .**55** A1
Piggott St HD6 . . . .**13** A1
Pighill Top La HD7 . . . .**72** B4
Pike Law La HD7. . . . . .**64** A3
Pike Law Rd HD7 . . . . .**64** A3
Pildacre Brow WF5 . . .**48** B4
Pildacre Croft WF5 . . .**48** B4
Pildacre Hill WF5. . . . .**48** A4
Pildacre La WF5,
  WF12 . . . .**48** A4
Pilgrim Ave WF13. . . . .**31** C1
Pilgrim Cres WF13 . . . .**31** C1
Pilgrim Dr WF13 . . . . . .**31** C1
Pilling La HD8 . . . .**92** B3
Pine Court Mews
  HD4. . . . .**82** B4
Pine Ct HD4 . . . .**82** B4
Pine Gr WF17. . . . .**19** B1
Pinehurst Ct HD3. . . . .**51** B3
Pine St HD1. . . . .**96** B3
Pines The WF12. . . . . .**47** A4
Pinewood Gdns
  HX4. . . . .**36** A2
Pine Wood Gdns
  WF14 . . . .**44** A3
Pinfold Cl
Dewsbury WF12. . . . . . .**58** A4
Mirfield WF14. . . . .**44** A3
Pinfold Hill WF13 . . . .**32** B1
Pinfold La
Brighouse HD6 . . . .**38** C3
Lepton HD8. . . . .**71** C1
Mirfield WF14. . . . .**44** B3
Pingle Rise HD8 . . . . . .**95** B4
Pioneer St WF12. . . . . .**46** B2
Piperwell Cl WF16 . . . .**18** A3
Pit La Batley WF13 . . . .**31** C4
Cleckheaton BD19 . . . . . **9** B4
Pits La BD19. . . . .**14** C4
Pitt St WF15 . . . .**30** B4
Plains HD7 . . . .**79** A4
Plains La Halifax HX5 .**23** C2
Marsden HD7 . . . .**79** A4
Plane St HD4 . . . .**68** A1
Plantation Dr HD4 . . . .**76** C3
Platt La HD7. . . . .**72** C3
Platt Sq 🅓 BD19 . . . . . **8** A1
Plover Dr WF17 . . . . . .**18** C3
Plover Rd HD3. . . . .**51** B2
Pog Hall HD7 . . . .**73** B2
Pollard Ave BD19 . . . . . **9** B3
Pollard Cl BD19. . . . . . . **9** B3
Pollard St S HD3. . . . . .**66** A2
Pollard St HD2 . . . .**53** B4
Pollard Way BD19. . . . . **9** B3
Pond Cl HD4 . . . .**76** B4
Pond Farm Dr HD6 . . .**12** B3
Ponker La HD8 . . . .**91** A2
Ponker Nook La
  HD8. . . . .**91** B2
Pontey Dr HD5 . . . .**70** A3
Pontey Farm Cvn Pk
  HD9. . . . .**82** B1
Pontey Mount HD5 . . .**70** A3
Ponyfield Cl HD2 . . . . .**52** B3
Popeley Rd WF16 . . . .**17** C4
Popeley Rise BD19. . . . **9** C2

Poplar Ave HD9. . . . . .**85** A3
Poplar Bank HD8 . . . . .**70** B1
Poplar Gr BD19 . . . . . .**15** C4
Poplar Rise HD8 . . . . .**92** A2
Poplar St
Huddersfield, Fartown
  HD2. . . . .**53** A3
🅓 Huddersfield,
  Moldgreen HD5. . . . . .**68** C3
Poplar Terr
Horbury WF4 . . . .**61** B2
🅓 Huddersfield HD5 . .**68** C3
Poplar View HX3 . . . . .**13** B4
Popley Butts HD9 . . . .**80** B1
Popley Dr HD9. . . . .**80** B1
Porchester Ho 🅓
  HD5. . . . .**68** C4
Porritt St BD19 . . . . **8** A3
Portal Cres WF14 . . . .**30** A2
Portal Dr WF14 . . . . . .**30** A2
Portland Cl HD3 . . . . . .**51** C1
Portland Ho 🅓 HX5. . .**23** C1
Portland St HD1 . . . . . .**67** B4
Post Office Row
  HD8. . . . .**93** A3
Post Office St BD19 . .**16** C4
Potters Wlk HD7. . . . . .**65** A2
Pottery St HD3 . . . .**50** B2
Powell St HD16 . . . .**18** B1
Pratt La WF14 . . . .**43** C4
Premier Way HX5. . . . .**24** A2
Preston St
Batley WF17 . . . .**19** C2
Dewsbury WF12. . . . . . .**47** A4
Prestwich Dr HD2 . . . .**39** B1
Prestwick Fold WF5 . .**35** A1
Pretoria St HD7. . . . . .**72** B3
Priestley Ave WF16 . . .**18** A4
Priestley Gdns
  WF16 . . . .**17** C3
Priestley Gr HD4. . . . . .**76** B3
Priestley Sq WF17 . . . .**10** B4
Primitive St 🅓 HD1. . .**96** B1
Primrose Gdns
  WF17 . . . .**20** B4
Primrose Gr HD4 . . . . .**67** C1
PRIMROSE HILL **67** C1
Primrose Hill WF17 . . .**20** A3
Primrose Hill Rd
  HD4. . . . .**67** C2
Primrose La
Kirkburton HD8. . . . .**88** C2
Liversedge WF15 . . . . . .**16** C3
Mirfield WF14. . . . .**30** C1
Primrose St HD4. . . . . .**67** C2
PRINCE ROYD **51** C4
Princes Gate WF14 . . .**61** C4
Princess Alexandra Wlk
🅓 HD1 . . . .**96** B1
Princess Ave WF12. . . .**34** A3
Princess Cl WF12 . . . . .**34** A1
Princess Cres WF12. . .**34** A1
Princess Gdns 🅓
  WF13 . . . .**32** B2
Princess La WF12. . . . .**34** A2
Princess Mary Stadium
  WF15 . . . .**16** C3
Princess of Wales Prec
  The 🅓 WF13. . . . .**33** A2
Princess Rd WF12 . . . .**34** A1
Princess St
Batley WF17 . . . .**19** C4
Brighouse HD6 . . . .**26** B4
Dewsbury WF12. . . . . . .**34** B2
🅓 Elland HX4. . . . .**23** A1
🅓 Huddersfield HD1. .**96** A1
🅓 Mirfield WF14. . . . .**43** C2
Princes St WF16 . . . . .**18** B2
Prince St
Batley WF17 . . . .**19** C4
🅓 Dewsbury WF13 . . .**33** A2

Prince St *continued*
Huddersfield HD4......**68** A2
Prince Wood La
HD2...............**51** C4
Priory Cl
Mirfield WF14......**43** A4
Ossett WF5.........**48** C2
Priory Croft WF5...**48** C3
Priory Ct
Cleckheaton, Birdacre
BD19..............**9** A3
Huddersfield HD3....**51** B3
Priory Pl HD2.......**41** B3
Priory Rd
Brighouse HD6......**26** C3
Ossett WF5.........**48** C3
Priory Way WF14....**43** A4
Priory Wlk WF14....**43** A4
Prospect Bsns Ctr
HD1...............**96** A1
Prospect Cotts HD5..**55** C2
Prospect La BD11....**2** B3
Prospect Pl
Brighouse HX3........**5** A4
2 Brighouse, Waring
Green HD6.........**26** A4
Holmfirth HD9......**86** A2
Ossett WF5.........**49** A3
Prospect Rd
Batley WF16........**17** C4
Cleckheaton BD19.....**8** A1
Huddersfield HD3....**65** B4
Liversedge WF15....**29** A4
Ossett WF5.........**48** C3
Prospect Sq HD8....**91** C3
Prospect St
Batley WF17........**19** C4
12 Cleckheaton BD19...**8** A2
Horbury WF4........**61** B2
Huddersfield HD1....**96** A1
Prospect Terr
3 Batley WF13......**31** C4
Cleckheaton BD19.....**8** A2
Liversedge WF15....**17** C3
Prospect View
WF15.............**29** B4
Prospect Way BD19..**13** B4
Providence Pl HD6...**26** C3
Providence St
Batley WF17........**19** C3
Brighouse BD12......**6** B3
2 Cleckheaton BD19...**8** B2
Dewsbury WF12......**33** C1
18 Elland HX5........**23** C1
Pulmans Pl HX3......**22** C4
Pumphouse La
WF14.............**44** A4
Pump La WF13......**31** C2
Punch Bowl Yd BD19..**7** C1
Purlwell Cres WF17...**19** B1
Purlwell Hall Rd
WF17.............**19** C2
Purlwell Inf Sch
WF17.............**19** C2
Purlwell La WF17.....**19** C2
Pussy La HD8........**89** C1
Putting Mill Wlk
HD8..............**95** C3
Pye Nest Ct WF15....**16** A2
Pyenot Ave BD19....**16** B4
Pyenot Dr BD19......**16** B4
Pyenot Gdns BD19...**16** B4
Pyenot Hall La BD19..**16** B4
Pymroyd HD4........**66** A1
Pynate Rd WF17.....**19** C4
Pyrah St WF13......**32** C3

Q

QBM Bsns Pk WF17..**10** C4
Quaker La
Cleckheaton BD19....**16** A4
Cleckheaton, Hightown
WF15.............**16** A3
Huddersfield HD1....**67** A3
QUARMBY........**51** A1
Quarmby Croft HD3..**51** A1
Quarmby Fold HD3...**51** A1
Quarmby Rd HD3....**66** A4
Quarry Cl HD9......**85** A4
Quarry Ct HD3......**50** C1
Quarry Dr HD5......**70** B3
Quarryfields WF14...**30** B2
Quarry Hill
Horbury WF4........**60** B3
Huddersfield HD5....**70** A2
Quarry Hill Ind Est
WF4..............**60** A3
Quarry La
10 Batley WF17......**10** C3
East Ardsley WF12....**21** A4
Huddersfield HD4....**75** B1
Kirkheaton HD5......**70** B3
Quarry Mount **4**
HD9..............**86** A3
Quarry Pl WF14......**42** C4
Quarry Rd
Cleckheaton BD19.....**8** A1
Cleckheaton, Gomersal
BD19..............**9** B1
Dewsbury WF13......**32** B1
Huddersfield HD4....**66** A1
Huddersfield, Marsh
HD1..............**67** A4
Liversedge WF15....**17** A2
Quarryside Rd WF14..**43** B3
Quarry View WF13...**31** C3
Quay St HD1........**96** B2
Quebec St HX5......**24** A1
Queen Elizabeth Gdns
HD1..............**67** B4
Queen St S HD1.....**96** B1
Queen's Cres WF5...**48** C3
Queen St BD19......**9** B4
Queen's Dr WF5.....**49** C3
Queen Dr Cl WF5....**49** B3
Queensgate HD1....**96** B1
Queen's Gdns WF5...**48** C3
Queens Mill WF13....**45** A4
Queens Mill Ind Est
HD1..............**67** C2
Queens Mill Rd HD1,
HD4..............**67** C2
Queen's Rd HD2.....**52** B2
Queens Rd W HD4...**66** A2
Queens Sq HD2.....**54** A3
Queens Square Bsns
Pk HD9............**83** B4
Queen St
Cleckheaton BD19....**9** B4
Dewsbury, Chickenley
WF12.............**34** B1
Dewsbury, Ravensthorpe
WF13.............**45** A4
Elland HX4.........**34** B4
Horbury WF4........**60** C3
Huddersfield HD1....**96** B2
Liversedge WF16....**17** C1
Mirfield WF14......**43** C2
Ossett WF5.........**48** C3
Skelmanthorpe HD8...**91** C3
Queen's Terr **6**
WF5..............**48** C3
Queensway HD8.....**89** C3
Queen's Wlk WF5...**49** B3
Queen Tap Yd **24**
HD1..............**96** A2

R

Rachael St WF4......**60** B3
Racton St HD7......**72** B3
Radcliffe Rd
Huddersfield HD3....**66** A2
Slaithwaite HD7.....**73** A4
Radcliffe St HD8.....**91** B3
Rafborn Ave HD3....**50** B3
Rafborn Gr HD3.....**50** B3
Raikes La WF17......**10** C4
Railway Ct HD8......**93** B4
Railway St
2 Brighouse HD6....**26** B3
Cleckheaton BD19.....**8** A1
Dewsbury, Scout Hill
WF13.............**45** C4
Dewsbury WF12......**33** A1
Huddersfield HD1....**96** A2
Liversedge WF16....**18** A1
Railway Terr
Brighouse HD6......**26** C4
Elland HX3.........**22** A4
Ramsden Mill La
HD7..............**65** A1
Ramsden St
Huddersfield HD1....**96** A1
Huddersfield, Leymoor
HD7..............**65** A2
Ramsey Cres WF4....**59** A1
Ramsey Ct WF4.....**59** A1
Ramsey Rd WF4.....**58** C1
Ramsey View WF4...**58** C1
Ranter's Fold WF4...**60** C3
RASHCLIFFE.......**67** B1
Rashcliffe Hill Rd
HD1..............**67** B2
RASTRICK........**25** C2
Rastrick Comm HD6..**26** A2
Rastrick High Sch
HD6..............**25** C3
Rastrick Prep Sch
HD6..............**25** C2
Rathlin Rd WF12.....**20** C1
Rattle Row **5** HD9...**86** A3
Ravens Ave
Dewsbury WF13......**45** C4
Huddersfield HD5....**69** A3
Ravensbridge Ind Est
WF13.............**45** B4
Ravenscliffe Cl HX3..**22** C4
Ravenscliffe High Sch
HX3..............**22** B4
Ravenscourt HD1....**66** C3
Ravens Cres WF13...**45** C4
Ravens Croft WF13...**45** C4
Ravensdeane HD3...**52** A2
Ravensfield Rd
WF13.............**45** C4
Ravens Gr WF13.....**45** C4
Ravenshall Sch
WF12.............**45** C2
Ravenshouse Rd
WF13.............**31** C1
Ravensknowle Rd
HD5..............**69** A3
Ravens Lodge Terr
WF13.............**45** C4
Ravens St WF13.....**45** B4
Raven St HD1.......**66** C3
RAVENSTHORPE....**45** A4
Ravensthorpe CE Jun
Sch WF13.........**45** A4
Ravensthorpe Ind Est
WF13.............**45** A4
Ravensthorpe Inf Sch
WF13.............**45** A4
Ravensthorpe Rd
WF12.............**45** C2
Ravensthorpe Sta
WF12.............**45** B2

Ravenstone Dr HX4..**36** B4
Ravens Way HD9.....**87** B2
Ravenswharfe Rd
WF13.............**45** C4
Ravens Wlk WF13....**45** C4
RAWFOLDS.......**18** A4
Rawfolds Ave WF17..**10** C4
Rawfolds Way BD19..**16** C4
Raw Hill HD6.......**25** C2
Raw Nook Rd HD3...**50** B2
Rawroyds HX4......**36** B3
RAWTHORPE......**54** C2
Rawthorpe Cres
HD5..............**54** B2
Rawthorpe High Sch
HD5..............**54** B2
Rawthorpe Jun Sch
HD5..............**54** A1
Rawthorpe La HD5...**54** B4
Rawthorpe St James
CE Inf Sch HD5.....**54** B2
Rawthorpe Terr
HD5..............**54** B2
Ray Gate HD3......**50** A2
Rayner Ave WF16....**18** A4
Rayner Dr HD6......**13** A2
Rayner Rd HD6......**13** A2
Rayners Ave WF15...**15** C2
Rayner St WF4......**60** C3
Raynor Cl HD3......**51** C1
Ray St HD1.........**96** B3
REAP HIRST.......**52** A4
Reap Hirst Rd HD2...**52** A4
Recreation La HX5...**37** A4
Rectory Cl HD7......**78** C3
Rectory Dr
Batley WF17........**11** A3
Huddersfield HD5....**55** B3
Rectory View WF12..**47** A1
Reddisher Rd HD7...**78** B3
Red Doles Ind Est
HD2..............**53** C3
Red Doles La HD2...**53** C3
Red Doles Rd HD2...**53** C4
Redfearn Ave WF16..**18** A3
Red House Mus The *
BD19..............**9** B3
Red Laithes Ct
WF13.............**45** A4
Red Laithes La
WF13.............**45** A4
Redland Dr HD8.....**88** B1
Redlands Cl WF14...**30** A1
Red Vale BD19......**9** B4
Redwing Cres HD3...**65** B3
Redwing Pk WF14...**43** C4
Redwood Dr HD2....**41** A3
Redwood Gr **7** HD5..**68** C4
Reed St HD3........**52** A1
Reeth Rd HD6.......**25** B2
Reform St
Cleckheaton BD19.....**9** B3
4 Dewsbury WF13....**32** A3
Regal Ct WF12......**33** B2
Regency Rd **1**
WF14.............**43** C2
Regent Cl HD6......**39** A4
Regent Ct HD1......**52** B3
Regent Ho **6** HX5...**23** C1
Regent Mews WF17..**20** C2
Regent Rd
Huddersfield HD1....**52** B1
Kirkheaton HD5......**55** C4
Regent St
Horbury WF4........**60** B4
Liversedge WF16....**17** C1
Mirfield WF14......**43** C1
Reid Park Ave WF4...**46** A3
Reins Rd HD6.......**25** B2
Reins Terr HD9......**83** B3
Reinwood Ave HD3..**51** B1

Reinwood Jun & Inf
Schs HD3..........**51** B1
Reinwood Rd HD3...**66** A4
Reservoir Pl WF13...**32** A3
Reservoir Rd WF17..**18** C2
Reservoir St WF13...**32** A3
Reservoir View HD8..**91** A3
Reuben St WF15.....**17** A3
Revel Garth HD8....**95** B2
Rhodes Ave WF16...**18** A4
Rhodes St WF15.....**17** C2
Rice St HD1.........**96** B1
Richard Pl **4** HD6...**13** A2
Richardson Sq **5**
HD1..............**96** A2
Richard St HD6......**13** A2
Richard Thorpe Ave
WF14.............**44** A3
Richmond Ave HD2..**53** A4
Richmond Ct HD4...**65** B1
Richmond Flats **7**
HD1..............**96** B3
Richmond Garth
WF5..............**49** B2
Richmond Gr BD19...**9** B4
Richmond Lea
WF14.............**43** C4
Richmond Park Ave
WF15.............**17** A1
Richmond Rd
Batley, Nunroyd
WF16.............**18** B4
Batley WF13........**33** A4
Richmond St BD19....**8** A1
RIDDINGS........**41** A1
Riddings Cl HD2....**40** C1
Riddings Rd HD2....**40** C1
Riddings Rise HD2...**41** A1
Ridge Ave WF4.....**58** C1
Ridge Cl
Huddersfield HD4....**67** C1
Skelmanthorpe HD8...**91** C2
Ridge Cres WF4.....**62** B4
Ridge Hill HD6......**25** B3
Ridge Lea HD6......**25** C3
Ridge Rd WF4......**62** B4
Ridge St HD4.......**67** C1
Ridge View HX5.....**38** B4
Ridge View Dr HD2...**52** A4
Ridge View Rd HD6..**26** A3
Ridgeway HD5......**54** B1
Ridgeway Cl HD5....**54** B1
Ridgeway Dr WF17...**11** A3
Ridgeway Gdns HD6..**12** B3
Ridgeways The HD7..**73** C2
Ridings La HD7.....**64** B2
Ridings Rd WF13....**33** A2
Riding St WF17......**18** B4
Ridingwood Rise
HD8..............**93** A3
Rifle Fields HD1.....**67** B4
Rifle St HD1........**96** B1
RILEY...........**89** A4
Riley La HD8........**89** A4
Riley Pk HD8........**89** B4
Riley St HD4........**68** A2
Rillside HD8.........**90** B3
Ring O'Bells Yd **9**
WF4..............**60** C3
Ringwood Edge
HX5..............**36** C4
Rink Par **7** WF17....**20** A1
Rink St WF17.......**20** A1
Rink Terr **6** WF17...**20** A1
Ripley Rd WF15.....**16** C2
Ripley St HX3.......**5** A1
Ripon Ave HD2.....**53** B4
Ripon Ho **5** HX5....**23** C1

Ripon Rd WF12 . . . . . . **33** C3
Risedale Ave WF17. . . . **11** B4
Risedale Cl WF17 . . . . . **11** B4
Rishworthian Ct
  HX3 . . . . **22** A3
Rishworth Rd WF12. . **33** A2
Rishworth St WF13 . . **33** A2
River Bank Ent Ctr
  WF13 . . . . **45** C4
River Bank Way HX5 . **24** B3
River Holme View
  HD9 . . . . **85** A4
River Pk HD9 . . . . **83** A3
Riverside HD8 . . . . **93** A4
Riverside Ct
  Denby Dale HD8 . . . . . **95** B3
  Huddersfield HD4 . . . . **67** C2
Riverside Dr BD19 . . . . **8** A3
Riverside Ind Est
  Dewsbury WF12 . . . . . **32** C1
  Horbury WF4 . . . . **60** A2
Riverside The HD7 . . **73** C4
Riverside Way WF13 . **45** A2
River St HD6 . . . . **26** C3
River Valley View
  HD8 . . . . **95** B3
River View WF14 . . . . **42** C4
Riverwood Dr HX3 . . **22** B4
RM Grylls Mid Sch
  WF15 . . . . **15** B2
Road End 4 HX4 . . . . **22** C1
Roaine Dr HD9 . . . . . . **86** B2
Roberson Terr BD19 . . **9** A2
Robert Ct WF15 . . . . . . **16** C1
Robertson Ave HD6 . . **26** A2
Robert's St BD19 . . . . . **7** C1
ROBERTTOWN **29** C4
Roberttown CE Jun &
  Inf Sch WF15 . . . . . . **29** B4
Roberttown Grange
  FW15 . . . . **29** B4
Roberttown La
  WF15 . . . . **29** C4
Robin Hill WF17 . . . . . **11** A2
Robin Hood Gr HD2. . **40** B2
Robin Hood Hill
  HD4 . . . . **76** B1
Robin Hood Rd HD2 . **40** B2
Robin Hood Way
  HD6 . . . . **27** B4
Robin La
  Batley, Heckmondwike
  WF13 . . . . **18** C1
  Batley WF13 . . . . **32** B4
Robin Rocks HD9 . . . . **85** A4
Robin Royd Ave
  WF14 . . . . **30** A2
Robin Royd Croft
  WF14 . . . . **30** A2
Robin Royd Dr
  WF14 . . . . **30** A2
Robin Royd Garth
  WF14 . . . . **30** A2
Robin Royd Gr
  WF14 . . . . **30** A2
Robin Royd La
  WF14 . . . . **30** A2
Robinson St HD1 . . . . **68** B3
Robin St HD1 . . . . **66** C3
Robsons Dr HD5 . . . . . **68** C4
Rochdale Rd HX4 . . . . **22** B1
Rochester Dr WF4 . . . **61** B4
Rochester Pl 5
  HX5 . . . . **37** C4
Rochester Rd WF17 . . . **3** C1
Rock Edge WF15 . . . . . **17** A3
Rock Fold HD7 . . . . . . **64** C2

Rockhill Cl WF17 . . . . **10** C3
Rock House Dr
  WF13 . . . . **32** C4
Rockley Cl HD5 . . . . . . **69** A2
Rockley St 5 WF13 . . **33** A2
Rockmill Rd HD9 . . . . **85** A4
Rock Rd HD3 . . . . **51** B4
Rock St
  15 Brighouse HD6 . . . **13** A1
  Huddersfield HD3 . . . **50** B1
Rock Terr HD1 . . . . **53** B3
Rock The HD7 . . . . **74** A3
Rock View
  Elland HX4 . . . . **36** B2
  Marsden HD7 . . . . **78** C2
Rock Villas HD8 . . . . . **92** C2
Rockwood Cl HD2 . . . **41** A4
Rockwood Rise HD8 . **95** B4
Roebuck Memorial
  Homes HD5 . . . . **69** B4
Roebuck St WF17 . . . . **10** C3
Roger La HD4 . . . . **68** B1
Rogerson Sq HD6 . . . . **13** A1
Roman Ave HD3 . . . . . **50** A3
Roman Cl HD3 . . . . **50** A3
Roman Dr HD3 . . . . . . **50** A3
Roman Rd 5 WF17 . . **10** C2
Romsey Cl HD3 . . . . . . **50** A3
Rookery Pl HD6 . . . . . . **13** B1
Rookes La HX3 . . . . **5** A3
Rookes View HX3 . . . . **5** A4
Rooks Ave BD19 . . . . . . **7** C2
Rooks Cl BD12 . . . . **6** A3
Rook St HD1 . . . . **96** A3
Rordin Hts HD2 . . . . . **40** B2
Rose Ave
  Huddersfield,
  Cowersley HD4 . . . . . **65** B1
  Huddersfield, Marsh
  HD3 . . . . **66** B4
Rosebank St WF17 . . **19** B4
Rosebery St
  Elland HX5 . . . . **37** B4
  3 Huddersfield HD2 . **52** C3
Rosedale Ave
  16 Huddersfield
  HD5 . . . . **68** C3
  Liversedge WF15 . . . . **17** A2
Rosedale Ho WF13 . . **32** C4
Rose Hill Dr HD2 . . . . **52** A3
Rosemary Cl HD6 . . . . **26** A3
Rosemary La HD6 . . . . **26** A3
ROSEMOUNT **38** A3
Rose Mount HD2 . . . . **52** A3
Rosemount Ave
  HX5 . . . . **37** C4
Rosemount Terr
  HX5 . . . . **37** C4
Rose Terr HD1 . . . . **53** B2
Roseville Terr WF12 . **33** C2
Roslyn Ave HD4 . . . . . **75** B1
Rossefield Ave HD2 . . **52** B3
Rosslyn Ct WF12 . . . . . **33** C1
Rotcher HD7 . . . . **72** A2
Rotcher La HD7 . . . . . . **72** A2
Rotcher Rd HD9 . . . . . **86** A3
Rothwell St HD5 . . . . . **69** A4
Round Hill Cl HD8 . . . **91** A3
Round Hill La HD5 . . **42** A1
Roundhay HD9 . . . . . . **83** B1
Roundwell Rd WF15 . **15** C3
Round Wood Ave
  HD5 . . . . **69** C4
Roundwood Rd
  WF5 . . . . **49** C2
Rouse Mill La WF17 . **20** A2
Rouse St 7 WF15 . . . **17** A2
Rowan Ave HD4 . . . . . **82** B4
Rowan Avenue Mews
  HD4 . . . . **82** B4
Rowan Cl WF17 . . . . . . **11** A4

Rowan Dr HD6 . . . . . . **13** C1
Rowlands Ave HD5. . . **69** B4
Rowley Ct HD8 . . . . **71** B1
Rowley Dr HD8 . . . . . . **70** C1
ROWLEY HILL **88** B4
Rowley La HD8 . . . . . . **88** B4
Row St HD4 . . . . **67** A2
Royal Acre HD7 . . . . . . **64** A3
Royal Terr HD3 . . . . . . **65** C3
Royd Ave
  Batley WF16 . . . . **18** A4
  Holmfirth HD9 . . . . . . **87** B4
  Huddersfield, Ainley Top
  HD3 . . . . **37** C1
Royd Croft HD3 . . . . . **66** A4
Roydfield St HD2 . . . . **53** B4
Royd Head Farm
  WF5 . . . . **48** B3
Royd House La HD7 . **73** C3
Royd Mill Bsns Pk
  HD6 . . . . **26** C4
Royd Mount HD9 . . . . **86** A3
Royd St Ave HD3 . . . . **65** C3
Royds Ave
  Birkenshaw BD11 . . . . **2** B3
  Brighouse HD6 . . . . **5** B2
  Holmfirth HD9 . . . . . . **87** A4
  Huddersfield HD3 . . . . **66** B3
  Ossett WF5 . . . . **34** C2
  Slaithwaite HD7 . . . . . **73** C4
Royds Cl HD9 . . . . **87** A4
Royds Cres HD6 . . . . . . **5** B1
Royds Dr HD9 . . . . **87** A4
Royds Edge HD9 . . . . . **80** C1
Royds Hall High Sch
  HD3 . . . . **66** B4
Royds Pk HD8 . . . . **95** B3
Royds St HD7 . . . . **78** C2
Royd St Batley WF17 . **20** B1
  Huddersfield HD3 . . . . **65** C3
  Slaithwaite HD7 . . . . . **72** B3
Royds The
  Clayton West HD8 . . . . **93** C4
  Holmfirth HD9 . . . . . . **86** A3
Royds View HD7 . . . . **73** C3
Royd Terr HD4 . . . . . . **76** A2
Royd Well BD11 . . . . . . **2** B3
Royd Wells WF14 . . . . **43** C4
Royd Wood BD19 . . . . **16** A4
Royle Fold WF16 . . . . . **18** A2
Royles Head La HD3 . **65** A4
Ruby St WF17 . . . . **11** A1
Rudding Dr WF17 . . . . **18** C1
Rudding St HD4 . . . . . **66** C2
Rufford Ct HD3 . . . . . . **65** B3
Rufford Rd
  Elland HX5 . . . . **37** B4
  Huddersfield HD3 . . . . **65** B3
Rumble Rd WF12 . . . . **33** C3
Rumbold Rd HD3 . . . . **52** A1
RUNTLINGS **48** B3
Runtlings WF5 . . . . **48** B3
Runtlings La WF5 . . . . **48** B2
Runtlings The WF5 . . **48** A3
Rushbearers Wlk
  HD5 . . . . **69** A1
Rushdene Ct BD12 . . . . **5** C3
Rushfield Vale HD8 . . **70** B2
Ruskin Gr HD2 . . . . . . **40** C1
Russell Cl
  Batley, Heckmondwike
  WF16 . . . . **18** B1
  Batley WF17 . . . . **19** C3
Russell Gr BD11 . . . . . . **2** B3
Russell St WF13 . . . . . **32** A3
Russet Fold WF15 . . . **17** A3
Russett Gr HD4 . . . . . . **68** B1
Rustless Cl BD19 . . . . **15** A4
Ruth St HD4 . . . . **76** C4

Rutland Rd
  Batley WF17 . . . . **20** A4
  Huddersfield HD3 . . . . **65** C3
Rutland Wlk 7
  WF13 . . . . **32** B2
Ryburn Rd HD3 . . . . . **51** B1
Rydal Dr HD5 . . . . **68** C4
Rydale Ct
  Cleckheaton WF15 . . . **16** A2
  Ossett WF5 . . . . **48** C2
Rydale Mews WF5 . . . **48** C2
Rydal Gr WF15 . . . . . . **30** A3
Rydings Ave HD6 . . . . **13** A1
Rydings Cl 11 HD6 . . **13** A1
Rydings Dr HD6 . . . . . **12** C1
Rydings Wlk HD6 . . . . **12** C1
Ryebank HD9 . . . . **86** B2
Ryecroft Dr HD3 . . . . . **51** B3
Ryecroft La
  Brighouse HD6 . . . . . . **26** C2
  Holmfirth HD9 . . . . . . **86** C1
Ryecroft St WF5 . . . . . **34** C1
Ryedale HD5 . . . . **55** B4
Ryedale Ho WF17 . . . . **19** C1
Ryefields HD9 . . . . **87** A2
Ryefields Ave HD3 . . . **51** A1
Ryefields Rd HD7 . . . . **65** A2
Ryndleside 4 HD3 . . **50** C3

S

Sabine Fold WF4 . . . . . **60** A3
Sackville St WF13 . . . . **45** A4
Saddleworth Rd
  HX4 . . . . **22** C1
St Aidan's CE Fst Sch
  HD8 . . . . **91** C2
St Aiden's Wlk WF5 . . **49** C2
St Alban's Ave HD3 . . **37** C1
St Andrew's CE Inf Sch
  HD6 . . . . **13** A1
St Andrews CE Jun Sch
  HD6 . . . . **13** A1
St Andrews Dr HD5 . . **55** C2
St Andrew's Dr HD6. . **13** A2
St Andrew's Rd HD1 . **53** C1
St Anne's Ave HD3 . . . **37** C1
St Anne's Cl WF12 . . . **46** C2
St Anne's Rd HD3 . . . . **22** C4
St Anne's Sq
  6 Holmfirth, Cliff
  HD9 . . . . **86** A3
  Holmfirth, Netherthong
  HD9 . . . . **84** A2
St Barnabas Rd
  WF15 . . . . **15** C3
St Chad's Ave HD6 . . . **12** B3
St Chad's CE Prim Sch
  HD6 . . . . **12** B3
St Francis Gdns
  HD2 . . . . **39** C3
St George's Ave
  HD3 . . . . **37** C1
St George's Rd HD9 . **87** A2
St George's Sq 18
  HD1 . . . . **96** A2
St George's St HD1 . . **96** A2
St Giles Cl HD6 . . . . . . **12** B3
St Hilda's Sch WF4 . . **60** C4
St Ignatius RC Prim
  Sch WF5 . . . . **49** A1
St James Ct HD6 . . . . . **13** B1
St James' Rd HD1 . . . . **52** A1
St James St
  Batley, Heckmondwike
  WF16 . . . . **18** A1
  Batley WF17 . . . . **19** C3
St James Way HD6 . . . **13** B1
St John Fisher RC High
  Sch WF13 . . . . **32** B3

St John Par WF13 . . . . **32** B1
St John's Ave
  Batley WF17 . . . . **19** A4
  Huddersfield HD4 . . . . **76** C4
  Kirkheaton HD5 . . . . . **55** C3
  Ossett WF5 . . . . **49** C3
St John's CE Inf Sch
  WF13 . . . . **32** A2
St Johns CE Jun & Inf
  Sch, Golcar HD7 . . . . **64** C3
St John's CE Prim Sch
  HD6 . . . . **27** B1
St Johns Cl
  Cleckheaton BD19 . . . . **8** B1
  Dewsbury WF13 . . . . . **32** B2
St John's Cl WF5 . . . . . **49** C3
St John's Cres
  Huddersfield HD1 . . . . **53** A2
  Ossett WF5 . . . . **49** C3
St John's Ct HD8 . . . . . **71** B1
St John's Dr HD1 . . . . **53** A2
St John's Pl
  Birkenshaw BD11 . . . . . **2** B4
  7 Cleckheaton BD19. . . **8** B1
St John's Rd
  Huddersfield HD1 . . . . **53** A2
  Kirkheaton HD5 . . . . . **55** C3
St John's St WF4 . . . . **60** A3
St John St
  Brighouse HD6 . . . . . . **26** A3
  Dewsbury WF13 . . . . . **32** B2
St John's View
  WF17 . . . . **19** A4
St John Wlk WF13 . . . **32** B2
St Joseph's RC Prim
  Sch
  Batley WF13 . . . . **32** A4
  Brighouse HD6 . . . . . . **12** C3
  Huddersfield HD5. . . . **69** B4
St Luke's CE Fst Sch
  BD19 . . . . **7** B1
St Lukes Cl
  Batley WF17 . . . . **20** B2
  Middlestown WF4 . . . . **59** A1
St Luke's Cl BD19 . . . . . **7** B1
St Luke's Hospl HD4 **66** B1
St Luke's Terr BD19 . . . **7** B1
St Mark's Rd HD1 . . . . **53** A2
St Marks View HD3. . **65** C4
St Martin's View 7
  HD6 . . . . **13** A1
St Mary's Ave
  Batley WF17 . . . . **19** B1
  Bradford BD12 . . . . **5** C4
  Holmfirth HD9 . . . . . . **84** A2
  Mirfield WF14 . . . . **44** B4
St Mary's Cl BD12 . . . . **5** B4
St Mary's Cres
  Bradford BD12 . . . . **5** B4
  Holmfirth HD9 . . . . . . **84** A2
St Mary's Ct HD9 . . . . **84** C2
St Mary's Dr BD12 . . . . **5** C4
St Marys Fold HD5 . . **55** C2
St Marys Gate 12
  HX5 . . . . **23** C1
St Mary's Gdns 1
  BD12 . . . . **5** C4
St Mary's La HD5 . . . . **55** C1
St Mary's Mews
  HD9 . . . . **83** A3
St Mary's Mount
  BD12 . . . . **5** B4
St Mary's Pl WF14 . . . **46** C4
St Mary's RC Prim Sch
  WF17 . . . . **19** B4
St Mary's Rd
  Holmfirth HD9 . . . . . . **84** A2
  Honley HD9 . . . . **84** A2
St Mary's Rise HD9 . **84** A2
St Mary's Sq
  Bradford BD12 . . . . **5** C4

St Mary's Sq *continued*
Honley HD9 . . . . **83** A3
St Mary's Way HD9 . . **84** A2
St Mary's Wlk WF14 . . **44** B4
St Matthew Rd
WF13 . . . . **32** B2
St Michael's Cl
WF12 . . . . **58** A3
St Michael's Mount
WF12 . . . . **58** A3
St Oswalds Pl WF5 . . **35** B1
St Patrick's RC Prim
 Sch
Batley WF17 . . . . **10** B4
Elland HX5 . . . . **36** C4
Huddersfield HD2 . . . . **52** B2
St Paulinus Cl WF13 . **32** B2
St Paulinus RC Primary
 Sch WF13 . . . . **32** A1
St Paul's Ave BD11 . . . **2** B3
St Pauls Rd HD5 . . . . **55** B2
St Paul's Rd
Birkenshaw BD11 . . . . . **2** B3
Mirfield WF14 . . . . **43** C2
St Paul's St HD1 . . . . **96** B1
St Paul's Terr [3]
WF14 . . . . **43** C2
St Peg Cl BD19 . . . . . . **8** B1
St Peg La BD19 . . . . . . **8** B1
St Peter's CE Jun & Inf
 Sch WF17 . . . . **10** B4
St Peters CE Jun Sch
WF4 . . . . **60** C3
St Peter's Cl
Batley WF17 . . . . **10** A3
[10] Mirfield WF14 . . . . **43** B3
St Peters Cres HD5 . . **55** B2
St Peters Ct WF4 . . . . **60** C3
St Peters Gate WF5 . . **35** A1
St Peter's Gdns
WF12 . . . . **33** C1
St Peter's Gr WF4 . . . . **61** A3
St Peter's Par WF12 . . **33** C1
St Peter's St HD1 . . . . **96** B2
St Philip's Cl WF13 . . **33** A3
St Philips Ct HD3 . . . . **51** B4
St Saviour's CE Jun Sch
WF17 . . . . **11** A3
St Stephens Ct HX3 . . **22** A4
St Stephen's Rd
HD1 . . . . **67** B2
St Stephen's St HX3 . **22** A4
St Thomas Gdns
HD2 . . . . **41** B4
St Thomas' Rd HD1 . . **67** B2
SALENDINE NOOK . . **50** C2
Salendine Nook High
 Sch HD3 . . . . **50** C1
SALFORD **76** B4
Salisbury Cl WF12 . . . **33** C2
Salisbury Rd BD19 . . . . **6** C2
SALTERHEBBLE **23** B4
Salter St WF17 . . . . . . **32** B4
Sampson St WF15 . . . **17** B2
Sandal Way WF17 . . . **10** C3
Sandbeds HD9 . . . . . . **83** A4
Sandbeds Trad Est
WF5 . . . . **35** B1
Sandene Ave HD4 . . . **75** B4
Sandene Dr HD4 . . . . **75** B4
Sandholme Dr WF5 . . **48** C3
Sandiway Bank
WF12 . . . . **46** C1
Sandringham Ct
HD2 . . . . **41** A3
Sands House La
HD4 . . . . **75** A3
Sands La
Dewsbury WF12 . . . . . **33** B1
Lepton HD5, HD8 . . . **71** B4
Mirfield WF14 . . . . **44** C1

Sands Rd WF12 . . . . . . **47** A4
Sand St HD1 . . . . **96** B1
Sandstone Cl HD9 . . **83** A1
Sandstone La HD4 . . . **66** A1
Sandwell St HD7 . . . . **72** B3
Sandwich Cres HD2 . . **39** B1
Sandyfield Terr
WF17 . . . . **19** B4
Sandy Gate HX7 . . . . **86** C2
Sandy La
Huddersfield HD4 . . . . **74** C1
Netherton WF4 . . . . . . **59** B1
Sandylands HD4 . . . . **82** B4
Sanford Ct [5] WF5 . . **48** C3
Sapphire Ct WF17 . . . **19** A4
Saunders Cl HD3 . . . . **51** C1
Savile Bsns Ctr
WF12 . . . . **33** A1
Savile Cl HD6 . . . . **14** A1
Savile Ct WF14 . . . . . **43** C4
Savile Dr WF4 . . . . . . **60** C4
Savile Gr WF12 . . . . . **32** C1
Savile Ho [7] HX5 . . . **23** C1
Savile La HD6 . . . . . . **14** A1
Savile Mews WF12 . . **46** B3
Savile Pit La WF12 . . **34** A2
Savile Pl WF14 . . . . . . **30** A1
Savile Rd
Dewsbury WF12 . . . . . **46** B4
Elland HX5 . . . . **37** B4
Huddersfield HD3 . . . . **51** C2
Savile Sq WF14 . . . . . **43** C3
Savile St
Batley WF17 . . . . **33** A4
Cleckheaton BD19 . . . . . **8** A3
Huddersfield HD3 . . . . **65** C3
SAVILE TOWN **46** C4
Savile Town CE Inf Sch
WF12 . . . . **46** C4
Savile Way HX5 . . . . **24** A2
Savile Wlk [7] WF13 . . **32** C2
Savile Pk WF5 . . . . . . **49** B2
Saville Rd HD8 . . . . . **91** C3
Saville St
Clayton West HD8 . . . **92** C2
Ossett WF5 . . . . **49** B2
Saxondale Ct [1]
WF4 . . . . **61** A3
Saxton Pl HD5 . . . . . . **69** C2
Saxton St WF15 . . . . . **17** C3
Scafell Ct WF12 . . . . . **33** B4
Scale Hill HD2 . . . . . . **53** A4
SCAPEGOAT **64** B3
SCAPEGOAT HILL . . **64** B3
Scapegoat Hill Jun &
 Inf Sch HD7 . . . . . . **64** A4
Scape View HD7 . . . . **65** A2
Scarboro Mdws
WF14 . . . . **43** C3
Scarborough St
WF12 . . . . **46** C4
Scarborough Terr
WF12 . . . . **46** C4
Scarbro Terr HX5 . . . . **37** B4
Scar Fold HD9 . . . . . . **86** A3
Scar Gr HD4 . . . . **76** B4
Scarhouse La HD7 . . **65** A2
Scar La HD3, HD7 . . . **65** B2
Scarr End La
Batley WF13 . . . . **31** C4
Dewsbury WF12 . . . . . **47** B3
Scarr End View
WF13 . . . . **31** C4
Scarr Green Cl HD9 . . **80** C2
Scar Top HD7 . . . . . . **65** A2
Scar Top La HD4 . . . . **82** B4
Scarwood Terr [7]
HD3 . . . . **65** C2
Schofield La HD5 . . . **68** C4
SCHOLES Brighouse . . . **6** C2
Holmfirth **87** A1

Scholes Fst Sch BD19 . **6** B2
Scholes Jun & Inf Sch
HD9 . . . . **87** A1
Scholes La
Brighouse BD19 . . . . . . **6** C1
Elland HX4 . . . . **22** A3
Scholes Rd
Holmfirth HD2, HD7,
 WF10 . . . . **87** B1
Huddersfield HD2 . . . . **53** A4
Scholey Ave HD6 . . . **26** A2
Scholey Rd HD6 . . . . **26** A2
School Ave WF13 . . . **31** C3
School Cres WF13 . . . **31** C3
School Gn HD6 . . . . . . **26** A2
School Gr WF13 . . . . . **31** C3
School Hill
Huddersfield HD4 . . . . **74** C1
Kirkburton HD8 . . . . . . **89** B4
School La
Denby Dale HD8 . . . . . **95** B3
Dewsbury WF13 . . . . . **31** C3
Horbury WF4 . . . . **60** C3
Huddersfield HD4 . . . . **76** B2
Huddersfield, Hill Side
 HD5 . . . . **55** B1
Huddersfield, Paddock
 HD1 . . . . **67** A3
Liversedge WF15 . . . . **29** A4
Slaithwaite HD7 . . . . **64** A4
School Rd HD7 . . . . . . **64** A4
School St W HD3 . . . . **51** B2
School St
[7] Batley WF17 . . . . . **10** C3
Cleckheaton BD19 . . . . **7** B1
Dewsbury, Chickenley
 WF12 . . . . **34** B2
Dewsbury, Ravensthorpe
 WF13 . . . . **45** A3
Elland HX4 . . . . **22** B1
Holmfirth HD9 . . . . . . **86** A3
Honley HD9 . . . . **83** A3
Huddersfield HD5 . . . . **68** C3
Liversedge, Norristhorpe
 WF15 . . . . **30** B4
Liversedge WF15 . . . . **29** C4
Ossett WF5 . . . . **34** C3
School Terr
Clayton West HD8 . . . **93** B3
Shelley HD8 . . . . **89** C1
School Yd WF4 . . . . . . **61** B4
SCISSETT **93** A2
Scissett CE Fst Sch
HD8 . . . . **92** C3
Scissett Mid Sch
HD8 . . . . **92** C3
Score Croft HD8 . . . . **91** C3
SCOTGATE **82** A2
Scotgate Rd HD9 . . . **82** C2
Scotland St WF17 . . . . **9** C4
Scott Ave WF16 . . . . **18** A4
Scott Hill HD8 . . . . . . **93** B4
Scott La
Cleckheaton BD19 . . . . **8** B2
Cleckheaton, Gomersal
 BD19 . . . . **9** B3
Scott's Cotts HD8 . . . **93** B4
Scott Vale HD2 . . . . . **40** C1
Scotty Bank [7] HD6 . . **26** A4
Scotty Croft La HD6 . **26** A3
SCOUT HILL **46** A4
Scout Hill Rd WF13 . . **45** C4
Scout Hill Terr [2]
WF13 . . . . **45** C4
Scout Hill View [1]
WF13 . . . . **45** C4
Sculptor Pl [14] HD6 . . **13** A1
Seagrave Rd HD4 . . . . **66** B1
Second Ave
Cleckheaton WF15 . . . **15** B2

Second Ave *continued*
Horbury WF4 . . . . **60** B3
Huddersfield, Dalton
 HD5 . . . . **54** C1
Huddersfield HD7 . . . . **64** C2
Kirkheaton HD5 . . . . . **55** C3
Sedgewick St [3]
WF17 . . . . **10** B3
Seemore Ctr WF5 . . . **48** C4
Sefton Ave HD6 . . . . . **12** C3
Sefton Cres HD6 . . . . **12** C3
Sefton Dr HD6 . . . . . . **12** C3
Sefton La HD9 . . . . . . **80** B2
Sefton Rise WF12 . . . **46** C2
Selbourne Ave
WF12 . . . . **46** B3
Selbourne Dr WF12 . . **46** B3
Selbourne Rd WF12 . . **46** B3
Selene Cl BD19 . . . . **9** C3
Sellerdale Ave BD12 . . **6** A3
Sellerdale Dr BD12 . . . **6** A4
Sellerdale Rise BD12 . **6** A3
Sellerdale Way BD12 . **6** A3
Selso Rd WF12 . . . . . . **33** C3
Senior St
Dewsbury WF13 . . . . . **32** B1
Huddersfield HD5 . . . . **69** A3
Sentry HD9 . . . . **83** A3
Sergeantson St [14]
HD1 . . . . **96** A2
Serpentine Rd BD19 . . **8** A1
Seventh Ave WF15 . . . **15** B3
Seymour Wlk HD9 . . . **80** C2
Shaftesbury Ave
HD6 . . . . **26** B1
Shakespeare Bldgs
HD1 . . . . **66** C4
Shambles The [11]
HD1 . . . . **96** B2
Shannon Cl HD6 . . . . **25** B1
Shannon Dr HD3 . . . . **50** A3
Shannon Rd HD6 . . . . **25** B1
Sharehill HD7 . . . . **64** B2
Share Hill HD7 . . . . . . **64** B1
Sharon Cotts WF5 . . . **35** A1
Sharpe St WF16 . . . . . **18** A1
Sharp Royd HD5 . . . . **69** C2
Sharp St WF13 . . . . . . **33** A3
Shaw Bsns Pk HD1 . . **68** B4
Shaw Cl HX4 . . . . **36** B2
SHAW CROSS **34** A4
Shawcross Bsns Pk
WF12 . . . . **34** A4
Shaw Cross Inf Sch
WF12 . . . . **21** A1
Shaw Gr HD9 . . . . **82** C2
Shaw La
Elland, Holywell Green
 HX4 . . . . **36** A2
Elland HX5 . . . . **24** C2
Huddersfield HD7 . . . . **66** A2
Shaw St
Cleckheaton BD19 . . . . **7** B1
Elland HX4 . . . . **36** B2
Mirfield WF14 . . . . **43** C3
Shaw's Terr HD7 . . . . **78** C3
Shearburn Cl WF5 . . . **35** A2
Sheardale HD9 . . . . . . **82** C2
Shearing Cross Gdns
[1] HD1 . . . . **53** B2
SHEEPRIDGE **40** B1
Sheepridge Gr HD2 . . **40** B1
Sheepridge Rd HD2 . . **40** B1
Sheffield Rd HD9 . . . . **87** B1
Sheila Terr WF16 . . . . **17** C1
Shelley Ave WF16 . . . **31** B4
Shelley Coll HD8 . . . . **91** A3
Shelley Ct WF4 . . . . . . **61** B4
Shelley Fst Sch HD8 . **89** C1
Shelley La HD8 . . . . . . **89** C3

SHELLEY
 WOODHOUSE **91** A4
SHEPHERD HILL **49** C4
Shepherds Gr HD2 . . . **41** A1
Shepherds Thorn La
HD2 . . . . **40** B4
SHEPLEY **90** B2
Shepley Bridge
WF14 . . . . **44** C2
Shepley Fst Sch
HD8 . . . . **90** A2
Shepley Mount
WF14 . . . . **30** B1
Shepley Sta HD8 . . . . **90** B3
Shepstye Rd WF4 . . . **60** C3
Sherburn Cl BD11 . . . . **2** B4
Sherburn Gr BD11 . . . . **2** B4
Sherburn Rd HD6 . . . **25** B2
Sheridan Ho LS27 . . . . **4** C4
Sherwood Ave
Cleckheaton BD19 . . . . **9** B2
Huddersfield HD2 . . . . **41** B3
Sherwood Cl
Batley WF13 . . . . **18** C1
Cleckheaton BD19 . . . . **9** B2
Sherwood Dr HD4 . . . **75** B1
Sherwood Rd HD6 . . **26** C4
Shibden Dr WF17 . . . . **18** C4
Shill Bank Ave
WF14 . . . . **44** C4
Shill Bank La WF14 . . **44** B4
Shillbank View
WF14 . . . . **44** B4
Ship St HD6 . . . . **26** B4
Shires Fold [4] HD3 . . **52** A1
Shires Hill [4] HD1 . . . **67** A3
Shirley Ave
Batley WF17 . . . . **10** B4
Bradford BD12 . . . . **5** C3
Cleckheaton BD19 . . . . **9** B2
Shirley Cres BD12 . . . . **5** C3
Shirley Gr
Brighouse HX3 . . . . **5** A1
Cleckheaton BD19 . . . . **9** B2
Shirley Manor Gdns
BD12 . . . . **5** B3
Shirley Manor Prim
 Sch BD12 . . . . **5** C3
Shirley Mount BD19 . . **9** B2
Shirley Par BD19 . . . . . **9** A2
Shirley Pl
Bradford BD12 . . . . **5** C3
Cleckheaton BD19 . . . . **9** B2
Shirley Rd BD19 . . . . . **9** B2
Shirley Sq BD19 . . . . . **9** B2
Shirley Terr BD19 . . . . **9** B2
Shirley Wlk BD19 . . . . **9** B2
Shop La HD5 . . . . **55** C2
Short St WF12 . . . . . . **34** A1
Shutt The WF4 . . . . . . **61** A2
Sickleholme Ct HD2 . **41** A1
Sickle St BD19 . . . . **8** B2
Siddon Dr HD5 . . . . . . **69** C1
Side La HD3 . . . . **65** B4
Sidings The WF12 . . . **46** B4
Sigott St HD3 . . . . **65** B4
Sike Cl HD9 . . . . **87** A3
Sike La HD9 . . . . **87** A3
Sikes Cl HD5 . . . . **69** B2
Silver Birch Ave
BD12 . . . . **6** A4
Silver Birch Cl BD12 . . **6** A4
Silver Birch Dr BD12 . . **6** A4
Silver Birch Gr BD12 . . **6** A4
Silver Court Ind Est
HD5 . . . . **68** B3
Silver St E HD5 . . . . . . **68** B3
Silver St W HD5 . . . . . **68** B3

Silver St HD5 . . . .**68** B4
Simon Fold BD12 . . . . .**5** C4
Simon Green Rd
HD7. . . . .**64** A1
Sixth Ave WF15 . . . . .**15** B3
SKELMANTHORPE . .**92** A3
Skelmanthorpe Bsns
Pk HD8. . . . .**91** C3
Skelmanthorpe Fst Sch
HD8. . . . .**91** C4
Skelmanthorpe Sta★
HD8. . . . .**91** C4
Skelton Cres HD4 . . . .**66** A1
Skipton Ave HD2. . . .**53** B4
Skipton St WF17 . . . .**32** C4
Skircoat Gn HX3. . . . .**22** C4
SKIRCOAT GREEN. . .**22** C4
Skircoat Lodge HX3 . .**22** C4
Skopos Motor Mus★
WF17. . . . .**20** A2
Slack La HD9. . . . .**86** B2
Slade La HD6 . . . .**39** B4
Slades La HD9. . . . . . .**80** C4
Slades Rd HD7 . . . .**64** A2
Slade Wlk WF17 . . . . .**10** C3
Slaids HD7 . . . .**74** B3
SLAITHWAITE **72** C4
Slaithwaite Ave
WF12 . . . .**46** B2
Slaithwaite CE Jun &
Inf Sch HD7 . . . .**72** A2
Slaithwaite Cl WF12 .**46** B2
Slaithwaite Rd
WF12 . . . .**46** C2
Slaithwaite Sta HD7 .**72** B3
Slant Gate
Huddersfield HD7. . . .**74** A4
Kirkburton HD8. . . . . . .**88** B1
Slead Ave HD6 . . . . . .**12** C4
Slead Cres HD6. . . . . .**12** C2
Slead Ct HD6 . . . .**12** C2
Slead Gr HD6. . . . .**12** C2
Slead Royd HD6 . . . . .**12** C2
Slead View HD6. . . . . .**12** C2
Slipper La WF14 . . . . .**29** B1
Small La HD7. . . . .**64** C2
Smallwood Gdns
WF12. . . . .**21** A1
Smallwood Rd
Batley, Chidswell
WF12. . . . .**21** A1
Batley, Chidswell
WF12. . . . .**34** A4
Smith Art Gallery★
HD6. . . . .**13** A1
Smith Cres HD6 . . . . .**25** B2
Smith House Ave
HD6. . . . .**13** A4
Smith House Cres
HD6. . . . .**13** A3
Smith House Gr
HD6. . . . .**13** A3
Smith House La
HX3. . . . .**13** A4
Smithies Hill Ind Est
WF17 . . . .**10** C2
Smithies La
Batley WF17 . . . .**10** B3
Liversedge FW16 . . . . .**31** A4
Smithies Moor Cl
WF17 . . . .**10** C1
Smithies Moor Cres
WF17 . . . .**10** C2
Smithies Moor La
WF17 . . . .**10** B1
Smithies Moor Rise
WF17 . . . .**10** C2
Smith Rd WF13 . . . . . .**31** C3

Smiths Ave HD3 . . . . .**52** A1
Smith St WF15. . . . . . .**17** B1
Smith Way WF5 . . . . . .**35** B1
Smithy Carr La HD6. .**13** A2
Smithy Cl HD8. . . . . . .**91** C2
Smithy La
Huddersfield HD5. . . . .**68** B3
Netherton WF4. . . . . . .**62** A4
Skelmanthorpe HD8. . .**91** C2
Smithy Par WF12 . . . .**58** B3
Smithy Pl HD9. . . . . . .**83** C1
Smithy Place La
HD9. . . . .**84** C4
Smithy Wlk WF12. . . .**58** B3
SNAKE HILL **43** B2
Snapes Fold HD5 . . . .**69** B2
Snelsins La BD19 . . . . .**7** C3
Snelsins Rd BD19 . . . . .**7** C3
Snowdon St WF17 . . .**19** B2
SNOW LEA **50** A2
Solid HD4 . . . .**76** B4
Solway Rd WF17 . . . . .**20** C3
Somerset Ave HD6. . .**26** B3
Somerset Cres HD5. .**68** B3
Somerset Rd HD5. . . .**68** C2
Soothill Hall WF17 . . .**20** B2
Soothill La
Batley WF17 . . . .**20** B3
East Ardsley WF17 . . . .**21** A3
Sorbus Way HD8. . . . .**71** A1
South Ave
Horbury WF4 . . . .**61** B3
Huddersfield, Cowlersley
HD4. . . . .**65** B1
Huddersfield, Sheepridge
HD2. . . . .**53** B4
South Bank Rd
WF17 . . . .**19** A4
South Croft Ave
BD11. . . . .**2** A4
South Croft Gate
BD11. . . . .**2** A4
South Crosland CE
Junior Sch HD4 . . . .**75** C1
South Cross Rd HD2 .**52** C4
Southdale CE Jun Sch
WF5 . . . .**49** A2
Southdale Gdns
WF5 . . . .**49** A3
Southdale Rd WF5. . .**49** A3
Southdene HD5 . . . . .**69** A3
Southern Rd HD4. . . .**65** C1
Southfield Cl WF4 . . .**61** A2
Southfield Ct HD8 . . .**88** C1
Southfield Fold
WF4 . . . .**61** A2
Southfield La WF4. . .**61** A2
Southfield Rd HD5. . .**69** C2
Southfields View
WF4 . . . .**61** A2
Southfield Terr BD11 . .**2** A4
Southgate
16 Dewsbury
WF13. . . . .**32** C2
Elland HX5 . . . .**37** B4
Honley HD9. . . . .**83** A2
Huddersfield HD1. . . . .**96** B2
South Gr HD6 . . . .**12** B3
South La
Elland, Blackley
HX5. . . . .**37** B2
Elland HX5 . . . .**37** B3
Holmfirth HD9. . . . . . .**86** A3
Netherton WF4. . . . . . .**63** B2
Southlands HD5 . . . . .**55** B3
Southlands Dr HD2 . .**39** C1
South Lane Gdns
HX5. . . . .**37** B3
SOUTH OSSETT. **49** A1
South Ossett Inf Sch
WF5 . . . .**49** A3

South Par
Cleckheaton BD19 . . . . .**7** C1
Elland HX5 . . . .**37** B3
Ossett WF5. . . . .**49** C2
South Parade Inf Sch
WF5 . . . .**49** B2
South Parade Jun Sch
WF5 . . . .**49** B2
South Royd HD5 . . . . .**69** C2
South St
Brighouse HD6 . . . . . .**13** A1
Dewsbury, Savile Town
WF12. . . . .**46** C4
Dewsbury WF13 . . . . .**32** C2
Elland HX4 . . . .**36** A2
Holmfirth HD9. . . . . . .**86** C4
Huddersfield, Netherton
HD4. . . . .**82** B4
Huddersfield, Paddock
HD1. . . . .**66** C3
6 Liversedge WF15 . . .**17** B2
2 Mirfield WF14 . . . . .**43** C1
Ossett WF5. . . . .**48** C2
South Terr
Dewsbury WF12 . . . . .**47** A4
Ossett WF17 . . . .**49** A1
South View
1 Batley WF17 . . . . .**10** C3
Dewsbury WF12 . . . . .**46** C4
Holmfirth HD9. . . . . . .**87** C1
Huddersfield HD1. . . . .**66** C3
Slaithwaite HD7. . . . . .**64** A4
South View HX3 . . . . .**12** A4
South View Gr BD19 . . .**9** B1
South View Terr
Dewsbury,
Ravensthorpe
WF13. . . . .**45** A4
4 Dewsbury WF13 . . .**32** B4
Southway
Huddersfield HD3. . . .**51** C3
Mirfield WF14 . . . .**29** C1
Southwell Ave HD3 . .**51** B1
Southwell La WF4 . . .**60** C2
Southwood Ave
HD9. . . . .**83** C3
Sovereign Bsns Ctr 5
HD4. . . . .**67** B2
Sovereign Cl WF17. . .**10** C3
Sovereign's Way
WF12 . . . .**46** A1
Sowood Ave WF5 . . . .**49** A1
Sowood Ct WF5 . . . . .**49** B1
Sowood Gdns WF5. . .**49** B1
Sowood Grange
WF5 . . . .**49** B1
Sowood La WF5 . . . . .**49** B1
Sowood View WF5 . . .**49** B1
Spa Bottom HD8. . . . .**70** B3
Spa Croft Rd WF5. . . .**49** C2
Spa Ctyd HD8. . . . . . .**70** B2
Spa Fields HD7 . . . . . .**73** A3
Spa Fields Ind Est
HD7. . . . .**73** A3
Spa Hill WF17 . . . .**20** A3
Spaines Rd HD2 . . . . .**53** A3
Spa La Ossett WF5. . . .**49** C2
Sparks Rd HD3 . . . . . .**51** B1
Spark St HD3 . . . .**50** C1
Sparrow Rise HD9 . . .**80** B2
Spa St WF17. . . . .**20** A3
Spa Terr HD8 . . . .**70** B3
Speakers Ct WF13 . . .**32** B2
Speedwell St HD1 . . .**66** C3
Spen Bank BD19 . . . . . .**8** C1
Spenborough Ind Est
WF15 . . . .**17** A3
Spenborough Sports
Complex WF15 . . . . .**16** C3

Spencer St
4 Mirfield WF14 . . . .**43** C1
Skelmanthorpe HD8. . .**91** C3
Spencer Terr HD2 . . . .**40** C1
Spenfield Ct WF15. . .**30** A4
Spen La BD19 . . . .**9** A2
Spen Trad Est BD19 . . .**8** B4
Spen Vale St WF16 . . .**31** A4
Spen Valley Ind Pk
BD19. . . . .**16** C4
Spen Valley Rd
WF13 . . . .**45** B4
Spen Valley Sports Coll
WF15 . . . .**17** B1
Spen View WF16 . . . . .**31** C3
Spinkfield Rd HD2 . . .**52** C2
Spinkwell Rd 4
WF13 . . . .**32** C3
Spinners Way
Brighouse BD19 . . . . . .**6** C2
Mirfield WF14 . . . .**43** C1
Spinneyfield HD2 . . . .**39** C1
Spinney The HD6 . . . .**13** A3
Spire Ct
Huddersfield HD1. . . . .**52** B1
Huddersfield, Marsh
HD3. . . . .**52** A1
Spout Hill HD6 . . . . . .**39** A4
Spout House La
HD6. . . . .**12** B4
Spring Bank
Batley WF15 . . . .**30** C4
Kirkburton HD8. . . . . . .**88** B1
Springbank Cres
HD2. . . . .**54** A3
Spring Bank Dr
WF15 . . . .**30** B4
Springbank Rd HD2. .**54** A3
Spring Dale HD9. . . . .**83** A3
Springdale Ave HD1 .**67** B2
Springdale St HD1 . . .**67** B2
Springfield Ave
Batley WF17 . . . .**19** B3
Clayton West HD8. . . . .**93** A3
Honley HD9. . . . .**83** A1
Slaithwaite HD7. . . . . .**72** A1
Springfield Cl HD8. . .**93** A3
Springfield Dr WF15 .**15** C3
Springfield Gr HD6 . .**13** A3
Springfield House 3
BD19. . . . .**8** B1
Springfield La
Cleckheaton FW15 . . . .**16** B3
Kirkburton HD8. . . . . . .**88** B1
Springfield Mills
HD8. . . . .**95** A2
Springfield Pk
WF14 . . . .**44** A3
Springfield Rd HX5 . .**24** B1
Springfield Terr
Brighouse BD19 . . . . . .**6** C3
Cleckheaton WF15 . . . .**15** C3
Dewsbury WF13 . . . . .**32** C3
Spring Gdns
Batley WF17 . . . .**19** B3
Birkenshaw BD11. . . . . .**3** C4
Spring Gr HD8. . . . . . .**93** A3
Spring Grove Jun & Inf
Sch HD1. . . . .**67** B3
Spring Grove St
HD1. . . . .**96** A1
Spring Head La HD7 .**78** C4
Springhouses HD8. . .**95** A2
Spring La
Batley WF17 . . . .**11** B1
Elland HX4 . . . .**22** A1
Holmfirth, New Mill
HD9. . . . .**87** B3
Spring Mill La WF5 . .**49** B4
Spring Side Rise
HD7. . . . .**64** C3

Spring St
Brighouse HD6 . . . . . .**26** A4
Dewsbury WF13 . . . . .**32** C3
7 Huddersfield HD1 . .**96** A2
Liversedge WF15 . . . . .**17** B2
Marsden HD7 . . . .**78** C2
Slaithwaite HD7 . . . . . .**72** B2
Springstone Ave
WF5 . . . .**35** A1
Spring Valley Cl 5
WF15 . . . .**17** A3
Spring Valley Sq 3
WF15 . . . .**17** A3
Spring Valley St 4
WF15 . . . .**17** A3
Spring View WF5. . . . .**49** B4
Springwell Cl WF15 . .**30** C4
Springwell Rd WF5 . .**49** A3
Springwell View 4
WF17 . . . .**10** C3
Springwood Ave
HD1. . . . .**67** B3
Spring Wood Ave
HX3. . . . .**22** B4
Spring Wood Dr
HX3. . . . .**22** B4
Springwood Gdns
HX3. . . . .**22** B4
Springwood Hall Cl
HD1. . . . .**67** A4
Springwood Hall Gdns
HD1. . . . .**67** B4
Springwood Sq 6
HD1. . . . .**96** A2
Springwood St HD1. .**96** A2
Spruce Dr HD4 . . . . . .**82** B4
Spruce Drive Mews
HD4. . . . .**82** B4
Spruce Hts HD6 . . . . .**13** A4
Spurr St WF17 . . . .**20** A2
Square Hill HD5 . . . . .**55** B2
Square The
Batley WF17 . . . .**18** C4
Shepley HD8. . . . .**90** A2
Squirrel Cl WF13. . . . .**19** A1
Squirrel Ct HD2. . . . . .**51** C4
Squirrel Ditch HD4 . .**68** B1
Squirrel End WF13 . . .**32** A4
Squirrel Hall Dr
WF13 . . . .**18** C1
Squirrel Wlk WF13 . . .**19** A1
Stable Cl HD7 . . . .**72** C3
Stable Fold BD12 . . . . .**6** A4
Stableford Gdns
HD2. . . . .**52** A4
Stableford Manor
HD7. . . . .**65** A3
Stackgarth HD6 . . . . .**26** A2
Stadium Way HD1 . . .**53** C1
Stafford Hill La HD5 .**55** C2
Staincliffe CE Jun Sch
WF17 . . . .**19** A1
Staincliffe Cl 10
WF13 . . . .**32** A3
Staincliffe Cres 4
WF13 . . . .**31** C4
Staincliffe Hall Rd
WF17 . . . .**19** A2
Staincliffe Rd WF13. .**32** A3
Staincliffe View
WF13 . . . .**31** C4
Staincross Ave
HD4. . . . .**75** B4
Staines Croft HD5 . . .**69** A4
Stainland Rd
Elland HX4 . . . .**36** B4
Halifax HX4. . . . .**23** A3
Stake Lane Bank
HD9. . . . .**86** C2

Stakes Fold WF16.....**18** B2
Stalley Royd La HD9 .**87** C1
STANCLIFFE
COMMON.........**43** A2
Stancliffe Way HD5 ..**55** B3
Standard Dr HD4 .....**75** A4
Standiforth La HD5 ..**69** B4
Standiforth PI HD5 ..**69** B4
Standiforth Rd HD5...**68** C4
Stanhope St HD8 .....**92** C2
Stanley La WF15......**17** A3
Stanley Mills Bsns Pk
    HD3................**65** B2
Stanley PI
    Batley WF17 ....**20** A3
    Huddersfield HD7.....**64** C2
Stanley Rd
    Huddersfield, Ainley
    Top HD3 ....**37** C1
    Huddersfield HD3.....**51** C3
    Liversedge WF15 .....**30** A4
Stanley St
    Brighouse HD6 ......**13** B1
    Cleckheaton BD19 ....**8** A2
    Huddersfield HD1.....**67** A1
Stanley Terr WF17.....**20** A4
Stannard Well Dr
    WF4 ....**61** A4
Stannard Well La
    WF4 ....**61** B4
Stanningley Gr **7**
    WF16 ....**18** A1
Stanwell Ave HD2....**52** A3
Star Terr HD6........**25** B1
Station App HD9....**83** C3
Station Ct
    Clayton West HD8....**93** B4
    Lepton HD8..........**70** B1
Station La
    Birkenshaw BD11......**2** B4
    Huddersfield HD4.....**76** B2
    Huddersfield, Wellhouse
    HD7...............**64** C1
    Liversedge WF16 .....**18** A1
    Shepley HD8.........**90** B3
Station Rd
    Batley WF17 ....**20** A2
    Birkenshaw BD11......**3** B4
    Bradford, Wyke BD12...**5** B4
    Brighouse HD6 ......**26** C4
    Cleckheaton BD19 ....**8** B2
    Dewsbury, Earlsheaton
    WF12..............**47** B4
    Dewsbury WF12.....**46** B3
    Elland HX4 ....**36** B2
    Holmfirth HD9........**86** A3
    Honley HD9..........**83** B3
    Huddersfield, Bradley
    HD2...............**41** C1
    Huddersfield HD4.....**82** A4
    Huddersfield, Wellhouse
    HD7...............**65** A1
    Lepton HD8.........**70** C1
    Liversedge WF16 .....**18** A1
    Marsden HD7 ....**78** C3
    Meltham HD9 ....**86** A3
    Mirfield WF14.......**43** C2
    Ossett WF5.........**49** A2
    Shepley HD8.........**90** A2
    Skelmanthorpe HD8...**91** C3
    Slaithwaite HD7 .....**72** C3
Station St
    Huddersfield HD1.....**96** A2
    Meltham HD9 ....**80** B2
Station Terr HD8....**91** C3
Station Yd WF17.....**20** A3
Staynton Cres HD2...**41** B3
Stead La HD5........**55** B2
Steanard La WF14 ...**44** B1
Steeplands HD2.....**41** B4
Steeple View HD7....**64** C2

Stephenson CI
    WF12 ....**33** B3
Steps Ind Pk HD9....**83** B4
STILE COMMON **67** C1
Stile Common Inf Sch
    HD4................**68** A1
Stile Common Jun Sch
    HD4................**67** C1
Stile Common Rd
    HD4................**68** A1
Stirley Hill HD4......**77** A1
Stithy St WF5........**34** C2
Stockerhead La
    HD7................**72** C2
Stockhill St WF13....**32** A2
STOCKS BANK **43** A3
Stocksbank Dr
    WF14 ....**42** C4
Stocks Bank Rd
    WF14 ....**43** A4
Stocks Dr HD8.......**90** A2
Stocks La WF17......**19** C3
Stocks Wlk HD5 .....**69** B1
Stockwell Ct BD19 ....**6** C2
Stockwell Dr WF17 ...**20** A4
Stockwell Hill HD4...**76** B2
Stockwell Vale HD4 ..**76** B2
Stone Acre Hts HD9..**81** A1
Stonebridge Wlk
    HD8................**90** B3
Stonecliffe Dr WF4 ..**59** A1
Stonecroft Gdns
    HD8................**90** B2
Stonedene Ct WF16...**18** B1
Stonefield Ave HD4 ..**66** A1
Stonefield PI WF17 ...**10** C3
Stonefield Rd HD4....**66** A1
Stonefield St
    Cleckheaton BD19 ....**15** A4
    Dewsbury WF13......**32** C3
Stonefleece Ct HD9..**83** A1
Stone Fold HD9......**83** A2
Stonegate WF5......**49** B1
Stone Gate Ct HD4...**76** A4
Stonehurst Rd 2
    WF14 ....**43** C4
Stonehyrst Ave
    WF13 ....**33** A3
Stonelea Dr HD6.....**25** C1
Stoneleigh Ct
    Bradford BD19 ....**6** B3
    Shelley HD8 ....**90** C4
Stoneleigh Gr WF5 ..**48** C3
Stoneleigh Mews
    HD2................**52** A3
Stones La
    Huddersfield HD7.....**64** C1
    Linthwaite HD7......**73** B2
Stone St BD19.......**7** C1
Stoney Bank St
    WF13 ....**45** C4
Stoney Battery Rd
    HD1................**66** C2
Stoney Croft BD19 ....**9** B1
Stoney Cross St
    HD4................**76** B4
Stoney Ford La HD5..**55** B3
Stoney Hill HD6.....**26** A4
Stoney La
    Batley WF17 ....**20** A4
    Brighouse HX3 ....**13** A4
    Huddersfield, Blue Bell
    Hill HD4...........**76** B4
    Huddersfield, Longwood
    HD3...............**65** B4
    Mirfield WF14.......**31** A1
Stony La Elland HX4 ..**22** A2
    Honley HD9..........**83** A1
Stony Royd Terr
    HD7................**73** B2

Storrs Hill Rd WF4,
    WF5 ....**60** A4
Storth Ave HD4 ......**65** B1
Storth Pl HD2 ......**52** C3
Storths Rd HD2......**52** C3
Stralau St WF17 .....**19** C4
Strands Ct WF4......**63** C4
Stratford Cl HD7.....**65** A3
Stratton Cl HD6......**26** B3
Stratton Pk HD6 .....**26** B3
Stratton Rd HD6.....**26** C3
Strawberry Ave
    WF15 ....**17** A1
Strawberry Bank
    WF15 ....**17** A2
Strawberry Sq 2
    WF16 ....**18** A1
Street La LS27 ....**4** C4
Stretch Gate HD8.....**90** B3
Strike La HD8........**91** B4
Stringer La **5** WF4 ..**61** A3
Stringer's Yd 11
    WF4 ....**60** C3
Stuart Gr HD7 ....**72** C2
Stuart Pl HD2.......**41** B3
Stubbin La HD4......**95** C3
Stubbin Rd HD7 .....**79** B4
Stubley Farm Rd
    WF16 ....**18** A4
Stubley Rd WF16....**17** C4
Stubs Beck La BD19...**8** A4
Studleigh Terr HD6 ..**12** B3
Stunsteds Rd BD19 ...**8** A2
Stutely Gr HD2 ......**41** A3
Sude Hill HD9 ....**87** C4
Sude Hill Terr HD9 ..**87** C4
Suffolk Ave WF17.....**19** B1
Suffolk Cl WF5 ......**48** B2
Suffolk Rise HD2 ....**40** B2
Suffolk St WF17 .....**19** B2
Sufton St HD2 ....**52** C3
Sugar La WF12 ......**33** B2
Sugden Cl HD6......**26** A2
Sugdens Terr HD6 ...**25** A1
Sullivan Cl HD4......**66** C1
Summerbridge Cl
    WF17 ....**19** A4
Summerbridge Cres
    BD19................**9** C4
Summerdale BD19...**9** B4
Summerfield Ave
    HD6................**13** B4
Summerfield Gr
    HD8................**88** A4
Summer St
    Huddersfield, Netherton
    HD4...............**75** C1
    Huddersfield, Rashcliffe
    HD1, HD4 ....**67** B2
Summervale HD9....**86** A4
Sunbury Gr HD5 .....**69** A4
Sunderland Ct 6
    HD6................**13** A1
Sunfield Terr 11
    BD19................**8** B1
Sunningdale Croft
    HD2................**39** B1
Sunningdale Rd
    HD4................**66** C1
SUNNYBANK.......**36** A4
Sunnybank HD8 .....**95** A2
Sunny Bank HD4....**74** C1
Sunny Bank Ave
    WF14 ....**30** A2
Sunnybank Cl BD19...**6** C1
Sunnybank Cres
    HX4................**22** B1
Sunnybank Dr HX4 ..**22** B1
Sunny Bank Dr
    WF14 ....**29** C2

Sunny Bank Gr
    WF14 ....**30** A1
Sunnybank Grange 1
    HD6................**26** A4
Sunnybank La HX4...**22** B1
Sunny Bank Par
    WF14 ....**29** C2
Sunnybank Rd
    Elland HX4 ....**22** B1
    Huddersfield HD3.....**52** A2
Sunny Bank Rd
    Batley WF17 ....**20** A4
    Brighouse HD6 ......**26** A4
    Meltham HD9 ....**80** A2
    Mirfield WF14.......**30** A2
    Slaithwaite HD7 .....**64** A1
Sunnybank St WF5...**48** C3
Sunnybank Terr
    HD6................**13** A1
Sunnybank View
    HD3................**65** B4
Sunny Bank Wlk
    WF14 ....**30** A1
Sunnybank Woods
    WF17 ....**20** A4
Sunny Brow HD4 ....**76** B2
Sunnydale Ave 3
    HD6................**26** A2
Sunnydale Croft
    WF5 ....**49** A2
Sunnydale Pk WF5...**49** A3
Sunnydale Rd WF5...**49** B3
Sunnydale Terr
    WF5 ....**49** A3
Sunny Heys Rd HD9..**80** B3
Sunny Heys W HD9 ..**80** B3
Sunnyhill Ave HD5...**55** B4
Sunnylea HD7 ....**79** A3
Sunnymead HD8.....**93** A3
Sunny Mead HD5 ....**69** C4
Sunnymount Terr 5
    WF17 ....**10** C3
Sunnyside
    Batley WF16 ....**18** A1
    Brighouse HD6.......**27** A2
    Huddersfield HD2.....**52** B2
Sunnyside Ave
    WF15 ....**29** C4
Sunny View Cres
    HD2................**40** C1
Sunroyd Ave WF4....**61** A4
Sunroyd Hill WF4 ....**61** A4
Sunways WF14 ......**29** C1
Surat Rd HD7........**72** B4
Surrey St WF17 ......**20** A3
Sussex St WF17......**20** A3
Sussex Wlk **2** WF13 .**32** B2
Sutherland Dr HD4 ..**75** B4
Sutton Ave HD5......**55** A1
Sutton Dr HD5.......**55** A2
Swaledale Ho WF17..**19** C1
Swallow Gr HD4 .....**82** C4
Swallow Hill WF17 ...**11** A2
Swallow La HD7......**64** B3
Swallow St
    1 Huddersfield
    HD1...............**96** A1
    Liversedge WF16 .....**18** A1
Swan Bank Ct HD9...**86** A2
Swan Bank La HD9...**86** A2
Swan Ct HD1 ....**67** A1
Swan La HD1.........**67** A1
Sweep La HD9.......**86** B1
Swift's Fold HD9.....**83** A3
SWINCLIFFE.......**2** B1
Swincliffe Cl BD19.....**2** B2
Swincliffe Cres BD19 .**2** B1
Swincroft WF5 ....**49** A3
Swindon Rd WF13 ...**32** C2
Swithenbank Ave
    WF5 ....**35** A2

Swithenbank St
    WF5 ....**34** C3
Sycamore Ave
    Huddersfield HD3,
    HD7...............**65** B3
    Meltham HD9 ....**80** B1
Sycamore Cl
    Batley WF12 ....**33** C4
    Lepton HD8..........**71** B1
Sycamore Ct
    Huddersfield HD3.....**65** B3
    Kirkburton HD8......**88** C1
Sycamore Dr
    Brighouse HX3 ....**13** A4
    Cleckheaton BD19 ....**7** B1
    Elland HX5 ....**36** C4
Sycamore Gn HD8 ...**94** C3
Sycamore Grange
    HD7................**65** A3
Sycamore Ind Est
    WF16 ....**31** A4
Sycamores The
    Dewsbury WF13......**32** B4
    Horbury WF4 ....**61** B3
Sycamore Terr
    Honley HD9..........**82** C1
    Horbury WF4 ....**61** B2
Sycamore View HD6 .**12** C1
Sycamore Way
    WF17 ....**10** C3
Sydney St WF15 .....**17** B1
Syke Ave WF12 ......**33** C2
Syke Fold BD19.......**8** A1
Syke Gr WF12........**33** C2
Syke Ing WF17 ......**34** A1
Syke Ing Terr WF12...**34** A1
Syke La WF12........**33** C1
Syke Rd WF12 ....**33** C2
Sykes Ave
    Batley WF16 ....**18** B3
    Mirfield WF14.......**44** B4
Sykes Cl WF17 ......**20** B4
Sykes La WF12.......**21** A2
Sykes Rd WF17 ......**20** B4
Sykes St BD19 ....**8** A1
Syke St WF12 ....**33** C1
Sykes View WF17 ....**33** B2
Sylvan Ridge HD2....**40** B2
Syringa St HD1 ......**52** A1

T

Tabbs Ct BD19 ....**6** C3
Tabbs La BD19.......**6** C3
Talbot Ave HD3 ......**51** C3
Talbot Ho **2** HX5 ...**37** B4
Talbot Row WF17 ....**20** A3
Talbot St WF17 ......**19** C2
Talbot View 1
    WF14 ....**43** C4
Tallow Mews HD8....**91** C2
TANDEM...........**70** A3
Tandem Ind Est
    HD5................**70** A4
Tandem Way HD5....**70** A4
Tanfield Rd HD1 .....**52** C2
Tanhouse St WF13 ...**45** B4
Tanners HD7 ....**72** B1
Tanner St WF15......**15** B3
Tannery Ct WF14....**43** A4
Tanyard Ave HD3 ....**51** A1
Tanyard Rd
    Huddersfield,
    Milnsbridge HD3.....**66** A2
    Huddersfield, Quarmby
    HD3...............**51** A1

Tateley Cl WF5 . . . .**35** A3
Tateley La WF5 . . . . . .**34** C3
Tate Naylor St WF13 .**32** B4
Taylor Cl WF5 . . . . . .**49** B2
Taylor Cres WF5 . . . . .**49** B2
Taylor Dr WF5 . . . .**49** B2
Taylor Hall La WF14 . .**29** C2
TAYLOR HILL **76** B3
Taylor Hill Rd HD4 . . .**76** A3
Taylor La HD7 . . . .**64** A3
Taylor's Bldgs HD4 . .**76** C4
Taylor St
  Batley WF17 . . . .**19** C2
  Cleckheaton BD19 . . . . .**7** C1
  Huddersfield HD7 . . . . .**65** A2
Teall Cl WF5 . . . .**49** C3
Teall's Croft WF5 . . . .**35** B1
Teall St WF5 . . . .**49** C3
Teasel Cl WF15 . . . . . .**15** C3
Technology Dr
  WF17 . . . .**20** B2
Teddington Ave
  HD5 . . . .**69** B4
Temperance Fields
  BD19 . . . .**6** C2
Templar Dr HD5 . . . . .**68** C3
Templars Cl HX4 . . . . .**22** A1
Temple Cl 16 HD1 . . . .**96** A2
Temple Rd WF13 . . . . .**32** A1
Temple St HD3 . . . . . .**51** B3
Tennyson Pl 5 BD19 . .**8** A2
Tenter Cl
  Batley WF17 . . . .**19** C4
  Skelmanthorpe HD8 . . .**91** C3
Tentercroft Ct
  WF13 . . . .**33** A3
Tenterfield Rd WF5 . .**49** A3
Tenter Fields WF12 . .**46** A4
Tenter Hill HD9 . . . . . .**87** C2
Tenter Hill La HD2 . . .**40** C2
Tenter House Ct
  HD8 . . . .**95** C2
Tenters Gr HD2 . . . . . .**40** B1
Tenth Ave WF15 . . . . .**15** C3
Terrace The HD9 . . . . .**82** C1
Tetley Dr BD11 . . . .**2** B2
Thackeray Gr HD4 . . .**66** C1
Thackray Ave WF16 . .**18** B3
Thanes Cl HD2 . . . . . .**52** B3
Thatchers Way BD19 . .**9** B3
Thewlis La HD4 . . . . . .**75** A3
THICK HOLLINS **81** A1
Thick Hollins HD9 . . .**81** A1
Thick Hollins Dr
  HD9 . . . .**81** A1
Thick Hollins Rd
  HD9 . . . .**84** B1
Third Ave
  Cleckheaton WF15 . . . .**15** B3
  Huddersfield HD7 . . . . .**64** C2
  Kirkheaton HD5 . . . . . .**55** C3
Thirlmere Ave
  Brighouse BD12 . . . .**6** B3
  Elland HX5 . . . .**24** B1
Thirlmere Rd WF12 . .**33** B4
Thirsk Cl HD2 . . . .**53** B4
Thirstin Gdns HD4 . . .**82** C3
Thirstin Rd HD9 . . . . .**83** A3
Thirteenth Ave
  WF15 . . . .**15** B3
Thistle Cl HD2 . . . . . .**52** B4
Thistle Hill HD6 . . . . .**70** B3
Thistle Hill Ave HD5 . .**70** B3
Thistle St HD1 . . . .**53** B2
Thomas St
  Batley, Heckmondwike
  WF16 . . . .**18** A1

Thomas St continued
  Batley WF17 . . . .**19** B4
  Brighouse HD6 . . . .**26** A3
  Elland, Holywell Green
  HX4 . . . .**36** A2
  Elland HX5 . . . .**37** C4
  Huddersfield, Lindley
  HD3 . . . .**51** B3
  Huddersfield, Yews Hill
  HD1 . . . .**67** A2
  9 Liversedge WF15 . .**17** A2
Thoresby Dr BD19 . . . .**9** B2
Thorgrow Cl HD8 . . . .**70** B2
Thorn Ave WF12 . . . . .**57** B4
Thornberry Dr WF15 .**15** B3
Thorncliffe Est
  WF17 . . . .**19** A1
Thorncliffe House Flats
  1 HD3 . . . .**51** B3
Thorncliffe Rd
  WF17 . . . .**19** B1
Thorncliffe St HD3 . .**51** B3
Thorne Rd HD1 . . . . . .**67** A2
Thornes Fold HD8 . . .**71** B1
Thornfield WF12 . . . . .**46** A4
Thornfield Ave HD4 . .**67** A1
Thornfield Cl HD4 . . .**67** A1
Thornfield Mount
  WF17 . . . .**11** A3
Thornfield Rd HD4 . . .**67** A1
Thornfield Rise 2
  HX4 . . . .**22** B1
Thornfield St 1
  HX4 . . . .**22** B1
Thorn Garth BD19 . . .**15** C4
THORNHILL **58** A4
Thornhill Ave HD3 . . .**51** C1
Thornhill Bridge La
  HD6 . . . .**13** A1
Thornhill Cl WF4 . . . . .**59** B4
Thornhill Jun & Inf Sch
  WF12 . . . .**58** A3
THORNHILL LEES . .**46** B2
Thornhill Lees CE Inf
  Sch WF12 . . . .**46** A3
Thornhill Park Ave
  WF12 . . . .**46** C2
Thornhill Pl 1 HD6 . .**26** A3
Thornhill Rd
  Brighouse HD6 . . . .**26** A3
  Dewsbury, West Town
  WF12, WF13 . . . .**32** B1
  Dewsbury WF12 . . . . . .**46** B3
  Huddersfield, Edgerton
  HD3 . . . .**52** A2
  Huddersfield HD3 . . . . .**65** C4
  Middlestown WF4 . . . . .**58** C2
Thornhills Beck La
  HD6 . . . .**13** B2
Thornhills La HD6 . . .**13** C2
Thornhill St WF12 . . .**46** C4
Thornie View WF12 . .**46** B2
Thornleigh HD2 . . . . .**46** C4
Thornleigh Dr WF15 . .**17** B3
Thornleigh Rd HD4 . .**66** B1
Thorn Rd WF12 . . . . . .**57** B3
Thorn St WF17 . . . . . .**10** B3
Thornton Cl WF17 . . . .**3** C1
THORNTON LODGE .**67** B2
Thornton Lodge Hall
  HD1 . . . .**67** A2
Thornton Lodge Rd
  HD1 . . . .**67** B2
Thornton Rd
  Brighouse HD6 . . . .**25** B2
  Dewsbury WF12 . . . . . .**46** B2
Thornton Sq 8 HD6 .**26** A4

Thornton St
  Cleckheaton, Hartshead
  Moor Side BD19 . . . . .**15** A4
  Cleckheaton, Marsh
  BD19 . . . .**16** C2
  Dewsbury WF13 . . . . . .**32** B2
Thorntonville BD19 . .**16** C4
Thorn View HX5 . . . . .**37** C4
Thornville Mount 3
  WF13 . . . .**45** C4
Thornville Pl WF13 . . .**45** C4
Thornville St WF13 . . .**45** C4
Thornville Terr
  WF13 . . . .**45** C4
Thornville Wlk
  WF13 . . . .**45** C4
Thorp Ave HD9 . . . . . .**86** B2
Thorpe Green Dr
  HD7 . . . .**65** A4
Thorpe La HD5 . . . . . .**69** C2
Thorpes Ave HD8 . . . .**95** B4
Thorpes Cres HD8 . . .**95** C2
Thorpe View WF5 . . . .**35** A2
Thorp Pyn Croft
  HD5 . . . .**54** B1
Threadneedle St
  HD1 . . . .**96** A2
Three Sisters Sq 1
  HD1 . . . .**53** A2
Threshfield Cres
  BD11 . . . .**2** A4
Throstle Nest WF17 . .**19** A2
Thurgory Gate HD8 . .**71** A1
Thurgory La HD8 . . . .**71** A2
Thurstonland Bank Rd
  HD9 . . . .**85** B3
Tichborne St FW15 . .**16** B2
Tichbourne St WF17 .**18** C2
Tidswell St HD6 . . . . .**18** B2
Tile Terr HD6 . . . .**26** A3
Till Carr La HX3 . . . . . .**5** A2
Timber St 3 HX5 . . . .**37** B4
Tinderley Gr HD5 . . . .**69** B2
Tinker La HD9 . . . .**80** B1
Tinsel Rd WF12 . . . . . .**33** C3
Tintern Ave HD3 . . . . .**65** B3
Titan District Ctr
  BD12 . . . .**5** C4
Tithe Barn St
  Dewsbury WF13 . . . . . .**33** A2
  Horbury WF4 . . . .**60** C3
Tithe Barn View
  HD6 . . . .**26** C2
Tithefields HD8 . . . . . .**70** B2
Tithe House Way
  HD2 . . . .**41** A4
Toby Wood La HD8 . . .**94** B2
Tofts Ave BD12 . . . .**5** C4
Tofts Gr HD6 . . . .**25** C1
Tofts Grove Gdns
  HD6 . . . .**25** C1
Tofts Grove Pl HD6 . . .**25** C1
Tofts Rd BD19 . . . .**8** A1
Tolson Cres HD5 . . . . .**54** C1
Tolson Grange HD5 . .**69** B3
Tolson Mus ⭐ HD5 . .**69** A4
Tolson St
  Dewsbury WF13 . . . . . .**32** C3
  Ossett WF5 . . . .**34** B2
Tolson's Yd 12 HD5 . .**68** C3
Tom La HD4 . . . .**66** A1
Tomlinson's Yd HD1 . .**96** B2
Tommy La HD7 . . . . . .**74** A3
TOOTHILL **26** A1
Toothill Ave HD6 . . . . .**26** A1
Toothill Bank HD6 . . . .**26** A1
Toothill La HD6 . . . . . .**26** A1
Toothill La S HD6 . . . .**39** B4
Topaz Cl HD2 . . . .**53** C4
Top Headlands WF5 . .**48** B3

Top Mdw WF14 . . . . . .**56** C4
Top of Carr 1
  WF17 . . . .**32** B4
TOP OF
  COWCLIFFE **39** A1
Top of the Hill HD9 . .**85** C3
Top O'Th' Bank
  HD9 . . . .**85** C3
Top o'The Hill HD7 . . .**72** A1
Top Rd HD8 . . . .**94** C4
Top Row HD4 . . . .**76** A2
Tor Ave BD12 . . . .**5** C3
Torcote Cres HD2 . . . .**40** B3
Torridon Rd WF12 . . . .**33** B4
Tor View HD9 . . . .**85** A4
TOTTIES **87** A3
Totties La HD9 . . . .**87** A3
Tower Bldgs 1
  WF16 . . . .**18** A1
Town Ave HD1 . . . .**53** C2
Town Cres HD1 . . . . . .**53** C2
TOWN END **64** B2
Town End
  Huddersfield,
  Almondbury HD5 . . . . .**69** B2
  Huddersfield, Town End
  HD7 . . . .**64** C2
  Ossett WF5 . . . .**48** C3
Town End Ave HD9 . . .**86** C4
Town End La HD8 . . . .**71** C1
Town End View HD9 . .**86** C4
Town Fields Rd HX5 . .**37** A4
Townfold WF5 . . . .**49** A4
TOWNGATE **44** A4
TOWN GATE **80** C2
Towngate
  Brighouse, Clifton
  HD6 . . . .**27** B4
  Holmfirth HD9 . . . .**86** A3
  Huddersfield HD4 . . . . .**76** C4
  Mirfield WF14 . . . .**44** A4
  Ossett WF5 . . . .**49** B4
Town Gate
  Brighouse BD19 . . . .**6** C2
  Holmfirth, Netherthong
  HD9 . . . .**84** A2
  Kirkburton HD8 . . . . . .**88** B2
  Lepton HD8 . . . .**71** C2
  Marsden HD7 . . . .**78** C3
Towngate Ave HD6 . . .**14** A1
Towngate Gr WF14 . . .**44** A3
Towngate Ho 1
  HX5 . . . .**23** C1
Towngate Prim Sch
  WF5 . . . .**49** B4
Towngate Rd WF17 . . .**19** A3
Town Gn WF12 . . . .**33** B1
Town Hall Bldgs 2
  HX5 . . . .**37** C4
Town Hall St
  4 Elland HX5 . . . .**37** B4
  1 Holmfirth HD9 . . . . .**86** A3
  4 Mirfield WF14 . . . . .**43** C2
Town Hall Way
  WF12 . . . .**33** A2
Town Head HD9 . . . . . .**83** A3
Town Pl HD1 . . . .**53** C2
Town Rd HD5 . . . .**55** C3
Town St Batley WF17 . .**32** C4
  Birkenshaw BD11 . . . . . .**2** A4
  Dewsbury WF12 . . . . . .**33** C1
Town Terr HD1 . . . .**53** C2
Town The WF12 . . . . . .**57** C4
Town Top HD5 . . . .**55** C3
Track Mount WF17 . . .**32** B4
Track Rd WF17 . . . .**19** B1
Trafalgar Cl HD2 . . . . .**40** A2
Trafalgar Rd HD3 . . . .**32** B3
Trafalgar St WF17 . . . .**19** A2
Transvaal Terr
  WF17 . . . .**11** B1

Travis Lacey Terr 8
  WF13 . . . .**32** B3
Trenance Gdns HX4 . .**22** A1
Trenton Rd WF17 . . . . .**20** C1
Tresham St WF12 . . . .**33** C4
Trevelyan St
  Brighouse HD6 . . . .**13** A3
  9 Huddersfield HD5 . .**68** C3
Triangle Bsns Pk
  WF17 . . . .**4** A1
Triangle The 2
  HD1 . . . .**67** A3
Triath Ct WF17 . . . . . .**18** B4
Trinity Ct HD9 . . . .**83** A2
Trinity Dr HD8 . . . .**95** A2
Trinity Gr 2 HD6 . . . .**13** A2
Trinity Ho WF13 . . . . . .**32** C4
Trinity St
  Batley WF17 . . . .**32** C4
  Huddersfield HD1 . . . . .**52** C1
  Mirfield WF14 . . . .**43** C2
Trinity View WF5 . . . .**35** A1
Troon Dr HD2 . . . .**39** B3
Trueman Ave WF16 . .**18** B3
Tubby La HD2 . . . .**53** B3
Tudor Croft HD2 . . . . .**41** B3
Tudor St HD7 . . . .**72** C2
Tudor Way WF12 . . . . .**46** A1
Tumbling Cl WF5 . . . . .**49** A4
Tunnacliffe Rd HD4 . .**68** A1
TUNNEL END **78** B4
Tunnel St HD4 . . . .**75** B1
Turnbridge Rd HD1 . .**68** B4
Turner Ave WF17 . . . . .**19** C3
Turner Cl 4 WF5 . . . .**48** C4
Turnip La WF17 . . . . . .**57** C4
Turn o The Nook
  WF5 . . . .**48** B4
Turnpike Cl BD11 . . . . .**2** A2
Turnpike St 2 HX5 . .**24** A1
Turnshaw Rd HD8 . . .**89** C4
Turnsteads Ave BD19 .**7** B2
Turnsteads Cl BD19 . . .**7** C2
Turnsteads Cres
  BD19 . . . .**7** C2
Turnsteads Dr BD19 . . .**7** C2
Turnsteads Mount
  BD19 . . . .**7** C2
Tweedale Gdns
  WF13 . . . .**32** B2
Tweedale St 1
  WF13 . . . .**32** B2
Tweed Cl WF17 . . . . . .**11** A3
Twelfth Ave WF15 . . . .**15** B3
Twitch Hill WF4 . . . . . .**61** B3
Two Gates HD7 . . . . . .**72** A3
Tyndale Ave WF4 . . . . .**61** B4
Tyndale Wlk WF16 . . .**18** B3

U

Ullswater Ave WF12. .**20** B1
Ullswater Cl
  Batley WF12 . . . .**33** B4
  Elland HX5 . . . .**24** B1
Ullswater Rd WF12. . .**20** B1
Una Pl HD2 . . . .**52** B2
UNDER BANK **86** A2
Underbank End Rd
  HD9 . . . .**86** B1
Underbank Old Rd
  HD9 . . . .**86** B2
Union Gr WF15 . . . .**17** B1
Union Rd WF15 . . . . . .**17** B1
Union St
  8 Batley WF17 . . . . . .**10** C3
  Dewsbury WF13 . . . . . .**33** A2
  6 Elland HX4 . . . .**23** A1
  8 Huddersfield HD1 . .**96** B3
  Huddersfield, Oakes
  HD3 . . . .**51** B2

Union St *continued*
Liversedge WF16 . . . . .**17** C1
Mirfield WF13 . . . .**45** A3
Ossett WF5. . . . .**48** C4
Slaithwaite HD7 . . . . . .**72** B3
Unity Ct WF13 . . . .**32** B2
Univ of Huddersfield
HD1. . . . .**96** B1
Unna Way HD1 . . . . .**96** A3
Uplands HD2 . . . .**52** B3
Uplands Dr WF14 . . .**43** C4
Upper Bank End Rd
HD9. . . . .**86** B2
Upper Barker St
WF15 . . . .**17** C2
UPPER BATLEY **11** C1
Upper Batley La
WF17 . . . .**11** B2
Upper Batley Low La
WF17 . . . .**11** C2
Upper Battye St
WF16 . . . .**18** A2
Upper Bonegate
HD6. . . . .**13** B1
Upper Brow Rd HD1 .**66** C3
Upper Butts HD5 . . . . .**8** A1
Upper Camroyd St
WF13 . . . .**33** A3
Upper Carr St WF15 . .**17** A3
UPPER CLOUGH **73** C2
Upper Clough Rd
HD7. . . . .**73** C2
Upper Commercial St
WF17 . . . .**17** C3
Upper Common La
HD8. . . . .**93** B1
Upper Croft Rd
WF17 . . . .**19** B2
UPPER CROSSLEY . .**30** B2
Upper Cross St 2
WF13 . . . .**32** C3
Upper Ellistones Ct
HX4. . . . .**22** A1
Upper Exley HX3. . . . .**23** B3
Upperfield Dr HD7. . .**64** B2
Upper Fold HD7 . . . . .**83** A2
Upper George St
Batley WF16 . . . .**18** A2
3 Huddersfield HD1 . .**96** A2
Upper Green Ave 10
BD19. . . . .**6** C2
Upper Green La
HD6. . . . .**13** A1
Upper Hagg HD9 . . . .**84** C4
Upper Hagg Rd HD9 .**84** C4
Upper Haughs HD7 . .**64** B3
Upperhead Row 11
HD1. . . . .**96** A2
UPPER HEATON **42** A1
Upper Heaton La
HD5. . . . .**55** B4
UPPER HEY **80** B4
Upper Hirst HD3. . . . .**50** A2
UPPER HOPTON **56** B3
Upper House La
WF15 . . . .**15** C2
Upper La
Cleckheaton BD19 . . . . .**9** B1
Netherton WF4. . . . . . .**63** B2
Upper Martin Gn
HX4. . . . .**22** A1
Upper Mills View
HD9. . . . .**80** A2
Upper Mount HD9 . .**81** A1
Upper Mount St
Batley WF17 . . . .**19** C1
Huddersfield HD1. . . . .**67** B2
Upper North St
WF17 . . . .**19** B2
Upper Peel St 1
WF13 . . . .**33** A3

Upper Quarry Rd
HD2. . . . .**41** C4
Upper Rd WF17 . . . . .**32** B4
Upper Reins HD9 . . . .**83** B3
Upper South St
WF13 . . . .**32** C3
Upper Station Rd
WF17 . . . .**20** A2
Upper Sunny Bank
Mews HD9. . . . .**80** A2
Upper Wellhouse Rd
HD7. . . . .**64** B1
Upper West St
WF17 . . . .**20** B3
Upton St WF17. . . . . .**19** B4

V

Vale Cl HD5 . . . .**69** B1
Vale St HD6 . . . .**13** A1
Valley Ave HX3 . . . .**5** A2
Valley Ct WF15. . . . . . .**17** B3
Valley Dr WF12 . . . . . .**58** A3
Valley Head HD2. . . . .**51** C4
Valley Rd
Cleckheaton BD19 . . . . .**8** B2
Dewsbury WF12 . . . . . .**58** B3
Liversedge WF15 . . . . .**17** B2
Ossett WF5. . . . .**48** C2
Valley Rd Bsns Pk
WF15 . . . .**17** A2
Valley View HX5 . . . . .**23** C2
Valley View Rd WF5 . .**48** C2
Varley Rd HD7 . . . .**72** B1
Venn St HD1. . . . .**96** B2
Ventnor Cl
Cleckheaton BD19 . . . . .**9** B4
Ossett WF5. . . . .**48** C3
Ventnor Dr WF5 . . . . .**48** C3
Ventnor Way WF5. . . .**48** C3
Vermont Cl HD7 . . . . .**64** B3
Vernon Ave HD1 . . . . .**52** C1
Vernon Cl HD1. . . . . . .**52** C1
Vernon Rd WF15 . . . . .**17** C2
Viaduct St
Huddersfield HD1. . . . .**96** A3
Slaithwaite HD7 . . . . . .**72** C3
Vicarage Ave LS27 . . . .**4** C4
Vicarage Cl BD12 . . . . .**5** C4
Vicarage Ct BD19 . . . . .**8** A2
Vicarage Dr HD9. . . . .**80** B1
Vicarage Gdns
Birkenshaw BD11. . . . . .**2** A3
Brighouse HD6 . . . .**25** C2
Vicarage Mdw
WF14 . . . .**44** B3
Vicarage Mdws HD9 .**86** B2
Vicarage Rd
Dewsbury, Savile Town
WF12. . . . .**46** B3
Dewsbury WF12. . . . . .**33** A2
Huddersfield HD3. . . . .**66** A4
Vicarage Terr WF17 . .**11** A1
Vicar La WF5 . . . .**49** A1
Vicar St 11 WF15. . . . .**17** A3
Vickerman Cres
HD4. . . . .**76** B3
Victoria Ave
Batley WF17 . . . .**19** C2
Brighouse HD6 . . . .**13** C1
Cleckheaton BD19 . . . . .**8** A1
Elland HX5 . . . .**37** A4
Victoria Chase HX3 . . .**5** B2
Victoria Cl HD4 . . . . . .**76** B2
Victoria Cres
Dewsbury WF13 . . . . . .**32** A4
Elland HX5 . . . .**37** B4
Victoria Ct WF17 . . . . .**10** C3
Victoria Dr WF12 . . . .**46** B2
Victoria La
Huddersfield HD1 . . . . .**96** B2

Victoria La *continued*
Huddersfield, Town End
HD7 . . . .**64** B2
Victoria Mills WF17 . .**19** B4
Victoria Pl
Brighouse HD6 . . . .**26** B3
Honley HD9. . . . .**83** A2
Huddersfield HD4. . . . .**74** C3
6 Huddersfield,
Moldgreen HD5. . . . . .**68** C3
7 Mirfield WF14 . . . . .**43** B3
Victoria Rd
Brighouse, Bailiff
Bridge HD6 . . . .**5** B1
Cleckheaton BD19 . . . . .**9** C2
Dewsbury, Thornhill Lees
WF12. . . . .**46** B2
Dewsbury WF13 . . . . . .**32** C3
Elland HX5 . . . .**37** A4
Huddersfield HD1. . . . .**67** B2
Liversedge WF15 . . . . .**17** A1
Meltham HD9 . . . .**80** B2
Victoria Spring Bsns Pk
WF15 . . . .**17** B2
Victoria Sq 12 HD9. . .**86** A3
Victoria St
Batley, Birstall
WF17 . . . .**10** C3
Batley, Carlinghow
WF17 . . . .**19** B4
Batley, Nunroyd
WF16 . . . .**18** A2
Brighouse, Clifton
HD6 . . . .**26** C4
Brighouse HD6 . . . .**26** B3
Clayton West HD8. . . . .**93** A3
Cleckheaton BD19 . . . . .**8** A2
Dewsbury WF13 . . . . . .**45** A4
Elland HX4 . . . .**23** A1
Holmfirth HD9. . . . .**86** A3
Horbury WF4 . . . .**60** B3
Huddersfield, Deighton
HD2. . . . .**41** A1
Huddersfield, Folly Hall
HD1. . . . .**67** C2
Huddersfield HD3. . . . .**51** C2
Huddersfield, Moldgreen
HD5. . . . .**68** C3
Marsden HD7 . . . .**78** C3
Victoria Terr
Clayton West HD8. . . . .**93** B3
Horbury WF4 . . . .**60** A3
Victor St WF17. . . . . . .**20** A3
Victory Ave HD3 . . . . .**66** B3
Viewlands HD2 . . . . . .**40** A2
View St HD5 . . . .**68** C3
Villa Gdns WF17 . . . . .**20** A1
Village St HX3 . . . .**5** A4
Villa Mount BD12 . . . . .**5** C3
Vine Ave BD19 . . . .**7** C2
Vine Cl HD6 . . . .**27** A4
Vine Cres BD19 . . . .**8** A2
Vine Ct HD6 . . . .**27** A4
Vine Garth HD6 . . . . . .**14** A1
Vine Gr HD6 . . . .**27** A4
Vine Ind Est HD6. . . . .**12** C1
Vinery Cl HD8 . . . .**93** B3
Vine St
Cleckheaton BD19 . . . . .**8** A2
Huddersfield HD1. . . . .**53** C2
Vineyard HD7. . . . .**64** C3
Virginia Rd HD3 . . . . .**51** C1
Vista Ct HD7 . . . .**65** B2
Vulcan Cl WF13. . . . . . .**32** C2
Vulcan Gdns WF13. . . .**32** C2
Vulcan Rd WF13 . . . . . .**32** C2
Vulcan St HD6 . . . .**26** C3

W

Wadman Rd HD9 . . . .**87** A1
Wain Brow HD4. . . . . .**76** B2
Wain Ct HD4. . . . .**76** B2
Waingate HD4. . . . .**76** B2
Waingate Pk HD7 . . . .**73** C3
Wain Pk HD4 . . . .**76** B2
Wakefield Commercial
Pk WF4. . . . .**60** A2
Wakefield Cres
WF12 . . . .**33** C2
Wakefield Old Rd 6
WF12 . . . .**33** A2
Wakefield Rd
Birkenshaw BD11. . . . . .**4** A3
Brighouse, Clifton
HD6. . . . .**27** A3
4 Brighouse HD6 . . . .**26** B4
Clayton West HD8. . . . .**93** A3
Denby Dale HD8 . . . . . .**95** C4
Dewsbury WF12 . . . . . .**33** B2
Halifax HX3. . . . .**22** B4
Horbury WF4 . . . .**61** B4
Huddersfield HD1,
HD5. . . . .**68** C3
Lepton HD8. . . . .**70** C1
Liversedge HD6,
WF14. . . . .**28** A1
Liversedge, Mill Bridge
WF15. . . . .**17** B2
Ossett WF5. . . . .**35** C1
Walker Gn WF12. . . . .**58** A4
Walker La WF4 . . . .**61** A3
Walkers Mount
WF17 . . . .**19** C1
Walker St
8 Brighouse BD19 . . . .**6** C2
Cleckheaton BD19 . . . . .**8** A2
Dewsbury, Earlsheaton
WF12. . . . .**47** B4
Dewsbury, Ravensthorpe
WF13. . . . .**44** C2
Dewsbury, Thornhill Lees
WF12. . . . .**46** C1
Walkley Ave WF15 . . .**18** A1
Walkley Gr 10 WF16. .**18** A1
Walkley La WF16. . . . .**31** A4
Walkley Terr WF16 . . .**31** B4
Walkley Villas WF16 . .**31** B4
Wallroyds HD8 . . . . . .**95** A2
Walnut Ave WF12 . . . .**34** B1
Walnut Cl WF12. . . . . .**47** C4
Walnut Cres WF12 . . .**47** C4
Walnut Dr WF12 . . . . .**34** B1
Walnut Gr WF12 . . . . .**34** B1
Walnut La WF12 . . . . .**34** A1
Walnut Pl WF12. . . . . .**34** A1
Walnut Rd WF12 . . . . .**34** B1
Walpole Rd HD4 . . . . .**66** C1
Walsham Dr HD3 . . . .**50** C3
Walton Croft HD5. . . .**69** A4
Walton Dr BD11 . . . . . .**3** C3
Walton Garth BD11 . . .**3** C3
Walton La BD19. . . . . .**14** C4
Waltroyd Rd BD19 . . . .**7** C1
Wapping Nick La
HX4. . . . .**23** C1
Ward Bank Rd HD9 . .**86** A2
Ward Ct HD6 . . . .**25** C1
Wards Hill WF17 . . . . .**19** C3
Wards Hill Ct 11
WF17 . . . .**19** C3
Ward Sq 26 HD1 . . . . .**96** A2
Ward St WF13 . . . .**33** A3
Warehouse Hill Rd
HD7. . . . .**79** A3
Warehouse St WF17 .**20** A2
Warhurst Rd HX5 . . . .**24** A2
WARING GREEN **13** A1
Waring Way WF12 . . .**33** B3

Warneford Ave WF5. .**35** A1
Warneford Rd HD4. . .**65** C1
Warneford Rise
HD4. . . . .**65** C1
Warren Cl WF15 . . . . .**30** B4
Warrenfield Ct HD2. . .**40** C1
Warren House La
HD3. . . . .**37** C1
Warren Park Cl HD6 .**12** B3
Warren Pk HD6 . . . . . .**12** B3
Warrenside HD2. . . . . .**41** A2
Warrens La
Birkenshaw WF17 . . . . .**3** A1
Cleckheaton WF17 . . . . .**3** A3
Warren St WF12 . . . . .**46** C1
Warrington Terr
HD7. . . . .**78** B3
Warwick Ave HD7. . . .**65** A3
Warwick Rd WF17 . . .**20** A1
Warwick Road Jun &
Inf Sch WF17 . . . .**19** C1
Washpit New Rd
HD9. . . . .**86** B1
Wasp Nest Rd HD1. . .**53** A3
Waste La
Huddersfield HD5. . . . .**69** A2
Mirfield, Lower Hopton
WF14. . . . .**43** C1
Mirfield WF14. . . . .**43** B1
Waste The WF14 . . . . .**43** B1
Watercroft HD5. . . . . .**69** B1
Waterfall Cotts HD7 .**78** A4
Watergate HD1 . . . . . .**96** B2
Watergate Rd WF12. .**32** B1
Water La
Dewsbury, Scout Hill
WF12. . . . .**46** A4
Netherton WF4. . . . . . .**59** C2
Shelley HD8 . . . .**89** C1
Water Lane Cl WF4 . .**59** C2
WATERLOO **70** A4
Waterloo Fold 2
BD12. . . . .**6** A4
Waterloo Rd
Brighouse HD6 . . . .**13** A1
Huddersfield HD5. . . . .**70** A4
Waterloo Rise HD5 . .**69** C3
Water Mill Ct HD9 . . .**87** B4
Water Row HD9 . . . . .**87** C1
Water Royd Ave
WF14 . . . .**43** C4
Water Royd Cres
WF14 . . . .**43** C4
Water Royd Dr
WF14 . . . .**43** C4
Water Royd La
WF14 . . . .**43** C4
Waterside
Huddersfield HD1. . . . .**67** B3
Huddersfield, Salford
HD1. . . . .**76** B4
Slaithwaite HD7 . . . . . .**72** C3
Waterside The HD9 . .**85** A3
Waterside Wlk
WF14 . . . .**42** C3
Waters Rd HD7 . . . . . .**78** A4
Water St
Brighouse HD6 . . . .**13** B1
Clayton West HD8. . . . .**92** C2
Huddersfield HD1. . . . .**67** B3
2 Huddersfield,
Rashcliffe HD1,
HD4. . . . .**67** B3
Waterstone Ct
WF13 . . . .**18** C2
Waterwheel Rise
HD4. . . . .**66** C1

Waterworks Rd
WF17 . . . . .18 C2
Watroyd La HD7 . . . .73 A4
Watson Ave WF12. . . .34 B2
Waverley Rd
Elland HX5 . . . . .37 B3
Huddersfield HD1. . . . .52 C1
Waverley St
Dewsbury WF12 . . . . . .32 C1
Slaithwaite HD7 . . . . . .72 B3
Waverley Terr HD1. . .52 A1
Wayne Cl WF17 . . . . . .19 C4
WEATHER HILL 51 A4
Weatherhill Cres
HD3. . . . . .51 A4
Weatherhill Rd HD3. .51 A4
Weavers Croft BD19 .16 C4
Weavers Ct
Batley WF16 . . . . .18 C2
Meltham HD9 . . . . .81 A2
Weavers Wlk HD8. . . .95 C4
Weaving La WF12. . . .46 A4
Webster Hill WF13 . . .32 C2
Webster St 4 WF13. .32 C2
Weir Side HD7. . . . . . .78 C3
Welbeck Rd WF17 . . . .10 C4
Wellands Gn BD19 . . . .7 B1
Wellands La BD19 . . . .7 A1
Well Close St HD6 . . . .13 B1
Wellfield Bank HD4 . .75 C4
Wellfield Cl HD7 . . . . .74 A4
Wellfield Rd HD3 . . . .51 C1
Wellgate Elland HX4 . .22 C2
3 Ossett WF5 . . . . . . .48 C3
Slaithwaite HD7 . . . . . .64 A1
Well Gr
Brighouse HD6 . . . . . . .12 C3
Huddersfield HD2. . . . .40 B1
Well Green La HD6. . . .12 C3
Well Hill HD9 . . . . .83 A2
Wellholme 13 B1
WELLHOUSE 64 C1
Wellhouse WF14. . . . .30 B1
Wellhouse Ave
WF14 . . . . .30 B1
Wellhouse Cl WF14 . .30 A1
Wellhouse Court Mews
WF14 . . . . .44 A4
Wellhouse Gn HD7. . .64 C1
Wellhouse Jun & Inf
Sch HD7. . . . . .64 C1
Wellhouse La
Huddersfield HD5. . . . .55 A3
Mirfield WF14. . . . . . . .30 B1
Well Ings HD8. . . . . . .90 B3
Wellington Arc 7
HD6. . . . . .26 B4
Wellington Bsns Ctr
HX5. . . . . .24 A1
Wellington Ct BD11. . .2 A4
Wellington Rd
WF13 . . . . .32 C2
Wellington Rd E 11
WF13 . . . . .32 C2
Wellington St
Batley WF17 . . . . .19 C2
12 Dewsbury WF13 . . .32 C2
Huddersfield HD3. . . . .51 B2
3 Liversedge WF15 . .17 B1
Wellington Terr
HD7. . . . . .79 A3
Wellington Wlk 9
WF13 . . . . .32 C2
Well La Batley WF17 . .20 A3
Brighouse HD6 . . . . . . .27 B4
Dewsbury WF13 . . . . . .31 C2
Holmfirth HD9. . . . . . . .86 B2
Wells Ct WF5 . . . . .48 B3

Wells Green Gdns
HD9. . . . . .84 A1
Wells Rd WF12. . . . . . .58 A4
Well St
3 Dewsbury
WF12. . . . . .33 B3
3 Elland HX4. . . . . . . .36 A2
Huddersfield HD1. . . . .67 B3
Liversedge WF15 . . . . .17 A3
Wells Terr HX3. . . . . . .5 A4
Welwyn Ave WF17 . . .18 C4
Welwyn Rd WF12 . . . .20 C1
Wendron Cl WF15. . . .29 C3
Wensleydale Ho
WF13 . . . . .32 C4
Wensleydale Par 2
WF17 . . . . .10 C2
Wensley Gr HD6 . . . . .25 B2
Wensley St E 6
WF4 . . . . .60 C3
Wensley St 5 WF4. . . .60 C3
Wentworth Ct HD6. . .25 C1
Wentworth St HD1. . .52 C1
Wesley Ave HD9 . . . . .84 A2
Wesley Cl WF17. . . . . .10 B3
Wesley Ct WF5. . . . . . .48 B4
Wesley Pl WF5. . . . . . .32 C2
Wesley St
Cleckheaton BD19 . . . . .8 A2
Dewsbury WF13 . . . . . .32 C2
Ossett WF5. . . . . .48 B3
Wesley Terr HD8 . . . . .95 A1
Wessen Ct HD7 . . . . . .78 C3
Wessenden Head Rd
HD9. . . . . .80 B1
West Acre Dr WF17 . .20 B3
Westacres HD6 . . . . . .26 B2
West Ave
Brighouse HX3 . . . . .5 A1
Honley HD9. . . . . .83 A2
Horbury WF4 . . . . .61 B3
Huddersfield HD3. . . . .51 C3
West Bank WF17. . . . . .19 B4
WESTBOROUGH 32 A3
Westborough High Sch
WF13 . . . . .32 A2
Westbourne Rd
HD1. . . . . .52 A1
Westbrook Dr HD5. . .70 A4
Westbrook Terr
WF17 . . . . .19 B4
Westburn Pl BD19 . . . .7 C2
Westbury St HX5. . . . .24 A1
West Cl HD2. . . . . .53 B4
Westcliffe Rd BD19 . . .7 C1
Westcliffe Rise BD19. .7 C1
Westcroft HD9. . . . . . .82 C2
West Croft BD12. . . . . .5 C4
Westcroft Dr WF5. . . .34 C3
WEST END 7 C1
West End
Cleckheaton BD19 . . . . .7 C2
Holmfirth HD9. . . . . . . .84 A2
West End Ave HD9 . . .86 C4
West End Dr BD19 . . . .15 C4
West End Mid Sch
BD19. . . . . .7 C1
West End Rd HD7 . . . .64 B2
Westerley Cl HD8 . . . .89 C1
Westerley La HD8. . . .89 C1
Westerly Way HD8. . .89 C1
Western Ave WF17 . . .11 A3
Western Rd HD4 . . . . .65 C2
WESTFIELD 17 C3
Westfield Ave
Dewsbury WF12 . . . . . .34 A2
Huddersfield HD3. . . . .51 B1
Meltham HD9 . . . . .80 A3
Skelmanthorpe HD8. . .91 B2
Westfield Cl WF16 . . .17 C3
Westfield Cres WF5. . .48 C3

Westfield Ct
Horbury WF4 . . . . .60 B4
Huddersfield HD5. . . . .68 C4
Mirfield WF14. . . . . . . .43 C3
Westfield Dr
Ossett WF5. . . . . .48 B3
Skelmanthorpe HD8. . .91 B2
Westfield Farm
WF5 . . . . .48 B4
Westfield Gr WF13 . . .31 C2
Westfield La BD12,
BD19. . . . . .6 A3
West Field La HD9 . . .86 C4
Westfield Pl BD19. . . . .6 B3
Westfield Rd
Batley WF16 . . . . .18 A3
Horbury WF4 . . . . .60 B4
Westfields Ave
WF16 . . . . .44 A3
Westfields Rd WF14. .43 C3
Westfield St
Batley WF16 . . . . .17 C1
Ossett WF5. . . . . .48 B3
Westfield Terr 4
WF4 . . . . .60 C3
Westfield Villas
WF4 . . . . .60 B3
Westgate
Brighouse HD6 . . . . . . .27 B4
Cleckheaton BD19 . . . . .8 A1
Dewsbury WF13 . . . . . .33 A2
Elland HX5 . . . . .23 C1
Honley HD9. . . . . .83 A2
Huddersfield HD1. . . . .96 A2
Liversedge WF16 . . . . .17 C2
Meltham HD9 . . . . .80 B2
Westgate Terr 14
WF13 . . . . .32 C2
West Grove Ave
HD5. . . . . .68 C4
Westgrove Ct BD19 . . .7 C2
West Ho 2 HX5 . . . . . .23 C1
West La BD19. . . . . .9 B3
West Ley HD9. . . . . . . .82 C2
West Lodge Cres
HD2. . . . . .38 A2
Westminster Rd
HX3. . . . . .12 A4
Westmoor Jun Sch
WF13 . . . . .31 C3
West Moorlands Ave
WF13 . . . . .32 B3
West Moor View
WF9. . . . . .82 C2
West Park Gr WF17 . .19 A3
West Park Rd WF17 . .18 C2
West Park St
8 Brighouse HD6 . . . .26 B4
Dewsbury WF13 . . . . . .32 B3
West Park Terr
WF17 . . . . .19 A3
West Pl HD5. . . . . .68 C4
Westridge Dr HD4 . . .75 B3
Westroyd Ave BD19 . . .8 A4
West Royd Ave
WF14 . . . . .43 C4
West Royd Dr 3
WF14 . . . . .43 C4
West Royd Gr WF14. .43 C4
West Royd Pk WF14. .43 C4
West St
Batley, Lower Soothill
WF17. . . . . .20 B3
Batley WF17. . . . . .20 A3
Birkenshaw BD11. . . . . .3 B3
Brighouse, Bailiff Bridge
HD6. . . . . .5 B1
2 Brighouse, Waring
Green HD6 . . . . .13 A1
Cleckheaton BD19 . . . . .8 A1

West St continued
Cleckheaton, Gomersal
BD19. . . . . .9 B3
Dewsbury WF12 . . . . . .32 C1
Elland HX4 . . . . .36 A2
Huddersfield HD3. . . . .51 B3
WEST TOWN 32 B1
WEST VALE 23 A1
West Vale WF12 . . . . . .46 A4
West Vale Prim Sch
HX4. . . . . .23 A1
West View
Batley WF17 . . . . .32 B4
Brighouse BD19 . . . . . . .6 C3
Huddersfield HD1. . . . .66 C3
West View Rise HD1. .66 C3
Westward Croft
HD3. . . . . .51 C4
Westway
Batley WF17 . . . . .20 C1
Mirfield WF14. . . . . . . .29 C1
West Wells Cres
WF5 . . . . .48 B3
West Wells Rd WF5 . .48 C3
Westwood Ct HD4 . . .69 C1
Westwood Fold
HD7. . . . . .73 A4
Westwood Rd WF5. . .49 B3
Westwood St HD1. . . . .4 C2
West Yorkshire Ret Pk
WF17 . . . . .19 A2
Wetherall St WF17 . . .19 B3
Wetherill Terr 4
WF13 . . . . .18 C1
Wetlands Rd HD9 . . . .80 C1
Weydale Ave HD3. . . .51 A2
Weymouth Ave HD3. .51 B1
Wharf Cl WF12 . . . . . .33 A1
Wharfedale Cres
HD8. . . . . .92 A2
Wharfedale Ho
WF17 . . . . .19 C1
Wharf St
Brighouse HD6 . . . . . . .26 B4
Dewsbury WF12 . . . . . .33 A1
Wharton St 3 WF15 .17 B2
Wharton Terr 3
WF16 . . . . .18 A1
Wheat Cl WF13 . . . . . .31 C2
Wheatcroft Ave
WF17 . . . . .19 C2
Wheat Field Ave
HD3. . . . . .51 A2
Wheathouse Rd
HD2. . . . . .52 C3
Wheathouse Terr 5
HD2. . . . . .52 C3
Wheatings The WF5. .49 B3
Wheatlands Dr
WF15 . . . . .29 C4
Wheatley Dr WF14 . . .43 C1
Wheatley Hill La
HD8. . . . . .93 A1
Wheatroyd Cres
WF5 . . . . .48 C1
Wheelwright Dr
WF13 . . . . .32 B4
Wheelwright St 13
WF13 . . . . .32 C2
Wherwell Rd HD6. . . .26 C2
Whewell St 4 WF17 .10 B3
Whinberry Pl 1
WF17 . . . . .3 C2
Whingrove Ave HD9 .80 B1
Whinmore Gdns
BD19. . . . . .9 C1
Whinney Hill Pk
HD6. . . . . .13 B3
Whitacre Cl HD2. . . . .41 A1
Whitacre St HD2. . . . .41 A1
Whitaker St WF17. . . .20 A2

Whitby Ave HD2 . . . . .53 B4
Whitby Cres WF12 . . .33 C2
Whitby Ct HD8. . . . . . .90 C3
Whitcliffe Mount Coll
BD19. . . . . .7 B2
Whitcliffe Rd BD19 . . .8 A1
Whitcliffe Road Fst Sch
BD19. . . . . .8 A2
Whitcliffe Sq BD19. . . .8 A1
Whiteacre Rd HD2. . . .41 B1
Whitebeam Pk HD2. . .52 A4
Whitechapel Gr BD19 .7 A2
Whitechapel Mid Sch
BD19. . . . . .7 C2
Whitechapel Rd
Brighouse BD19 . . . . . . .7 A2
Cleckheaton BD19 . . . . .7 A2
White Cross HD2 . . . . .41 A3
White Cross Rd
WF12 . . . . .33 B4
White Gate HD9 . . . . .83 A3
Whitegate Rd HD4. . .68 C2
Whitegates Gr HD8 . .88 A4
Whitehall Ave
Bradford BD12. . . . . . . .5 C3
Mirfield WF14. . . . . . . .30 A1
Whitehall Ct 2
WF4 . . . . .61 A3
Whitehall Gr
Birkenshaw BD11. . . . . .2 B3
Birkenshaw, Drighlington
BD11. . . . . .3 A4
Whitehall Rd
Birkenshaw BD11. . . . . .3 B4
Bradford BD12. . . . . . . .5 C3
Linthwaite HD7. . . . . . .73 B2
Whitehall Rd BD19. . . .8 A4
Whitehall Rd E BD11. .2 B3
Whitehall Rd W BD11 .2 A2
Whitehall Way
WF13 . . . . .33 A2
White Hart Dr HD4. . .76 C4
WHITEHAUGHS 38 A2
Whitehead La HD4. . .67 C1
White Horse Cl
WF17 . . . . .11 B4
WHITE LEE 10 B1
White Lee Cl WF16. . .18 B4
White Lee Rd WF16 . .18 A4
White Lee Side
WF16 . . . . .18 B4
Whiteley St HD3. . . . .66 A2
White Rose Ave
HD5. . . . . .69 B4
White's Bldgs WF5. . .35 A1
White's Row WF4. . . .59 C3
Whitestone La 2
HD1. . . . . .53 B2
White Wells Gdns
HD9. . . . . .87 A1
White Wells Rd HD9 .87 A1
Whitfield St 10 BD19 . .8 A2
Whitley Rd WF12 . . . . .57 A3
Whitley Spring Cres
WF5 . . . . .49 B3
Whitley Spring Rd
WF5 . . . . .49 B4
Whitteron Cl HD3. . . .51 B3
Whitwell Ave HX5. . . .24 B1
Whitwell Dr HX5. . . . .24 B1
Whitwell Gr HX5. . . . .24 B1
Whitwell Green La
HX5. . . . . .38 A4
Whitwood La HD6 . . . .6 A1
Whitworth Rd 1
WF13 . . . . .32 B1
Wholestone Gate
HD7. . . . . .64 A3
Wickets The WF17 . . .32 B4
Wickham St BD19. . . . .6 C3

Wickleden Gate
HD9. . . . .**87** A1
Wiggan La HD2. . . . . .**40** C2
Wiggin Cross HD7 . . .**74** A3
Wilby St BD19 . . . .**8** A1
Wildspur Gr HD9 . . . .**87** B2
Wildspur Mills HD9 . .**87** B3
Willan's Rd HD13 . . . .**32** C3
Willerton Cl WF12 . . .**21** B1
William Henry Smith
Sch HD6. . . . .**25** B2
William Henry St 1
HD6. . . . .**13** A1
William Horsfall St
HD4. . . . .**66** B1
William Royd La
WF16 . . . .**18** B3
William St
Batley WF13 . . . .**18** C1
10 Brighouse HD6 . . . .**26** A3
Dewsbury, Ravensthorpe
WF13. . . . .**45** A3
Dewsbury WF12 . . . . . .**33** B2
Elland HX4 . . . .**36** C4
Huddersfield HD1 . . . . .**96** B3
Huddersfield, Paddock
Brow HD4 . . . .**66** B2
2 Liversedge WF15 . . .**17** B2
Willow Bank HD2 . . . .**52** C4
Willowbank Gr HD5. .**55** B3
Willow Cl
Cleckheaton BD19 . . . . . .**9** B1
Skelmanthorpe HD8 . . . .**91** C2
Willow Croft BD19 . . . .**7** C1
Willow Ct WF17 . . . . . .**19** C4
Willow Field HD8 . . . .**71** C1
Willow Gr
Huddersfield HD7 . . . . .**65** A3
Ossett WF5 . . . .**49** A1
Willow La HD1. . . . . . .**53** A2
Willow La E HD1. . . . .**53** B2
Willow Rd WF17 . . . . .**20** B2
Willow St BD19 . . . .**8** A3
Willows The WF4 . . . .**60** C3
Willow Terr WF17 . . . .**20** B2
Willow Wlk WF15 . . . .**17** A1
Willwood Ave HD3 . . .**51** B1
Wilman Dr WF5 . . . . . .**48** B4
Wilman Post WF5 . . . .**48** B4
Wilmar Dr HD3 . . . . . .**50** B3
Wilshaw Mill Rd
HD9. . . . .**84** C1
Wilshaw Rd HD9. . . . .**84** C2
Wilson Ave
Mirfield WF14 . . . .**43** B3
Ossett WF5 . . . .**49** C2
Wilson Gdns 5 HD3 .**65** C2
Wilson Rd WF14 . . . . .**43** B3
Wilson Terr WF14 . . . .**43** B3
Wilson Wood St
WF17 . . . .**32** C4
Wilton Ave HD2. . . . . .**41** A3
Wilton Ind Ct WF17 . .**10** C2
Wilton St
Brighouse HD6 . . . .**12** C1
Dewsbury WF12 . . . . . .**33** A1
Wilton Terr BD19 . . . . . .**8** A1
Winchester Ho 3
HD5. . . . .**68** C4
Windermere Rd
Batley WF12 . . . .**33** B4
Meltham HD9 . . . .**80** C1
Windermere Rise
BD19 . . . .**13** B4
Winding Rise BD19 . . .**5** B1
Windmill Cres HD8 . .**92** A2

Windmill Gr BD19. . .**17** B4
Windmill La WF17 . . .**11** A3
Windmill Terr HD4 . . .**76** B2
Windsor Cl WF12 . . . .**34** B4
Windsor Ct WF12 . . . .**34** A4
Windsor Dr
Huddersfield HD5 . . . . .**69** C4
Liversedge WF15 . . . . .**30** B4
Skelmanthorpe HD8 . . .**92** A2
Windsor Gdns WF12 .**34** B4
Windsor Pl HD2 . . . . .**41** A3
Windsor Rd
Batley, Chidswell
WF17. . . . .**34** B4
Batley, Copley Hill
WF17. . . . .**11** B4
Huddersfield HD4 . . . . .**65** B1
Windsor View WF12 . .**34** B4
Windsor Wlk
Batley WF17 . . . .**11** B4
Brighouse HX3 . . . .**13** A4
Windy Bank La
WF15 . . . .**15** B2
Windyridge St WF4 . .**60** B4
Winfield Dr HD3 . . . . .**50** C2
Winget Ave HD4 . . . . .**65** B1
Winney Bank La
HD9. . . . .**86** C3
Winsford Dr HD5 . . . .**55** B1
Winter Hill HD7 . . . . .**73** A1
Winton St HD1. . . . . . .**67** A1
Wistons La HX5. . . . . .**24** A1
Withens Rd WF17 . . . .**10** B4
Withyside HD8 . . . . . .**95** B3
Woburn Dr HD5 . . . . .**70** A4
Wood Ave WF16 . . . . .**18** A3
Woodbine Rd HD1 . . .**53** B3
Woodbine St WF5 . . . .**35** A1
Woodbine Terr HD8 . .**93** B4
Wood Bottom La
HD6. . . . .**12** B2
Wood Bottom Rd
HD4. . . . .**82** A3
Woodburn Ave
WF12 . . . .**47** B4
Wood Close Bottom
HD7. . . . .**73** B2
Wood Croft HD6 . . . . .**25** C3
Woodedge Ave HD5. .**69** C4
Wood End 4 HD4 . . . .**67** B1
Wood End Cotts
WF14 . . . .**43** B2
Woodend Rd WF14. . .**43** B2
Wood End Rd HD4 . . .**76** A2
Wood Farm La HD9 . .**85** A4
Woodfield Ave
Batley WF17 . . . .**19** A2
Elland HX4 . . . .**22** B1
Woodfield Ct HD2 . . .**52** C2
Woodfield Dr HX4 . . .**36** B4
Woodford Dr HD5. . . .**55** B1
Wood Gr WF5 . . . .**35** A2
Woodhall Cl WF4 . . . .**62** B4
Woodhall Dr WF17. . .**19** A2
Woodhead Cl
Huddersfield HD2. . . . .**40** B1
2 Ossett WF5 . . . .**48** C4
Woodhead Rd
Batley WF17 . . . .**11** B4
Brockholes HD9 . . . . . .**83** C1
Huddersfield HD4 . . . . .**76** A4
Woodhead St 14
BD19 . . . .**8** B1
WOODHOUSE **26** B2

Woodhouse Ave
HD2. . . . .**53** C4
Woodhouse Gdns
HD6. . . . .**26** C2
Woodhouse Gr HD2. .**53** C4
Woodhouse Hall Rd
HD2. . . . .**53** C4
Woodhouse Hill
HD2. . . . .**53** C4
Woodhouse La HD6. .**26** B2
Woodhouse Prim Sch
HD6. . . . .**26** B2
Woodkirk Gdns
WF12 . . . .**21** B4
Woodkirk Gr BD12. . . .**5** C3
Woodkirk Int Freight
Terminal WF12 . . . . .**21** B4
Wood La
Batley WF17 . . . .**20** A1
Brighouse HX3 . . . .**25** A4
Denby Dale HD8 . . . . . .**94** C3
Dewsbury WF13 . . . . . .**33** A3
Holmfirth HD9. . . . .**86** A4
Huddersfield HD4 . . . . .**68** B1
Kirkheaton WF14 . . . . .**43** A2
Netherton WF4,
WF12. . . . .**58** A1
Woodland Dr HD6 . . .**12** C1
Woodland Gr WF13 . .**31** C2
Woodland Mdws
HD8. . . . .**88** C1
Woodland Rd HD2 . . .**54** C4
Woodland Rise HD2 .**52** C2
Woodlands
Horbury WF4 . . . .**61** B4
Ossett WF5 . . . .**35** A1
Woodlands Ave
Cleckheaton BD19 . . . . . .**9** A3
Lepton HD8 . . . .**71** A1
Woodlands Cl
Denby Dale HD8 . . . . . .**95** B3
Huddersfield HD2 . . . . .**41** C4
Woodlands Cres
BD19 . . . .**9** A3
Woodlands Dr
Cleckheaton BD19 . . . . . .**9** A3
Lepton HD8 . . . .**88** B4
Skelmanthorpe HD8 . . .**92** A2
Woodlands End
HD8. . . . .**71** A1
Woodlands Fold
BD11 . . . .**2** B3
Woodlands La WF13 .**31** C2
Woodland Sq HD6 . . .**26** C3
Woodlands Rd
Batley WF17 . . . .**11** A2
Cleckheaton BD19 . . . . . .**9** A3
Halifax HX5. . . . .**23** C2
Lepton HD8. . . . .**71** A1
Woodlands Rd E
HD8. . . . .**70** C1
Woodlands The
HD9. . . . .**80** C1
Woodlands Way
HD8. . . . .**88** B4
Woodlea Ave HD3 . . .**66** B4
Woodleigh Gr HD4. . .**75** B3
Woodlock Cl HD2. . . .**40** B2
Woodman Ave
Elland HX5 . . . .**37** B3
Huddersfield HD2. . . . .**41** C3
Wood Mount WF4 . . .**62** A4
Wood Nook HD8. . . . .**95** A3
Wood Pit La HD9 . . . .**87** C1
Woodroyd HD7 . . . . . .**64** B3
Woodroyd Ave HD9 . .**83** C3

Woods Ave HD7 . . . . .**79** B3
Woodside HD8 . . . . . .**95** B3
Woodside Cotts 1
HD3. . . . .**65** C2
Woodside Cres
WF17 . . . .**19** A2
Woodside Gr HX4. . . .**36** C4
Woodside La HD2. . . .**40** A2
Woodside Rd HD4 . . .**75** C4
Woodside Terr 6
HX4. . . . .**36** C4
Woodside Veiw HD4 .**65** B1
Woodside View HX4 .**36** C4
Woods Mount HD7. . .**79** B3
Woodsome Ave
WF14 . . . .**43** A4
Woodsome Dr
Lepton HD8 . . . .**88** A4
Mirfield WF14. . . . .**43** B4
Woodsome Est
WF17 . . . .**19** B2
Woodsome Lees La
HD8. . . . .**88** A1
Woodsome Pk HD8 . .**88** A4
Wood St
Batley WF17 . . . .**19** C3
Brighouse HD6 . . . .**26** B4
Clayton West HD8 . . . . .**92** C2
Cleckheaton BD19 . . . . . .**7** C1
Dewsbury WF13 . . . . . .**33** A3
Elland HX5 . . . .**37** C4
Huddersfield HD1. . . . .**96** A2
Huddersfield, Longwood
HD3. . . . .**65** C3
Huddersfield, Moldgreen
HD5. . . . .**68** C4
Ossett WF5 . . . .**35** A2
Skelmanthorpe HD8 . . .**91** B3
Slaithwaite HD7 . . . . . .**72** B3
Woods Terr HD7 . . . . .**79** B3
Woodstock Cres
HD3. . . . .**51** B2
Wood Terr HD4 . . . . . .**67** C1
Woodthorpe Terr
HD1. . . . .**67** B3
Wood Top
Brighouse HD6 . . . .**12** B3
Marsden HD7 . . . .**78** C2
Wood Vale Office Pk
HD6. . . . .**13** B2
Woodvale Rd HD6 . . .**13** B1
Wood View HD2 . . . . .**52** A3
Wood View Gr HD6. . .**12** C2
Woodville Ave HD7 . .**65** A2
Woodville Pl HD2. . . .**41** A4
Woodville Rd WF12 . .**33** A2
Woodward Ct WF14. .**30** B1
Woolcroft Gr HD7 . . .**86** C4
WOOLDALE **86** C4
Wooldale Cliff Rd
HD9. . . . .**86** B3
Wooldale Jun Sch
HD9. . . . .**87** A4
Wooldale Rd HD9. . . .**86** C4
Wool Pl HD8. . . . .**92** A2
Woolrow La HD6. . . . .**13** C4
Wool St WF16 . . . .**18** A1
Worcester Gr HD4 . . .**68** A1
Workhouse La HX4 . .**36** C4
Wormalds Bldgs 3
HD1. . . . .**53** A2
Wormald St
Dewsbury WF13 . . . . . .**32** C2
Huddersfield HD5. . . . .**69** B1
Liversedge WF15 . . . . .**17** C1

Wormalds View
WF12 . . . .**46** A4
Wray's Bldgs WF4 . . .**60** C3
Wren Hill WF17 . . . . . .**11** A2
Wren St HD1 . . . .**66** C3
Wrexhall Rd WF12 . . .**33** B4
Wrigley Ct HD4 . . . . . .**82** B3
Wroe St WF13 . . . .**31** C3
Wycliffe St WF5 . . . . .**35** A1
WYKE **5** C4
Wyke Cres BD12 . . . . . .**6** A4
Wyke Old La HD6. . . . . .**5** B1
Wynmore Dr HD3. . . .**50** C3
Wynthorpe Rd WF4 . .**61** A3
Wyvern Ave HD3. . . . .**66** B4
Wyvern Cl WF17 . . . . .**19** C4
Wyverne Rd HD7 . . . .**65** A2

Y

Yard Four 1 WF17 . . .**10** C2
Yard No 4 WF16. . . . . .**18** C2
Yarn Ct BD19 . . . .**5** B1
Yates La HD3 . . . .**66** A2
Ye Farre Cl 3 HD6. . .**13** A2
Yew Gr HD4 . . . .**65** B1
Yew Green Ave HD4. .**67** A1
Yew Green Rd HD4. . .**67** A1
Yew Pk HD6 . . . .**12** B3
YEWS HILL **67** A2
Yews Hill Rd HD1,
HD4. . . . .**67** A2
Yews Mount HD1 . . . .**67** B2
Yew St HD2. . . . .**53** A3
Yew Tree HD7. . . . .**72** B1
Yew Tree Ct 6
WF15 . . . .**17** A3
Yew Tree La
Huddersfield HD4,
HD7. . . . .**65** B1
Slaithwaite HD7 . . . . . .**72** B1
Yew Tree Rd
Huddersfield HD2,
HD3. . . . .**38** A1
Shepley HD8 . . . .**90** B3
York Ave HD2. . . . .**53** A4
York Ct WF17 . . . .**19** C4
York Dr
Batley, Bank Foot
WF17. . . . .**20** A4
Batley, Nunroyd
WF16. . . . .**18** A4
York Gr Batley WF17 . .**20** A4
4 Mirfield WF14 . . . . .**43** B3
York Ho 4 HX5. . . . . . .**23** C1
York Pl 9 BD19 . . . .**8** A2
York Rd Batley WF17 . .**19** C4
Dewsbury WF12 . . . . . .**33** C2
5 Mirfield WF14 . . . . .**43** B3
Yorkshire Mill Village
WF17 . . . .**20** A3
York St HD6 . . . .**26** A3
Yorkstone HD4 . . . . . .**66** A1

Z

Zakaria Muslim Girls
High Sch WF17 . . . .**20** A2
Zetland St HD1 . . . . . .**96** B2
Zion Cl HD3 . . . .**51** B3
Zion St WF5 . . . .**34** C3

List of numbered locations

In some busy areas of the maps it is not always' possible to show the name of every place.

Where not all names will fit, some smaller places are shown by a number. If you wish to find out the name associated with a number, use this listing.

The places in this list are also listed normally in the Index.

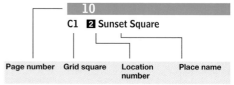

C1 **2** Sunset Square

| Page number | Grid square | Location number | Place name |

3
C1 **1** Whinberry Pl
2 Birstall Park Ct

5
C3 **1** Cameron Ave
2 Methuen Oval
3 Greengates Ave
C4 **1** St Mary's Gdns
2 Griffe Head Cres

6
A4 **1** Greenacre Cl
2 Waterloo Fold
3 Binks Fold
4 Hobson Fold
5 Albert Terr
6 East Croft
7 New Rd
C2 **3** Walker St
5 Naylor's Bldgs
6 Greenfield Dr
8 Acer Way
9 Cowdray Dr
10 Upper Green Ave
11 Lower Green Ave
12 Paddock The
13 Industrial St

8
A1 **1** Carlton Cl
2 Carlton Way
3 Gladstone St
4 Baden Terr
5 Cross Crown St
6 Holdsworth Ct
7 Platt Sq
8 Butts Yd
9 Old Robin
A2 **1** Beatrice St
2 Alice St
3 John William St
4 Canary St
5 Tennyson Pl
6 Lynton Terr
7 Crowther St
8 Claremont St
9 York Pl
10 Whitfield St
11 Caroline St
12 Prospect St
B1 **1** Market Pl
2 Horncastle St
3 Springfield House
4 Church Grange
5 Central Arc
6 Central Par
7 St John's Pl
8 Cross Church St

9 Fairfield Terr
10 Ashfield Terr
11 Sunfield Terr
12 Mayfield Terr
13 Beechfield Terr
14 Woodhead St
15 Pavement St
B2 **1** Coach La
2 Providence St

10
B3 **1** College St
2 Musgrave St
3 Sedgewick St
4 Whewell St
5 John St
6 Bond St
C1 **1** Bower The
3 Lonsdale Ave
C2 **1** Yard Four
2 Wensleydale Par
3 Brookroyd Gdns
4 Oak View Terr
5 Roman Rd
C3 **1** South View
2 Coronation Terr
3 Alexandra Ave
4 Springwell View
5 Sunnymount Terr
6 Chapel La
7 School St
8 Union St
9 John Nelson Cl
10 Quarry La
12 Moon Cl

13
A1 **1** William Henry St
2 West St
3 East Mount
4 East Mount Pl
5 Firth Ave
6 Sunderland Ct
7 St Martin's View
8 Back New St
9 Frances St
10 Back Charles St
11 Rydings Cl
13 Albion Pl
14 Sculptor St
15 Rock St
16 Haigh St
17 Barton St
18 Knightsbridge Ct
19 Larkfield Ct
A2 **1** Trinity Gr
2 Ye Farre Cl
4 Richard Pl
B1 **1** Barber St
2 Old Lane Ct

3 Crescent The
4 Empsall Row
5 Alfred St
6 Lane Court No 1
7 Lane Court No 2
8 Eastwood St
B2 **1** Croft Pl
2 Bottomley St
3 Oddfellows St

17
A2 **4** Alexandra St
5 Churchfield Cl
6 Churchfield Terr
7 Rouse St
8 Lonsdale Terr
9 Thomas St
10 George St
A3 **1** Garden Par
2 Garden Wlk
3 Spring Valley Sq
4 Spring Valley St
5 Spring Valley Cl
6 Yew Tree Ct
7 Cartwright House
8 Luddite House
9 Arkwright Ct
10 Lee Ct
11 Vicar St
B1 **1** John William St
2 Birchwood Ct
3 Wellington St
4 Melbourne St
5 Frederick St
B2 **1** Albion St
2 William St
3 Alfred St
4 Wharton St
5 Bennett St
6 South St
C2 **1** Centre St
2 Greenside

18
A1 **1** Tower Bldgs
2 Strawberry Sq
3 Wharton Terr
4 Alfred St
5 Brewery St
6 Garden St
7 Stanningley Gr
8 Brooke St
9 John St
10 Walkley Gr
A2 **1** Grosvenor Terr
2 Lewes Fold
3 Hove Ct
4 Clarydon Pl
5 Park Rd
6 Frank Peel Cl

A3 **1** Milton St
2 Grosvenor St
C1 **2** Hillary St
3 Churwell Ave
4 Wetherill Terr

19
C3 **1** Churchfield St
2 Henrietta St
3 Back Henrietta St
4 Back Providence St
5 Market Sq
6 Market Pl
7 Brunswick St
8 Hume Crest
9 Cobden Cl
10 Bayldons Pl
11 Wards Hill Ct

20
A1 **1** Back Warwick Terr
2 Cedar Gr
3 Mount Ave
4 Back Mount Ave
5 Cross Rink St
6 Rink Terr
7 Rink Par

22
B1 **1** Thornfield St
2 Thornfield Rise
B2 **1** Goldfields Cl
2 Goldfields View
3 Moorlands Ct
C1 **1** Lindwell Pl
2 Lindwell Gr
3 Lower Wellgate
4 Road End
5 Lindwell Ave
6 Hollyns Terr

23
A1 **1** Elizabeth St
2 Lambert St
3 Princess St
4 North St
5 George St
6 Union St
7 Cross St
8 High St
9 Garswick Terr
C1 **1** Towngate Ho
2 West Ho
3 Mexborough Ho
4 York Ho
5 Ripon Ho
6 Regent Ho

7 Savile Ho
8 Eland Ho
9 Marlborough Ho
10 Calder Ho
11 Croft Ho
12 St Marys Gate
13 Church Ho
14 Portland Ho
15 Coniston Ho
16 Cornwall Ho
17 Castlegate Ho
18 Providence St

24
A1 **1** Back Bower Rd
2 Turnpike St
3 Back Springfield Rd
4 Heathfield Grange

25
C2 **1** Castle Terr
2 Castle Pl
3 Orchards The
4 Holly Bank Ho
5 Jumble Dyke
6 Raw Hill
7 Ogden La

26
A2 **3** Sunnydale Ave
A3 **1** Thornhill Pl
2 Closes Rd
3 Longroyde Rd
4 Denham St
5 Bryan St
6 Ash Grove Terr
7 Harley St
8 Laura St
9 Back William St
10 William St
11 Bramston Gdns
12 Fentham Ind Est
A4 **1** Sunnybank Grange
2 Prospect Pl
3 Church La
4 Heaton St
5 Daisy St
6 Croft St
7 Scotty Bank
8 Thornton St
B3 **1** Back Gooder La
2 Railway St
B4 **1** Hutchinson La
2 Hangram St
3 Clifton Rd
4 Wakefield Rd
5 Hall St
6 Park Row

7 Wellington Arc
8 West Park St

PHILIP'S MAPS
the Gold Standard for drivers

◆ **Philip's street atlases cover every county in England, Wales, Northern Ireland and much of Scotland**

◆ Every named street is shown, including alleys, lanes and walkways

◆ Thousands of additional features marked: stations, public buildings, car parks, places of interest

◆ Route-planning maps to get you close to your destination

◆ Postcodes on the maps and in the index

◆ Widely used by the emergency services, transport companies and local authorities

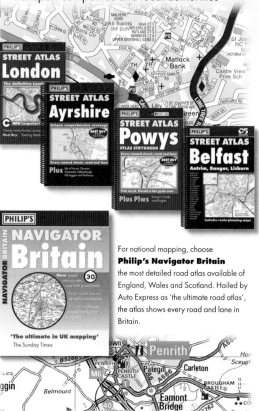

For national mapping, choose **Philip's Navigator Britain** the most detailed road atlas available of England, Wales and Scotland. Hailed by Auto Express as 'the ultimate road atlas', the atlas shows every road and lane in Britain.

Street atlases currently available

England
Bedfordshire and Luton
Berkshire
Birmingham and West Midlands
Bristol and Bath
Buckinghamshire and Milton Keynes
Cambridgeshire and Peterborough
Cheshire
Cornwall
Cumbria
Derbyshire
Devon
Dorset
County Durham and Teesside
Essex
North Essex
South Essex
Gloucestershire and Bristol
Hampshire
North Hampshire
South Hampshire
Herefordshire Monmouthshire
Hertfordshire
Isle of Wight
Kent
East Kent
West Kent
Lancashire
Leicestershire and Rutland
Lincolnshire
Liverpool and Merseyside
London
Greater Manchester
Norfolk
Northamptonshire
Northumberland
Nottinghamshire
Oxfordshire
Shropshire
Somerset
Staffordshire
Suffolk

Surrey
East Sussex
West Sussex
Tyne and Wear
Warwickshire and Coventry
Wiltshire and Swindon
Worcestershire
East Yorkshire Northern Lincolnshire
North Yorkshire
South Yorkshire
West Yorkshire

Wales
Anglesey, Conwy and Gwynedd
Cardiff, Swansea and The Valleys
Carmarthenshire, Pembrokeshire and Swansea
Ceredigion and South Gwynedd
Denbighshire, Flintshire, Wrexham
Herefordshire Monmouthshire
Powys

Scotland
Aberdeenshire
Ayrshire
Dumfries and Galloway
Edinburgh and East Central Scotland
Fife and Tayside
Glasgow and West Central Scotland
Inverness and Moray
Lanarkshire
Scottish Borders

Northern Ireland
County Antrim and County Londonderry
County Armagh and County Down
Belfast
County Tyrone and County Fermanagh

How to order
Philip's maps and atlases are available from bookshops, motorway services and petrol stations. You can order direct from the publisher by phoning **0207 531 8473** or online at **www.philips-maps.co.uk**
For bulk orders only, e-mail philips@philips-maps.co.uk